PIONEERS:

THE STORY OF

OSWEGO COUNTY'S

SEARCH AND RESCUE

TEAM

Jim Farfaglia

To Jim Smith

Jim [signature]

Also by Jim Farfaglia

<u>Poetry</u>

Country Boy

People, Places & Things: The Powerful Nouns of My Life

Reach Out in the Darkness: How Pop Music Saved My Mortal Soul

The Best of Fulton (2017)

<u>Local History</u>

Voices in the Storm: Stories From The Blizzard of '66

In Pursuit of Clouds: The Journey of Oswego's Weatherman Bob Sykes

Of the Earth: Stories From Oswego County's Muck Farms

Camp Hollis: The Origins of Oswego County's Children's Camp (co-written by Jane Spellman and Alysa Koloms)

To Douglas Legg

Here but for a moment,

inspiring us still.

Preface

To the Mountains

July 10, 2016. Predawn. I'm taking my usual morning walk in a quiet Fulton, New York neighborhood, watching for the emerging light to offer a hint of what the day will bring. Today, however, the sun doesn't show up at its scheduled time and last night's thunderstorms have left behind low, slow-moving clouds. Even in a light shirt and shorts, I'm already sweating. It looks to be another of those triple-H days in Central New York: hazy, hot and humid.

Figuring out how to endure another day of this summer's oppressive heat isn't the only thing on my mind as I return home from my walk. Before temperatures begin their steady climb, I'll be making my way to the Adirondack Mountains, the roads leading to them rising a substantial 1,300 feet above my hometown. I've been told that atmospheric conditions where I'm headed can be vastly different from Fulton's, and so I've packed both sunscreen and a rain jacket in my backpack. I don't want anything to distract me on this trip to the Adirondack's Santanoni Preserve. Once regarded as the grandest of that region's Great Camps, today the Preserve's estate lies vacant, quietly embedded in a dense forest. Within that wilderness, a mystery is contained and it is the reason I am travelling to Santanoni.

Though I can drive to its foothills in a few hours, the times I've visited the Adirondacks have always felt like a journey to a different world. Sure, there are plenty of trees where I live and hiking trails within minutes of my home, but they are nothing like the expanse of forest I'll soon be entering. Today's trip feels especially otherworldly, though, because not only will I be making my way through challenging terrain, but also into the Santanoni mystery which began on this day – July 10 – forty-five years ago. Yes, today is an anniversary of sorts, but not one anybody cares to celebrate. For on this date in 1971, a tragedy occurred on the Santanoni Preserve, its horrific details still echoing through those Adirondack Mountains.

The tragedy bears a name: Douglas Legg. Even with nearly a half-century's passing, many residing in northern New York State have not forgotten Douglas's name or what happened to him that July day. And once those with no recollection of the boy hear the sad details, they too cannot forget: While the Legg family was vacationing at the Santanoni Preserve, eight-year-old Douglas, in a series of events which have never been completely substantiated, vanished into his wilderness surroundings. His family never saw him again.

In the days that followed, the heartbreaking story of Douglas's disappearance became front-page news. Media coverage carried it far and wide, with newspaper headlines reflecting the shifting hope and despair in the first days after the youngster went missing: "Throngs Join Hunt for Douglas." "Rains Slow Search for Boy." "New Scent May Lead to Doug." Concern for the boy's well-being resulted in an onslaught of people who volunteered to search the Adirondack woods for him. Fueled by an instinctive need to reunite child with family, but with a naïve concept of the harsh realities of wilderness searching, they came by the hundreds. Most did their best to help, but their ill-preparedness and inexperience ended up hindering the search. Three weeks after Douglas was last seen, after following footprints leading nowhere and bloodhounds chasing scents that dissolved into thin air, the search ended. But the questions remained.

Today, I'm bound for the Santanoni Preserve, not in hopes of solving this mystery — those much more familiar with the Adirondacks' precarious environment have tried to no avail. Rather, I'm travelling to the tragedy's epicenter because I want to walk into the forest where the many questions of Douglas Legg's fate still linger. I want to spend time there thinking about a man who never stepped foot on Santanoni soil, but somehow managed to provide a meaningful response to those questions. And I want to reflect on how this man inspired others to join him as he created a resource for anyone hopelessly lost in the wilderness.

His name was Bart Bartholomew, and while the frantic search for Douglas Legg was taking place, a couple hundred miles from the Adirondacks in my hometown of Fulton, Bart considered the harsh reality lying ahead for the Legg family. Reading each day's newspaper coverage of the search, he discussed the complexities of it with his wife, saying aloud what many had been thinking: "What if Douglas was our son? What more could have been done? What *must* be done so this will never happen again?"

Bart began to imagine what was needed to address the lack of reliable support for Douglas's family during their time of need, a service which had never been available in Fulton, or in New York State, or anywhere in the eastern United States. The time had come, he resolved, for the creation of a professional search and rescue team. Bart envisioned a group of volunteers who would respond quickly and skillfully when a child, or a person of any age, went missing. Within a month of Douglas Legg's disappearance, the result of this man's vision, aptly named the Oswego County Pioneer Land Search and Rescue Team, had been established in Fulton. Forty-five years later, it remains the most respected emergency service organization of its kind in New York State.

Though a lifelong Fultonian, I had only learned about the creation of the Pioneer team in 2015, while working with our city's library on a project to help people write local history memoirs. Two Fultonians with ties to the search and rescue team participated in the project and I found their stories compelling. I was pleased to bring their memories of the team to the attention of others, knowing theirs was a story that deserved to be told.

After the project ended, though, I found myself unable to let go of the Pioneers' saga. I was curious to know more about how the team managed to establish itself without any preexisting search and rescue organizations to emulate. I wanted to hear how today's Pioneers managed to adapt their founders' principles to our technologically-savvy world. Most of all, the writer in me was hungry to dig deeper into the team's near-half-century-old history to learn more about its successes and struggles. From my curiosity, the inspiration to write this book was born.

While researching the details of the Pioneer team, I was privileged to meet and interview founding members and their families. Old newspapers offered me heart-wrenching backstories of the missing people they sought to rescue. I was able to witness the current team's training programs which maintain their founder's stringent search standards. Yet, while navigating my way through the evolution of the Pioneers, what I learned kept propelling me back to the fate of one little boy forever lost in the Adirondacks. In order to properly tell the Oswego County Pioneer Land Search and Rescue Team's story, I realized that I must begin with Douglas Legg. So, today I make a pilgrimage into the mountains, ready to walk the path which began with a tragedy, but ends with a triumph.

Chapter One

The Adirondacks:
Playground or Treacherous Trap?

Though Bart Bartholomew did not take part in the search for Douglas Legg, he was well aware of how someone could have gone missing in the Adirondack Mountains. No stranger to the region, Bartholomew had been a frequent visitor on family camping vacations and hunting trips with friends. He knew the dangers inherent in those mountains and had learned how to safely navigate its unpredictable terrain.

The same could not be said for me, however, and with no experience in areas as remote as the Santanoni Preserve, common sense prevailed. Safety first, after all. So, while planning my visit to the location of Douglas Legg's disappearance, I asked my friend and experienced Adirondack hiker, Vince Markowsky, to serve as my guide.

In the early morning light, I pull into Vince's driveway and he fits his solidly-built 5' 11" frame into my subcompact Toyota Corolla, looking every bit like a man ready for an Adirondack hike. Indeed, hiking has been a part of my guide's life since he was 15. By the time he'd turned 46, five years ago, Vince had accomplished something in the Adirondacks that many only dream of. "There are 46 peaks above 4,000 feet in the Adirondack Park," Vince explains as we begin our drive to Santanoni, which is home to several of those peaks. "It's become a popular goal for hikers to climb them all. If they do, they become part of the 46er Club." Vince assures me he finished all 46, but with the added challenge of completing them in the wintertime. "So, I'm a winter 46er," he says.

As we head toward those peaks, our talk turns to Douglas Legg. I'm assuming Vince's winter expeditions added an extra challenge to his hiking, so, since Douglas went missing in the middle of summer, I'm also assuming that fair weather conditions should have been in the boy's favor when he got lost. Not so, according to Vince, who easily lists a number of pitfalls no matter what the weather: "Adirondack terrain is so unique, primarily because its mountains are much older than other ranges, such as the Rockies and Himalayas. Sections of Adirondack high peaks are bare granite rock, and some of these areas are quite steep. With all the foot travel on the trails, there are exposed roots and those can be tripping hazards. Trees in some sections grow very tightly together, and if you happen to lose the trail or hit a blowdown area, where extremely high winds have taken down sections of trees, you can easily get lost."

I'm starting to understand the challenges for any Adirondack visitor, let alone an eight-year-old, but Vince isn't finished with the realities of wilderness hiking. "There's always a chance for hypothermia," he states. I remind Vince that Douglas got lost in mid-July; surely bitter-cold conditions couldn't have been a factor in his disappearance. "Even summer rain," Vince continues, "can become dangerous. Strong winds in high altitudes can strip heat right out of a soaking wet hiker."

There are other inclement weather concerns: "In snow, heavy rain or even fog, the painted markers maintained to help people keep on the trail can become hidden," Vince says, promising to point out these markers when we hike today. "Not all of the high peaks have these markers and several are trail-less. The New York State Parks system has purposely left them in their natural condition as part of the challenge to completing the 46 peaks. Instead, parts of the mountains have what are known as herd paths, which are made by hikers themselves." The Santanoni Preserve, Vince makes sure to note, is in one of the Park's unmarked areas.

Things get quiet in our car as we drive out of the more populated areas of Oswego County. The tree cover along our travel route thickens, and with the sun still low in the eastern sky, it feels like we're driving back into the dark of night. This shadowy view mirrors my thoughts as I try to process the picture Vince has painted of what lies ahead for us. I'm adding his warnings to what my research about the Adirondacks has already made clear. Hiking its lush forests, which seem so appealing in travel brochures and TV ads, has a dangerous flip side. Getting lost in all that greenery, history shows us, has been a cruel reality ever since the first person decided to visit those mountains.

Indeed, for the first 200 years after Europeans settled in America, the area which eventually became known as The Adirondack Park was considered a mammoth and unnavigable wilderness. Covering more than one-fifth of New York State, the territory's dense forests and towering mountains were seen as a part of this new country to be viewed with respect, but always from a distance. It wasn't until the mid-1800s, when naturalists such as Henry David Thoreau wrote the praises of wilderness, that the common man first ventured into the Adirondacks. People hungry to experience what they'd read started exploring the outer edges of the region. The expansion of railroad systems allowed those enthusiasts to more deeply penetrate the mountainous backwoods, and by 1875, more than 200 hotels were offering inquisitive travelers a destination.

Great Camps, like the one we're headed to on the Santanoni Preserve, were sprawling summer getaways for the wealthy, and they began sprouting up on cleared land alongside lakes and rivers. Soon, those sweeping cuts into the area's forests and America's increasing demand for Adirondack hardwood lumber spurred nature conservationists to lobby for an end to this "progress." By 1894, their demands became law and the Adirondack Park was established as forever wild. Today, more than 2,000 miles of trails wind through the Park's six million acres, annually drawing upwards of ten million visitors. Most enjoy their favorite outdoor activity – fishing, boating, hiking, camping – and safely head home. But not everyone does.

Whether safety is foremost in the minds of those visiting the Park is unclear, but it certainly should be, as journalist Adam

Federman noted in his *Adirondack Life* article, "Lost." "Not long after the Adirondacks had been mapped, people were losing their way in it," Federman wrote. He revealed the park's dangers by offering the firsthand account of writer Charles Dudley Warner's trip to the region. In 1878, Warner was hiking the Adirondacks in pursuit of the bountiful fishing areas he'd heard about and ventured off the main trail to access a nearby river.

Adirondack fire towers are an example of the lofty attempts made to keep people safe while visiting the Park.

"So sure was I of my whereabouts," Warner told of his adventure, "that I did not note the bend of the river, nor look at my compass." The lone hiker was then met with darkening skies, thunder and rain. Eventually, he found his way back to the trail, but only after meandering three miles from his original starting point. The experience clearly humbled the amateur explorer and even modified his view of nature. "The rapture on the lonely shore," Warner advised future hikers, "is agreeable only when you know you can, at any moment, go home." As I journey to the wilderness where Douglas Legg disappeared, I add a postscript to Warner's statement: "...or only when you know your child will safely return home."

About 300 people get lost or injured in the Adirondack Park each year. The vast majority of them find their way, as Warner did, back to their starting point. But some do not. For instance, between 1988 and 1998, 21 people who were lost in the Adirondacks never found their way back to the trails that would lead them home. Syracuse's *Post-Standard* reported on this decade of loss, offering profiles of those unfortunate visitors to the Park. Most were adult hunters or hikers, with the exception of a few teenage boys who had joined their fathers on hunting trips. The lone child mentioned was, in fact, Douglas Legg, who was included on the list because, in 1993, yet another attempt to find an answer to his disappearance took place. Again, searchers came up empty-handed.

Considering the dangerous situations one can encounter in the wilderness, I was struggling to understand why visiting the Adirondacks is still so popular. As we pass a road sign announcing our entrance into the foothills of the Park, I ask Vince why people continue to take such risks. His response is reassuring:

"Being in the Adirondacks creates an overall wellness in me. There's the physical benefit of getting exercise, which produces endorphins; the mental satisfaction of being in nature; and the fact that when I'm concentrating on my hike, I'm very present. There's also the social aspect of going through challenges, which can be both painful and joyful, with others. When I rough it, I appreciate what I've got back home. Most of us live day after day in our modern comforts and we forget how fortunate we are to have food ready to eat, or that we can get cleaned up whenever we want. Even the flat surfaces we have to walk on – these things are not readily available in nature and I've known such gratitude for them after coming back from being in the wild."

Vince's words soften the realities of what can happen to the not-so-fortunate in the Adirondack Park, and his list of positives awaiting those who safely maneuver the area remind me of another fact I learned in my research: Much of the Park – about sixty percent of it – is privately owned. There are families who have made a home within its forest for generations, as well as vacationers who spend summers there to escape the trappings of crowded city life. This was the case for Santanoni Preserve, so named because of its proximity to the Santanoni Mountain range.

Arriving at the Preserve's gravel parking lot, we head over to a visitors center located in one of the estate's original buildings. Now maintained by the New York State Department of Environmental Conservation, the property has been designated a National Historic Landmark. A brochure on the registration table proclaims it "one of the great treasures of the region." It's a five-mile hike to the main estate area, which gives Vince and I plenty of time to discuss the brochure's history of Santanoni.

Established in the late-1800s by the family of wealthy Albany banker Robert C. Pruyn, the 13,000-acre property remained primarily pristine forests. As we hike to the main area, we are surrounded by the thick Adirondack tree cover Vince had earlier described. The road, not much wider than a hiking trail, is not open to vehicular traffic. It rises gradually in elevation, cutting a single path through a sea of green. I notice the humidity of my early morning walk has disappeared, replaced with some soft cloud cover and a steady breeze. It's a beautiful sight to behold, but I can't help noticing to my left and right all the places where someone could easily get lost.

Santanoni Preserve, the location of one of Adirondack Park's Great Camps, was once the summer home of Douglas Legg and his family.

When we reach the main estate area, I am struck by the majesty of this Great Camp. Though sorely in need of repair, the layout of the buildings is striking. We are lucky to visit Santanoni on a day when tours are being offered. In 1993, the Adirondack Architectural Heritage was formed to advocate for the estate's restoration, and each summer, it hires interns to give tours and help a local contractor restore the buildings to their original stateliness. Our intern, an architect major from William & Mary College, includes the story of Santanoni's construction as he conducts the tour.

The main estate area reflects a strong influence of Japanese design, which is, no doubt, due to the fact that a member of the Pruyn family served as an ambassador to Japan under President Lincoln. In 1953, the Preserve was purchased by brothers Myron and Crandall Melvin, prominent bankers from Syracuse whose extended family included Douglas Legg. Our tour guide makes no mention of Douglas's disappearance, and when I mention my reason for visiting the Preserve and the significance of today's date, our guide says he knows of the Legg boy's tragic demise. It does not, however, warrant a place in his tour's narrative.

The Melvin family's association with the Santanoni Preserve focused on maintaining the beauty of its natural surroundings and the architectural integrity of the Great Camp. We step into the main gathering space of the estate, its walls lined with a birch bark "wallpaper" and Japanese rice paper. I spot a large granite fireplace and recall an interview I'd conducted a few weeks prior to today's visit.

"Oh, that fireplace in the main building; you could almost stand up inside it," remembered Estella (Mahle) Harvey. Estella's father had worked as a caretaker for the Melvin family's Syracuse home and sometimes helped out during the summer when they were staying at Santanoni. Occasionally, young Estella got to go along with her dad. "The poker tables were made out of deer legs," she explained, walking me room to room with her memories. "There was a vase given to them by the Ambassador of Japan that was over four feet tall. It was a beauty."

In the late '60s, after nearly two decades of maintaining the Preserve, the Melvins expressed an interest in turning it over to New York State. Attempts were made to sell the expansive property, with the family looking to maintain rights to a 50-acre section that surrounded the estate's buildings. Though their first attempts failed, the Melvins heard about a new organization, The Nature Conservancy, a nationwide not-for-profit devoted to conserving biological diversity through land protection.

After several meetings between Conservancy officials and the Melvin family, a $1.5 million deal was in the works when Douglas Legg went missing. The immensity of their loss rapidly advanced the Melvins' closure of the land transfer, but only after the grieving family relinquished their final 50 acres. Everyone understood – how could any member of Douglas's family ever imagine returning to the Santanoni Preserve?

The estate tour ends and Vince and I head off to find the Boathouse Trail, which, according to reports I'd read about Douglas's disappearance, is where the boy was last seen. We manage near buildings and trails, but when I step a few feet into the woods, I am hopelessly disoriented.

Vince obviously has a better sense of direction and he eventually locates the estate's boathouse. Through its grimy windows, we eventually spot a few weathered canoes and rowboats; the rest of the building offers no sign of the estate's once vibrant life. We poke around outside, but find no clear trail until Vince imagines where one might have been based on new tree growth and patches of what appear be the remains of a footpath.

I follow Vince's lead and we quickly end up surrounded by towering trees. With sunlight now greatly diminished, as we venture deeper into the woods, everywhere I look offers the same shaded-green vista. For a moment, I forget that Vince is nearby and stop dead in my tracks. A shiver of fear runs through me. The word "petrified" comes to mind. Is this how it was for young

Douglas Legg, I wonder, who 45 years ago stood where I now stand?

Chapter Two

The Search for Douglas Legg

Depending on who you talk to, the circumstances of how Douglas Legg vanished from his family's estate can be strikingly different. One version of the story, often used in books and articles that recap his disappearance, begins with the boy and his uncle, Myron Melvin, heading out for an early afternoon hike. Preparing to enter the woods from the Boathouse Trail, Myron noticed that Douglas was in shorts and a T-shirt. Knowing their hike would meander through thickets and areas of overgrown poison ivy, he told his nephew to return to the estate and put on long pants and shirt. The boy headed back to change and somewhere between where his uncle waited for him and the estate's main lodge – a mere 50 or 60 yards – Douglas vanished.

When I learned of this explanation for the Legg boy's disappearance, I had a strong, immediate reaction: How could an adult send an eight-year-old off on his own? Who would assume such a young child could manage alone on an Adirondack trail? Then it hit me: Douglas Legg did not disappear in today's world, where children are never farther than a few feet from a responsible adult. He disappeared in a different era, when children felt free to explore their surroundings and adults trusted they would return home safely.

Despite the more innocent world of 1971, there are additional details from this version of Douglas's disappearance that add to its mystery. Statements by the Melvins noted that after Douglas left his uncle's immediate sight, other family members were in close proximity. His twelve-year-old brother Paul was playing on the entry road into the estate and several adults were relaxing in the lodge's spacious rooms. All were within earshot of the child. So, when Douglas did not return to his uncle, Myron assumed his nephew had changed his mind about the hike. Anxious to get on his way, he set off into the woods.

There's another version of what happened to Douglas on that July day, but you won't find any written accounts of it. Alternate stories of his disappearance were told to me by people who were part of the subsequent search or who lived in Newcomb, the closest town to the Santanoni estate. They described Douglas as a stubborn and independently-minded lad who, on that sunny afternoon, heard that his Uncle Myron was heading off for a hike. After inquiring if he could accompany his uncle, Myron sent Douglas back to the estate lodge, upsetting the boy. Angry at not being allowed to participate, instead of returning to his family, Douglas stormed off into the woods alone.

No matter what version you believe, when Myron returned from his hike by mid-afternoon, the family realized Douglas was nowhere to be found. They were concerned, but in those first moments of awareness, the Melvins weren't ready to think that one of their family could be missing. They also knew that Douglas, in many ways, defied his young age. Those who referred to him as stubborn also mentioned his confidence as a hiker, describing him as "a husky mini-woodsman" and "a thinker." With hope, his family spread out across the estate's open areas, but when repeated calls for Douglas went unanswered, they knew they needed help.

In 1971, if someone went missing in the Adirondacks – or anywhere in New York State – there was no 911 Center to call.* In the days before people automatically dialed those three numbers, the most a frantic caller might have to rely on was a brightly-colored sticker with emergency contact numbers affixed to their telephone. Even then, especially if the caller resided in a remote area like the Adirondacks, available resources were probably quite limited. At best, without an organized search and rescue team, if a person went missing near a village or town, there may have been a volunteer fire department to contact.

But were firemen equipped to handle a missing person case? What about police? Did law enforcement get involved in searches, and if so, since Douglas went missing near state-owned land, shouldn't a forest ranger be called? As precious minutes ticked away, the decision of who was the most qualified to help Douglas's family complicated their dilemma.

While confusion on who would take charge of the search for Douglas ensued, it didn't take long for word of the boy's disappearance to reach Newcomb. The hamlet of several hundred people had a single police officer – a town constable – and when he got word that the Legg boy was missing on the Santanoni Preserve, he knew the first person to call: Gary Carter. As captain of Newcomb's ambulance corps and a lifelong woodsman, it was the logical call to make. Carter knew his way around emergencies and he was well aware of the challenges of searching for a missing person in the Adirondacks, having been part of makeshift search teams since he was younger than Douglas Legg.

"When I got the call about Douglas, I was at the estate in

---

* Though the first 911 system was launched in Alabama in 1968, it wasn't until the mid-'90s that they began operating in Upstate and Northern New York.

17

twenty minutes," Gary explained. "In the first twenty days of the search, I only came out of the woods once before dark. I'd come home to sleep, but it wouldn't be until ten or eleven o'clock; one time it was 3:30 in the morning."

Gary told me his memories of the search for Douglas during our interview at his current home in Corinth, New York. The town supervisor of Newcomb had put me in contact with Gary, who welcomed my request to talk about the events he played a key role in 45 years ago. From his modern-day log cabin overlooking the Hudson River on the easternmost edge of Adirondack Park, Gary was anxious to explain how he ended up playing an important role in trying to find young Douglas. Sitting with the person who'd logged more hours on the search than anyone else, Gary Carter was the perfect person to answer my many questions about what actually happened. I knew exactly where to start.

Every newspaper article, essay and book I'd read about Douglas Legg described the search for him as highly disorganized, so I was anxious to hear how Gary remembered the scene. He answered with one word: "Chaotic." At my urging, he elaborated: "It became a big fight over who was in charge of organizing things, the state police or the sheriff. It finally boiled down to them getting the law books out and finding where it said the sheriff of the county is in charge of all search and rescue work. But then the police came back saying it might be more than a search and rescue; there might be something criminal involved. So they were constantly going back and forth."

Aside from territorial squabbling, when he'd heard a boy was lost on Santanoni Preserve, Gary knew that search organizers were going to have a major roadblock to overcome – literally. "Nobody knew the Santanoni area because it was private property," Gary explained. "The roads into the area were gated and people were not allowed to hike there as they could in much of the rest of the Adirondacks. Even the state police and troopers did not have a key to open those gates."

With the estate's 13,000 acres to cover and most people having never set foot on it, the search got off to a rough start. But that didn't stop people once they heard a little boy was missing in those woods. Word of the Santanoni emergency quickly circulated from neighbor to neighbor and a few dozen people showed up that first night to volunteer, though none had the search experience of 31-year-old Gary Carter. Before anyone else had arrived, Gary had already begun scoping out the estate's boathouse area where the boy was last seen. He was assigned a couple of guys to work with him, and as Gary noted, they were not terribly helpful:

"Douglas hadn't been gone all that long, so we searched about a mile and a half beyond the boathouse that first night. It was pitch dark as we got further out, and the two guys I had with me were scared. I knew we needed to fan out and cover more area, but they just stayed right beside me." It was well past midnight when Carter returned home without finding a clue of the boy's whereabouts.

By daylight on Sunday, July 11, according to newspaper accounts, more than one hundred people arrived anxious to help, the thought of a little boy having to spend the night alone in the woods deeply troubling all who heard the news. Volunteers checked the estate's buildings and walked up and down every trail in and around the Melvin's property. Troopers searched nearby Newcomb Lake by canoe. Gary Carter's neighbor, Frank Porter, a more skilled searcher than his helpers from the night before, volunteered to help, but when the two men got there, state police wouldn't let them on the Preserve.

" 'Nobody can go in there,' Gary recalled the authorities saying. "They told us, 'We've got dogs coming.' I knew we had to get started, but they kept us waiting until the afternoon. The police sent us to an area I knew from my search last night wasn't where the boy would have been." Summing up the search's first full day," Gary proclaimed it "a waste of time."

A youngster lost in the wilderness was big news in 1971, just as it is today. But getting word of it back then wouldn't have been instantaneous, as our superfast cyber-world now allows. It was Monday, July 12, when newspapers throughout New York State began the sad reports of Douglas Legg's disappearance. *The Palladium-Times*, the local paper of choice for many in Oswego County, including Bart Bartholomew, published its first article with this headline: "Hunt Continues For Missing Syracuse Boy." Addressing the daunting challenge ahead for searchers, a police officer familiar with Santanoni described it as "one of the most isolated areas in the state."

Also attracting media attention was the Melvin family patriarch, Crandall, Sr., who sent out a statement on behalf of Douglas's loved ones: "They'll find him. Douglas can't be far away and he is a sturdy boy accustomed to being outdoors." That night, though, temperatures starting dropping, and by early morning, they'd reached an uncomfortably-chilly 42 degrees. Those life-threatening weather conditions added to the public's concern for the boy, and volunteer numbers grew to 300.

July 13's newspapers reported that tracks made by a child had been found, though the excitement about their discovery met with some doubt. When the location of the tracks was revealed, Lake Harris, people wondered about an eight-year-old making such a trek. The good-sized body of water was five miles from Santanoni, and since the tracks were found on the opposite side of the lake, that added another mile and a half to Douglas's travels. Along the way, he would've had to traverse dense, swampy terrain, at least some of the time in near-total darkness. Could Douglas have made such a journey? Authorities in charge were betting that he could.

Bloodhounds were brought in and Gary Carter told me he worked with their dog handlers. The canines quickly picked up

Douglas's scent, followed it a mile and a half, and promptly lost it. A newspaper report mentioned one dog, aptly named for this forest search, Woody. Described as "a hound with a super-sensitive nose," Woody's specialty was old scents, and he travelled all the way from Buffalo, New York to "second-guess other bloodhounds and assist hundreds of searchers." Woody may have been successful on his other hunts, but even a powerful sense of smell couldn't bring up anything of significance in the Legg search.

Officials prepared to enter the Adirondack woods in hopes that search dogs could lead them to Douglas Legg.

Helicopters began sweeping the area that would have been feasible for a young boy to traverse in two days. Three volunteers dredged the Upper Duck Hole, a swampy pond noted for its extremely poor visibility and dangerous "quicksand-like" bottom. But land searches, which were how the majority of volunteers helped, were the most challenging; closely-growing trees and thickets of the Preserve made navigation a slow and frustrating task.

"That Santanoni Preserve is a huge piece of property," Rod Richer pointed out when he and I discussed the Legg case. I had met Rod after an event at a bookstore, where I made mention of my research for this book. He stopped by to share his memories of being on the search for Douglas and what the terrain was like: "One of the Preserve's borders is state-owned land and another is a mining company, so it's all pretty much wilderness."

Born and raised in Baldwinsville, Douglas's hometown, Rod and his father were a part of a group of volunteers from Central

New York who made the trip to the Adirondacks to offer their help. "I got lost on one of the days I was searching," Rod admitted. "A guy I was walking with suggested we take a certain turn and that was a bad move. My dad had to end up finding us, but not before *he* got lost while searching for me. It wasn't so bad walking through the hardwoods, but if you became caught up in the pine trees and got disoriented, you'd be good and lost. The branches on those pines are so low to the ground that you just couldn't keep track of which direction you were heading. I could be from me to you and not even be able to see you."

It was hard for me to imagine trying to search while moving through such dense tree cover, but Gary Carter helped by explaining how he and his search partner attacked the thickest sections they were navigating: "I would lie on top of the bushes to hold them down and Frank would step over me. Then he'd lie down and I'd go over him. We'd be yelling out in case Douglas could hear us and trying to look carefully at the areas we were covering. It would take two and a half hours to go a couple hundred feet."

When I learned that an experienced hiker like Gary was frustrated by the challenging Santanoni terrain, I wondered how the other volunteers, whose numbers had grown to nearly 500, were faring. As could be expected, those with little or no experience in Adirondack searching struggled with doing their part. In fact, as Oswego County Pioneer Search and Rescue Team member Dale Currier explained to me, many well-meaning citizens had no clue what "doing their part" meant.

"What I remember most of the Douglas Legg search was busloads and cars full of people wearing shorts and nice polo shirts," Dale said. "They were dressed for a summer resort in the Adirondacks, not for the wilderness of that area." Much like Gary Carter, Dale knows what he's talking about when it comes to the Adirondacks. Born and raised in Port Henry, New York, an hour's drive northeast of Newcomb, he'd grown up in dense woods much like the search site.

"My uncles had a hunting camp in the area where Douglas went missing and a forest ranger there was a good friend of the family," Dale continued. "When I offered to help, the ranger told me, 'Take some of these people and walk along the woods on the road, but don't lose sight of them.' He didn't want to tell these crowds they couldn't participate, but he also didn't want to have to organize another search to find missing volunteers."

Besides thick foliage, steady rain made already-limited travel more difficult. Mid-summer daytime temperatures created humid swamp conditions, turning the area into a breeding ground for mosquitoes and black flies. "I'd go home after a day's search, take a shower and the stall would be full of mosquitoes caught in my hair," Gary Carter remembered.

There was another dangerous aspect to the Santanoni Preserve that challenged searchers: bogs. People were struggling in areas around these wetland sink holes, as Dick Kaulfuss recalled. Dick was a student at the State University at Oswego when Douglas went missing, and as a member of the college's outing club and with many years of scouting during his youth, he decided to help. He travelled to Newcomb three times, and one of those times he ended up searching a bog.

"With bogs, the ground actually grows over an area of water in the form of mosses and such," explained Kaulfuss. "From time to time on that search we'd see a hole with water maybe a foot wide, but there was actually a lot more water — say six feet of it — underneath where we were standing. The ground would actually move, so we had to be very careful where we stepped."

In order to thoroughly search the bogs, volunteers were instructed to use sticks, so Kaulfuss brought ski poles from home. "We used them when we were walking along the bog and came up on one of the water holes. We'd poke around with the poles to see if something — or someone — was under all that water."

One hundred and fifty men and women from the Plattsburgh Air Force Base helped push the search numbers over a half thousand. Liverpool schoolteachers who were colleagues of

Douglas's father, several deputy sheriffs from Onondaga County, and 85 staff and students from the Syracuse School of Forestry joined in. Not everyone from the region who was troubled by the daily reports of the search could manage to make their way to the Adirondacks. A Liverpool woman donated $100 to the cause, money her family had been saving for a vacation.

As the search approached the one-week mark, hope for Douglas's safe return began to fade. Everyone knew that, while an adult can survive several weeks without food, they can't last even a week without water. But, what about a little boy, separated from his family in dangerous surroundings? Search efforts intensified, with dozens of volunteers re-inspecting roads and pathways already thoroughly searched numerous times. Some carried bullhorns, calling out "Douglas" into the silence of the forest. Alan Van Auken, president of the Newcomb Volunteer Fire Department, spoke for many when he told a newspaper reporter: "I'd go home each night and see my eight-year-old youngster and it would make me want to go back out and find this missing boy."

By the first weekend following Douglas's disappearance, volunteers numbered nearly one thousand, most of them untrained in search and rescue. When the large group became unmanageable from the makeshift headquarters at the edge of Santanoni Preserve, authorities moved their operation first to Newcomb's Town Hall, and then to the school's cafeteria. There, each new recruit was assigned a task. Some, like making meals and preparing lodging for searchers, didn't feel a lot like help for an emergency situation. But Newcomb, with one general store and no motel, was sorely unprepared to handle the onslaught of volunteers who more than doubled its population. "Food came from all over; truckloads from stores and restaurants," Gary Carter pointed out. Families opened their homes, but some still ended up sleeping on gym floors, in cars, or in tents under foreboding trees.

It wasn't just Adirondack-born volunteers who proved helpful to authorities as they tried to organize throngs of people. Also joining the search for Douglas was Hugh Parrow, an Oswego County man who wound up playing a pivotal role in the county's Pioneer Search and Rescue Team. Over the course of my research for this book, Huey and I met several times and he proved to be a wealth of search and rescue information. At each meeting, he would show up with a folder of newspaper clippings and Pioneer paperwork. As we discussed the evolution of the team, Huey would read from pages of handwritten notes he'd compiled in anticipation of our talks. He wanted me to know every detail of his involvement with the Pioneers, including how he came to participate in the Legg search.

"I'd been a sportsman since my early days growing up in Bundyville, in Oswego County," Huey explained. "I picked up a lot about the woods from my 14 years in the Boy Scouts and from my father, Hubert Parrow, who took me hunting once I turned 18. So I learned my way around the woods with map and compass. I had never done anything like the Adirondack search, but, having hunted at Tupper Lake and Osceola, I knew those woods. A buddy and I decided we wanted to help."

Even today, at 80 years old, Huey's solid build, his awareness of his surroundings, and his alert, inquisitive eyes exemplify the years he spent as a woodsman. It wasn't long before those charged with finding Douglas Legg realized the value of Huey's abilities. Assigned to volunteer under the direction of Forest Ranger Robert Bailey, Huey's group was supposed to be looking for clues in an area marked off with string.* In their naivety and

----

* Rod Richer remembered witnessing a less-orthodox technique for creating search area perimeters: "Those in charge of the search also used rolls of toilet paper to designate the area's borders."

over-enthusiasm, people kept breaking the string. "Finally," Huey told me, "Ranger Bailey got upset because he was losing time. He said, 'Is there anybody here who can follow a damn string line!' Well, I'd been watching what the ranger was trying to do and saw how important it was for the search, so I called out, 'I can.' "

Huey was quickly moved up the ranks and ended up not only helping Bailey maintain order that day, but he also ran into the ranger later that evening. The tired searchers ended up having dinner together and the forest ranger requested that Huey join his team the following day. A friendship was formed that lasted until Bailey's death in 2014, but at the time, Huey had no idea how important this new friendship would be to his future. Just a few weeks later, back in Oswego County, Huey would strike up another friendship with someone else inspired to help after Douglas Legg disappeared: Bart Bartholomew.

Helicopters were helpful when Douglas's search organizers utilized the new technology of infrared photography, which had previously proven effective on military operations. This type of aerial photography creates images of search areas, which are shown in black, with any heat-generated sources, such as a human being, noted by bright dots. This offered direction for those searching on land, but when the

"We searched places far from Santanoni," said Gary Carter, a lead searcher for Douglas Legg. "In one case, we were helicoptered to a spot 23 miles from where the boy was last seen."

dots turned up to be only warm-blooded wildlife or fires built by volunteers camping in the woods, hopes were dashed. Discouraged that even modern technology could not help, the Melvin family decided to take matters into their own hands.

On July 18, eight days into the search, 29 members of California's Sierra Madre Search and Rescue Team arrived at the Newcomb headquarters. This highly-trained group, considered by many to be the best search and rescue unit in the country, was the nearest professional resource the Melvins could find. Founded in 1952, the Southern California team had a track record of success, including a search just a year previous to Douglas's disappearance, when the west coast team spent six days hunting for a lost Boy Scout. They found him, unconscious but alive. Encouraged by this information, the Melvins eagerly paid the team's airfare to Upstate New York.

The Californians had worked in eleven western states, but this was their first search in the Northeast. "Those men didn't have a clue how to search the dense area of the Adirondacks," Rod Richer pointed out. "Their idea of how to search was to climb to the top of one of their tall hills in California and look out in all directions to find the missing person. That wasn't going to work in this part of the country."

Huey Parrow remembered hearing about the California team while he was on the Douglas Legg search, recalling that not only were they unfamiliar with eastern United States mountain terrain, but they were also unprepared for equipment failure. "In many Adirondack areas, there are heavy iron lodes," Huey said. "This was affecting their compasses and their ability to hold direction."

Gary Carter was assigned to introduce the Sierra Madre group to New York State woodland searching and recalled their team leader saying he'd never seen anything like it before. "They'd been on so many searches and never had any trouble, but the first night they were here, bears ate all their food. They ended up saying that all they could do was the same thing we were already doing: beating the brush."

When people learned that even a professional rescue team couldn't help, hopes sank to a new low. Those who'd been searching steadily for more than a week began showing signs of fatigue. A Department of Environmental Conservation officer stated what many people were beginning to think: "I've been looking for people up here for more than ten years and there's always some sort of sign: a lost sneaker, maybe, or a torn tee shirt. Here there's none. After all this time, with all these people looking, there should have been something."

As the second weekend of searching ended, maneuvers began winding down. Only 100 volunteers remained, but they were steadfast in their commitment to the search and to the belief that Douglas could still be alive. By day 15, eight square miles of Adirondack forest had been thoroughly searched. In a final effort by the Melvins, the family paid to have four German Shepherd cadaver-hunting dogs brought in from Seattle. Gary Carter was also assigned to help that group.

"They used one dog at a time, because it was tiring work for the animals," Gary said. "We started the dogs with a circle around the estate lodge, moving out another hundred feet from the lodge and making another circle, and so forth. The dogs came upon a lot of things: wallets, socks, underwear, but nothing that belonged to the boy."

As information about Douglas's fate remained a mystery, rumors started spreading. Suggestions that he had been kidnapped rose and were quickly refuted by both family and officials. Emotions were wearing thin, and finally a newspaper suggested in print what many people had been doing since day one. The Geneva Times editorial staff appealed for prayers, comparing the boy's plight to that of the Apollo 13 astronauts, whose spaceship had been seriously damaged on its way to the moon just a little over a year before Douglas's disappearance. The successful overcoming of that tragedy was still fresh in the editor's mind when he wrote: "Prayers (for the astronauts) were sent from virtually all over the world and the prayers were answered."

By Monday, July 26, closing out two full weeks of searching, the number of volunteers had dwindled down to a handful. Still, Gary Carter wasn't ready to give up, despite all he'd endured. "I went through two pair of boots during the search and ended up having to use an old pair of sneakers. I lost 28 pounds and figure I walked pretty near 700 miles." Gary stopped the interview at this point. The look on his face indicated there was more he wanted to say, but wasn't sure how to proceed. Finally – maybe deciding he could confide in me – he continued:

"The authorities even brought in a psychic from Connecticut who had been helpful in three homicide cases in her home state. The hair on the back of my neck is standing up just talking about this. I worked with her for several days and she got a sense of where the boy had been, but was unable to find him."

There was no mention of this psychic to be found in my research sources and I suspect Gary hasn't told a lot of people about this facet of the search. But it showed me how he and others did everything they could to try to find young Douglas. Even after this failed attempt, Gary continued to search whenever new leads came in, and so did a few members of law enforcement and the armed forces, who pledged to not abandon the search until all agencies involved agreed to end it. On Sunday, August 1, that decision was made. An announcement followed: "The twenty-three day search for Douglas Legg will end tonight."

Gary Carter eventually logged 40 days looking for Douglas. Fortunately, the company he worked for saw what he was doing as meaningful community service and continued to pay his wages. But I wondered how a person could keep up such exhausting work for so long. Earlier in the interview, Gary had mentioned his current involvement with his town's over-55 hockey league. Clearly, even at 76 years old, he exhibits a robustness for the kind of physical challenges he'd encountered searching 45 years ago. How about his spirit, though?

Nothing Gary said during the interview specifically addressed how he felt about never finding Douglas Legg, but he did tell me that, in 1977, six years after spending all those days and nights searching for the boy, he and some other community members formed the Newcomb Search and Rescue Team. "We went on over 100 searches in the ten years we were together and found every single missing person except two. We always found them by the next morning; sometimes even by the first night," he proudly explained.

How different that must have felt for Gary Carter compared to his 40 days of searching, during which he was unable to find a single clue of what happened to Douglas Legg.

In some ways, the search for Douglas continues today. As every ardent search and rescuer I interviewed for this book told me time and again, a search never officially ends until the person is found – alive or dead. So, 45 years later, without a trace of Douglas Legg having ever been uncovered, his whereabouts and the story of his disappearance remain, in search and rescue terms, "open."

Over the years, there's been talk of erecting a monument in the boy's memory. That never occurred, perhaps because such a structure would make his demise too set in stone. Some people prefer to talk about Douglas as if he may still be among us. But especially for search and rescuers, an unsolved case such as Douglas Legg's plays over and over in their mind. People from Newcomb, his hometown of Baldwinsville, or wherever his disappearance impacted a community, still talk about what may have happened to the boy.

"It's a mystery," Rod Richer declared. "The dogs they had tracking his scent should have found him, but they didn't. They had the heat sensor airplanes flying over the area he would have been able to walk and they should have detected him. I think he may have fallen into some sort of swampy bog..."

Others familiar with the Santanoni bogs agree that this is

where Douglas met his demise. According to Estella (Mahle) Harvey, her father was among those believers. "Dad worked alongside the Preserve's caretaker Art Tummings, and both of those men always had a gut feeling about what happened to Douglas. They said that he had been upset about something, stormed off and got himself into a bog. Those bogs will swallow up things as big as a horse or a wagon, so why not a little boy?"

George Cannon, the Newcomb town supervisor who got me in touch with Gary Carter, has witnessed the resiliency of the Legg legacy. George always has his finger on the pulse of the people he serves and he shared this fact of the continued interest in Douglas Legg: "Every now and then – it's happened ten or twelve times since he disappeared – somebody will find a bone in those woods. It turns out to be animal bones, but it gets everyone excited. There'll be police cars and people checking to see if it might be from Douglas, but there's never ever been any sign of that boy."

One of the most credible tips in the aftermath of the search for Douglas occurred in 1973, when a man who was on leave from the Navy went hunting on the Santanoni Preserve. After chasing a deer across a peninsula leading to a 21-acre island in Newcomb Lake, he stumbled upon a small skull and partial skeleton, which he believed to be human. He told a hunting buddy about his find, but because he was worried about returning on time from his four-day Navy leave, he never reported it to the police.

In 1993, when a story about the renewed search for Douglas hit television and newspapers, the hunter called police to report his discovery from 20 years previous. Police had the man, now living in Montana, accompany them to the island, but after two decades, he could only give a general location of where he had hunted. Authorities searched the most likely area, a 50 x 50-yard section about a half mile from the Santanoni estate, but this failed to turn up Douglas Legg's remains, which authorities believed would have been tobacco-colored and buried under inches of sediment and moss.

Just like everyone who has lived in that part of the

Adirondacks, George Cannon is well aware of how easy it is to get lost in its harsh environment. "But still," he expressed, "it seems like somebody would have found a shirt or even a button. There were lots of rumors that he got picked up by a group of hippies and taken away. But nobody really knows."

Others who were on that search or who were following it are reluctant to have their opinions on what happened to Douglas included in this book. It's a sensitive subject for the Melvin/Legg family, and my requests to speak with Douglas's relatives were politely denied. I understood the family's reluctance to speak with me when I came across a 1981 article in Syracuse's *Herald-American* that quoted Mrs. Legg ten years after her son's disappearance: "There is absolutely nothing new to say about it. The family has persevered, and yet, we think of him every day." From Douglas's family to the extended family of those unable to let his memory fade, no one has figured out a proper way to find peace amid this tragedy...

Well, nobody but Bart Bartholomew, who never managed to get up to the Adirondacks during the three weeks of chaotic searching for Douglas. Bart was busy with his work and family back in Fulton, but each July day that passed without any success reported from Newcomb drew the boy's plight closer to him. The July 20 issue of *The Palladium-Times* stirred Bart's heart with an article quoting SUNY Oswego Professor Paul Wilbur, who'd spent three days on the search: "There is a crying need for volunteers and funds in the efforts to find the boy."

That emotional plea did not sit idly on the newspaper page for Bart; it lit up like a fire. The time had come to act: Something had to be done in the name of Douglas Legg.

Chapter Three

It Started With a Backyard Meeting

"If Bart saw a need, he wanted to be part of solving it," Barbara Bartholomew explained when I asked about her husband's motivation to found the Pioneers. I had gotten to know Barbara during the Fulton Library's memoir project when she submitted an essay about the search team. From her Florida home, through the wonders of the internet, she and I carried on an email conversation about Bart's commitment to forming the team.

"Starting the Pioneers was very typical of my husband," Barbara said. "The more he read and heard about the loss of little Douglas Legg and the failed efforts to find him, the more he thought about the need for professionally trained and qualified searchers."

Bart had plenty to reflect on in the days and weeks following Douglas's disappearance. Though he certainly wasn't the only person hanging on to every word about Douglas's fate, as Barbara pointed out, his reaction to the news was anything but typical:

"Once Bart made his mind up," she said, "he acted on it. The early '70s was a period of unrest in our country, with national events such as the Vietnam War and Kent State. We had already hosted at our home a very diverse group from SUNY Oswego and Syracuse who were pro and con on the war. We felt it was time to bring reconciliation, so we held the meetings. My focus was on that issue, while Bart was focused on getting a rescue team started. He wanted to see if others felt the same."

It wouldn't take long for Bart to get his answer. Before the Douglas Legg search was officially suspended by Newcomb officials, Bart had placed a brief press release in Fulton and

Oswego newspapers announcing a meeting at his home. Writing newspaper copy wasn't something Bart normally did, but fortunately, it was for Barbara: "From early 1970 until late 1976, I worked for *The Palladium-Times*. So, I gave the team a kick-start by writing that article." Barbara would lend her writing skills to the Pioneers throughout their recruitment and formation phases, and her first press release gave a voice to Bart's plans. The article hit papers on July 22, just twelve days after Douglas's disappearance. Its headline optimistically predicted: "Group Starts to Form Land (Search) and Rescue Team," with the future team leader clearly articulating his proposal:

> FULTON – Efforts are underway to form a volunteer search and rescue team in the Oswego County area, according to Robert Bartholomew, acting coordinator.
>
> Noting that he has been contemplating such an idea since hunting season last fall, Bartholomew states that the loss of the Baldwinsville youth in the heart of the Adirondack Mountains prompted him to pursue the idea further.
>
> Pointing out that the team's primary responsibility will be geared to land search and rescue in the event of emergencies such as lost children or hunters, he said the team would also be equipped to assist in the event animals are reported in trouble, such as deer marooned on ice floes on waterways.
>
> The group will work closely with all other rescue groups such as the U.S. Coast Guard, State Police, Sheriff's Department, Civil Air Patrol, city and

village police and fire departments, and rescue teams.

If sufficient interest is shown in developing this team, a training program will be implemented. "We are looking for 18 years or older males to get this team underway. Needed are persons with background experience as woodsmen. Desired skills would include first aid, map and compass, hiking, survival training and forms of rescue training," Bartholomew explained.

The article ended with a notification about the first meeting's location, Bartholomew's home, and date. People didn't have much time to ponder Bart's invitation, though; the press release hit his hometown paper the day of the proposed meeting. But he needn't have worried if anyone would heed his call. As the summer sun burned off into the cooler July evening, a group of people began congregating in the backyard of the Bartholomew house.

"We lived on 16 Whitaker Road," Bart's son Richard explained. "Our home was still in the city limits of Fulton, but as kids we spent most of our time in the woods not far from us." I spoke with Richard, who currently resides in Texas, by telephone after Barbara suggested I talk with the Bartholomew children regarding their dad's search and rescue work. I was fortunate that Richard, the third of the four Bartholomew boys, had clear memories of the 1971 meeting, when he was twelve years old.

"I was in our basement," Richard admitted, "because I didn't think I should be a part of this group of adults." Still, from a cellar window, Richard had a good view of the backyard as the meeting began: "Dad had a fire in the pit he'd made. Near that, under two apples trees we'd planted, was our picnic table."

Taking a seat at that table was 31-year-old Huey Parrow, the Bundyville man who had been on the Douglas Legg search where he befriended a North Country forest ranger. "I'd read about

Bart's call to discuss a search and rescue team, so I went to meet him," Huey said. "There was also a group of people who rode horses, a snowmobile club, members of the local sportsman club, a retired newspaper reporter from Syracuse and a few other woodsmen from around town."

Another of the 15 or so people gathered in the backyard was Steve Ives, from the town of Volney. Ives had also read Bart's press release, and as an outdoorsman, he was interested. Steve was young, just 24 years old, and he'd never attended that type of meeting, but as he found a seat and waited for the discussion to start, he noticed something he could relate to. "Bart had a canoe hanging up on the back of his house," Steve recalled during our first of many interviews about the Pioneers. After seeing the canoe, Steve settled back, remaining quiet through most of the meeting, keenly listening.

Barbara Bartholomew was home that night, and as the only woman at the first gathering, she admitted to being in attendance because it took place at her home. "I was probably serving cookies and coffee and staying in the background," she told me, but she also clearly recalled the conversations: "They were hunters who knew the woods and they were so enthusiastic. Some, including Huey Parrow, had firsthand stories of the confusion and chaos during the Legg boy's search and there was sincere motivation to respond constructively to the need for qualified, trained people in search and rescue."

From his cellar location, Richard Bartholomew listened to the voices rising from his backyard: "People were all talking at the same time and it was very confusing. They were saying something had to be done; they had to form some sort of team that could go in and work with law enforcement, Civil Defense and Red Cross. They knew they needed to work as a unit and function like the west coast rescue team for Douglas Legg. And they knew they needed to be trained. Finally, Dad got everyone quiet."

Steve Ives described what he experienced while listening as Bart addressed the group: "He presented what I was feeling.

Before he even said a word, you could see it on his face and in his body language. As Bart described what he thought should happen, he would almost tear up. He said, 'I don't know what we are going to do about this, guys, but this can't happen again. I don't know how you feel, but this is how I feel and that's why I put that notice in the papers.' One by one, each of the people gathered in that circle said, 'I know what you're talking about.' "

Bart's commitment struck a chord in Steve. Newly-married and anxious to take on responsibilities like he'd seen his parents do, he'd been looking for a way to volunteer for his community. While listening to Bart, something clicked for him. "At that point, I said to myself, this is what I'm supposed to be doing. This is what I want to put my efforts into." Steve wasn't alone. One by one, the other men in the circle began to speak their mind.

One of the key points the group heard was something Bart would repeat many times at future meetings and in press releases: "Why should anyone have to pay thousands of dollars to find a lost child?" Bart was referring to the Sierra Madre team flown in from California by Douglas Legg's family. Rumors about what the family had paid for the west coast team had stirred a lot of locals into agreeing they needed a search and rescue unit in New York. The men in Bart's backyard echoed that belief. "They pledged that they would be volunteers," Barbara said, "and they named themselves "The Pioneers," and that they were!"

Though silent through most of that first gathering, Steve Ives had plenty to say during our interview about what resulted from it: "We pledged from that point on that no one in New York State would ever have to find themselves in the situation the Legg family had been in, which has to be one of the worst feelings in the world. To think your child is missing – all the things going through your mind that come like a rush: *My child is lost.' 'What happened to them?' 'How can I find them?'* At such times, you need a highly-trained professional rescue team. We all said people would never have to feel there was no one to help them.

"We admitted that we really didn't know what we could do

37

differently than those who were on the Legg search. Bart said he'd checked around and found nothing related to search and rescue in New York State, and back then there were no computers to research it. But I do remember as we got up to leave, Bart saying to us all, 'We're not only going to form a search and rescue team, but we're going to form the *best* search and rescue team that ever was.' "

Bart, Huey, Steve and several others in the group committed to meet weekly, and a date was selected to begin the daunting process of creating a search and rescue team from scratch. As his backyard emptied, one can only wonder what was going on in Bart's mind. Without a preexisting team to look to for guidance or any step-by-step instructions on how to form such a team, who knew where to start?

As evening settled in, I can imagine that Bartholomew pondered those concerns. Stirring the embers in the fire pit, watching the sparks fly and burn away, he must have been replaying the events that had just transpired. Yes, it was clear he would need to be a strong leader for the Pioneers, but he was also assured of one thing: Bart Bartholomew would not be forming a search and rescue team on his own.

Chapter Four

What's It Take to Be a Pioneer?

The founding Pioneers at a celebration of the team's tenth anniversary. Kneeling, l to r: George McCulloch, Huey Parrow. Standing, l to r: Steve Ives, George Blount, Norm Hayden, John Knaizuk, Robert Halstead, John LaMay, Ralph Larkin, Bart Bartholomew.

On July 29, one week after the gathering at Bart Bartholomew's home, the Oswego County Pioneer Land Search and Rescue Team held their first official meeting. Some of the group that had shown up at Bart's chose not to continue on, such as "the horseback riders, who decided it wasn't for them," Huey Parrow said. "But most of us stayed together." A few new volunteers joined after hearing about the group's plans and the inaugural team of Pioneers was ready to move forward. The team roster changed as time went on, but during its formative years, there was a core group of men and women who remained committed to the Pioneers' goals.

When I first learned that only a few of the original Pioneers knew each other prior to the group forming, I thought it commendable how they quickly created such a strong bond. Ranging in age from their early twenties to mid-sixties, the members of this new team were at different stages of their careers and family obligations. And while most of them had already spent time volunteering, their chosen organizations greatly varied. In fact, other than enjoying time outdoors, there wasn't much about this group that would suggest they could function as a team. Soon, though, each Pioneer founder stepped forward with an attribute that would serve their search and rescue goals.

Compiled from interviews with original Pioneers, their family and friends; a review of scrapbooks covering the team's 45-year history; and newspaper reports and other archives regarding their searches, the following "mini-biographies" offer a glimpse into what made each founding member a true Pioneer.

Bart Bartholomew

"Dad was a sponge; he learned from everything around him," said Richard Bartholomew when I asked him to describe his father. "He shared his love of the outdoors with us: we camped, hiked, biked, canoed, hunted and fished. We learned about wild plants and vegetation you could eat, things like staghorn sumac, cattail roots and wild garlic. That's how Dad showed us his love; he did it by training us kids."

Hearing about Bart's knowledge of the outdoors and the ease with which he shared it, I assumed he must have grown up in a supportive environment, filled with recreational and social activities. But that wasn't the case, his wife Barbara explained: "Bart came from a very deprived family. As a Depression-era kid, he and his five siblings had moved many times all over Central New York and Pennsylvania in order for their father to find work. At 13 years old, finally settled into his family's first decent house, Bart and his twin brother Richard were profoundly affected when they were playing catch with their father and he suddenly dropped dead of a massive heart attack.

"After their father's death, the boys overheard talk by their mother of sending them to Boys Town in Nebraska. So they ran away, and by hopping train cars and walking, got all the way into Pennsylvania. Eventually, they were found and returned home, and then split up. Bart went with an aunt and uncle for three years and Richard ended up in the town of Sterling living with a chicken farmer family. Bart never graduated from high school, opting to go into the Army and serving three and a half years. He was granted early discharge when his mother took ill and returned to Fulton to care for her."

Bart found work as a millwright, met and married Barbara, and began making a better life for himself and his family. Whenever he wanted to learn something, he attended classes and read what he could on the subject. This was not only true of his work, but also of family activities and community volunteerism. "In the '60s," Barbara continued, "folks in our church talked about helping to build the first YMCA in Fulton. They'd chosen a church building on Oneida Street which had suffered from a bad fire and Bart was involved with the major and much-needed reconstruction, such as refinishing floors for what would be the Y's first gym. He then became its very first volunteer physical education director. In the 1970s, he started the Y's 'Wise Owls' Runner's Club, and later, a new group for cross-country skiing."

When Bart organized a "Sixth Ward Self-Help and

Improvement Project," which focused on cleaning up his neighborhood, its success caught the attention of the city of Fulton's mayor, Percy Pat-trick. Patrick appointed Bart to head the city's first Civil Defense Department, which would prove an important resource when the Pioneers first formed. Civil Defense, a national organization offering civilian support during World Wars I and II, shifted its focus in the 1960s to offering emergency aid following natural and manmade disasters. Again noting

Fulton's mayor, Percy Patrick (left), and Bart Bartholomew, circa 1972.

Bart's work in this position, Mayor Patrick asked him to fill the role of alderman when a vacancy occurred. In the next election cycle, he was defeated, but around that time Douglas Legg disappeared, and at age 40, he shifted his attention to search and rescue.

Bart's dedication to community service paved the way to his founding the Pioneers. Over the years, he exhibited attributes that proved his ability to lead, among them the welcoming way he promoted causes he believed in. Wayne Dealing, an early Pioneer member who spoke with me about the group, offered this memory of Bart: "He was always inspirational in the way he talked up the team, always getting their name out there. Wherever he went, he wore his search and rescue shirt with its patches."

Fred Seward, a coworker of Bart's at Miller Brewery, shared this story of how Bartholomew advocated for good health whenever he saw the opportunity: "My wife and I bought snowshoes when we moved to Fulton to give us something to do during the long winters. We didn't really know how to use them, so Bart offered to show us. We snowshoed the wooded area behind his house, and after walking a while, my wife's feet got really cold. She wasn't sure she could continue. Bart said, 'No need to turn back. I'll make a fire and we can warm up.' I didn't know how we were going to start a fire in the middle of nowhere, but Bart collected downed branches and tree limbs, laid them atop the snow and made a fire. We cozied up to it, got warm and then continued our hike."

I learned one more aspect of Bart's character, this one exemplifying his ability to overcome difficult challenges as well as expanding his example of leadership. In 1976, when diagnosed with early onset diabetes, Bart took a decidedly positive route to controlling it: he became a runner. Jim Crombach, who met Bart after joining the Pioneers in 1973, explained how the team's leader discovered he had diabetes and then chose a proactive way to deal with it: "Bart had gone fishing, and after he'd parked his truck, he wandered off through the woods to spend the day on a trout stream. While walking back to his truck, he went into a diabetic coma which left him on the ground for hours.

"Bart eventually came to, was able to get his feet under him and returned to his truck. He used his citizen's band ("CB") radio, which all the team members kept in their vehicles, to call for help. When his doctor automatically put him on insulin, Bart informed him, 'I'll be off this medicine in a year.' And sure enough, he was. He decided he'd become a runner, even though he'd never run a step before that incident. As soon as he could, he walked a block. Then he'd walk a block and run a block, and in a year's time, Bart was completely off insulin. That's the kind of man he was."

Bartholomew stayed involved with the Pioneers for about ten years. Once he felt the team was on solid ground with reliable leadership, he stepped down, staying involved in a lesser role. He found new ways to contribute to his community, but he also took time for hobbies, including judo classes. He even performed as a clown. "In 1978, Bart learned about a group in Fulton that was into clowning," Barbara said. "He studied it for years, and after attending a week of schooling at a clown camp, he named himself HoHo the Hobo. HoHo entertained at children's birthday parties and community events."

In 1981, at age fifty, Bart, his son John and a friend, Dave Dayger, took a 500-mile bicycle trip into the Adirondacks, continuing his commitment to good health, adventure and fellowship. After his career at Miller's Brewery ended, Bart combined his work ethic and passion for the outdoors by opening the Sea-way Trail Bicycle and Canoe Center in Wolcott, New York. By this time, he and Barbara had moved to Fair Haven, and when he wasn't working at the bike shop, he was planning an outdoor event, volunteering at the local fire department or the newly-forming Sterling Nature Center; in short, helping wherever he saw the need, no matter how big or small.

When the Bartholomews had enough of Upstate New York weather, they moved to Florida. Bart passed away April 20, 2014, and that summer, a memorial service was held for him in Fulton. "It was very special for me that several of the original Pioneer team came to his service," Barbara shared. "He came from a troubled family and was determined to make a better life, which motivated him to make something of himself, not only for his family, but for all that needed it, including the search and rescue team."

"Dad was in his element when he was teaching," Richard said, "especially with the rescue team. He could pull things out of nothing and make it something, like the everyday citizens he made into this incredible group of Pioneers. He was very proud of them, right until he passed away."

As proud as his family is of Bart, he himself never spoke of the Pioneers as *his* accomplishment. To him, it was a team effort, and how it formed and progressed is a testimony to each member. But it takes a leader with strong values to inspire others, and something I read about how Bart overcame diabetes illustrates that. Though he was explaining to a newspaper reporter his motivation for running road races, his comment also shows why, in my opinion, Bart Bartholomew was the right person to form and lead the Pioneer team: "I never won a race and probably never will. But when I was lying there in that hospital bed, I could have been dead. I was a loser then. Now, as long as I finish a race feeling good, I know I've won."

Hugh Parrow

As I compiled information about the founding Pioneers' childhoods, it didn't surprise me that most of them had grown up close to nature. This would have been more than likely for anyone raised in rural Oswego County several decades ago. Before television and electronics constituted the play worlds of today's youth, having fun meant being outdoors. If they weren't in school or performing daily chores, yesterday's children were learning about their world through natural settings. They were having fun, but for future Pioneers like Huey Parrow, their enjoyment would lead them to the work of saving lives.

Huey attributes his search and rescue skills to early woodsmen experiences like the Boy Scouts and hunting, and when he became responsible for training Pioneer volunteers, he included in his teaching some unconventional but valuable lessons, like this story from his early hunting days: "One of my father's friends had been in the Battle of the Bulge and I came up behind him once when he was unaware of me. I startled him and he turned on me with his gun pointed. He said, 'Don't ever do anything like that again.' Years later, the Pioneers went on several searches for lost hunters and we'd come upon some who'd been lost for several hours. These people were in shock and disoriented and still carrying their guns. We had to be very methodical on how we approached them."

This attention to the outdoors and survival skills was engrained in Huey, and they influenced the choices he made as an adult, including marriage. It's no surprise that Huey's wife, Barbara Jean (Jeannie), who grew up in Minetto, the next town over from where her future husband was raised, described her childhood this way: "I was always a tomboy. My grandfather was a hunter and I spent a lot of time with him. I always got involved with outdoor activities, including some that girls didn't normally do. Then I met Huey, and as we raised our family, we ended up spending a lot of time in the woods. He was the person who taught me map and compass."

With Huey's work at Crucible Steel and as a truck driver for the Teamsters, and Jeannie driving school bus and raising their family of three, neither had a lot of time for individual outdoor interests. But, whenever they found free time, they spent it in nature environments with their children, and as their son Hugh, Jr. remembered, there was always an element of learning:

"Our family was very involved in camping, hiking and hunting. When we'd go on a hunt, along with basic safety skills, we were taught how to use map and compass. We'd take a reading before

46

we went into the woods so we would always have a start point and be able to get back to our cabin. We also learned first aid, how to treat shock and other emergency skills. Dad taught those same skills for our Minetto Boy Scout troop, as well as how to work together and organize a large group of people. These were all part of scouting, and teaching and organizing them were things Dad naturally did. They easily transferred to the search and rescue team.

"Dad was a big part of the team being prepared for whatever the missing person situation was. Those early Pioneers never knew what they were facing when a call came. Was it a young person? An older person with dementia? Dad knew how to react in all those situations and how different seasons influenced rescue plans. As one of the founders, he shared all this with the group."

In Bart Bartholomew, the Pioneers had a leader; in Huey Parrow, they had a teacher. Several people who served on the Pioneers with him acknowledged the important role he played on the team. Steve Ives remembers that "Huey's map and compass was so important. Even though he wasn't trained to be an instructor, he did so when he needed to be."

Steve's son Derek, who became a part of the team as a teenager, saw Huey as a real role model: "He took me under his wing with his amazing skills. Huey could look at a map once, walk ten miles into the area the map covered and tell you exactly where every ridge was going to come up."

Huey Parrow, top right, discussing a search plan with New York State Police and other volunteers.

Huey's help while I researched this book affirmed what Derek told me about his role model's excellent memory. Huey has phenomenal recall of the many search details he dealt with, some over forty years ago. I once asked him for the date of a search the team had done in Pennsylvania. "I believe it was May 1985," he suggested, "but check the records." After digging through the files, I found the information I was looking for. The actual date: June 1985. After a 31-year lapse, Huey was off by a month.

Jim Crombach, an early Pioneer from Phoenix, described how many who trained under Huey saw him: "He was a jolly, likeable character, but he knew his stuff and there was never any question that he understood what was going on. He was a field officer for the team and when it came time for a search to set up, he was in charge. To use an example from the workplace, Huey was like the general officer on the floor."

Howard and Burnetta Bennett joined the Pioneers in the early 1990s, nearly two decades after Huey first began training the scores of people who ended up volunteering for the team. When I first ran across Burnetta's unusual first name in the Pioneers' archives, I was pretty sure she was someone I'd met years earlier in a writing class. A quick email to her confirmed she was. I scheduled a late-morning phone interview with Burnetta and her husband Howard after he'd finished his shift as an Oswego County sheriff. They traded memories of their time with the Pioneers, including those of Huey.

"When I joined the team," Howard explained, "Huey was the first person to show me how to use map and compass to get an idea of direction." "I had no sense of direction whatsoever," Burnetta added, "but when I learned how to use a map from Huey, it just opened up the world to me."

Somewhere in the mid-1990s, Huey and Jeannie stepped down from their leadership positions with the Pioneers, joining searches and trainings when possible. Over the years, Huey has continued to utilize his abilities with memory and detail, developing them in the field of genealogy. "I've found 3,500 people in my family tree," Huey proudly shared.

I was impressed with such an accomplishment, but initially I failed to notice the connection between Huey's family history and search and rescue. Eventually, it made sense. Mapping family history takes patience as a person digs through the facts for clues, following the trail each lead offers them, much like how the search for a lost person is conducted.

I also became the beneficiary of Huey's sharp genealogy skills. Once he knew I was attempting to track down all the original Pioneers, he took the lead on finding a few who had long ago left Oswego County. Huey kept hitting roadblocks and after several attempts on trying to locate one particular team member, I was ready to give up. But I'm not the Pioneer Huey Parrow is. He persisted until he eventually found his man, Chuck Blount.

Chuck Blount

Chuck Blount brought years of experience with both summer residential camps and year-round family camping to the Pioneers. Thirty-seven years old when the team formed, Chuck had already spent three decades learning to navigate some of the Adirondack's most primitive areas. At five years of age, he began attending a children's camp in the Adirondack Park, but it wasn't the type of summer camp many of us remember from our youth. Chuck's camp was set in a wilderness environment, one which could only be accessed by boat, offered no indoor plumbing or electricity, and taught survival skills through real-life experiences.

"The camp was called Tanager Lodge, and it was located on Upper Chateaugay Lake," Chuck explained as we begin our phone interview. I was only able to speak with Chuck after Huey Parrow tracked him down at an assisted living complex in Colorado. Happy to talk about the camp that helped shape his childhood and led to his involvement with the Pioneers, Chuck credited his positive experiences at Tanager to a man named Fay Welch, who he described as "an experienced naturalist and college professor."

Indeed, when I researched Tanager Lodge and Mr. Welch, I learned how important this man was to the early 20th century movement devoted to conserving wilderness. Desiring to share the wonders of nature with children, Welch developed a program that immersed youngsters in wilderness areas to help them develop survival skills. Tanager Lodge became the setting for achieving his goal and Chuck Blount was one of his most devoted campers.

Since he was born and raised in the northern Oswego County town of Lacona, I was curious how Chuck's family would have known about an Adirondack wilderness camp 20 miles from the Canadian border. He explained that his father, Floyd Blount, and Welch met at the Syracuse School of Forestry and became close friends. While Welch's college education led him to nature conservation and camping, Floyd ended up in the lumber industry as part of his hometown's Blount Lumber Company. As a recreational hunter and volunteer with his local Boy Scout troop, Floyd wanted his children to experience the same love of the outdoors he'd enjoyed. Remembering the friendship he'd formed with Welch, he inquired about his children attending Tanager Lodge.

"I went to Tanager for nine summers," Chuck explained. "The co-ed camp was a seven-week-long program. We lived in tents, took hiking trips all the time, and it was at the camp where I learned how to use map and compass."

When Chuck reached adulthood, he worked for his father's lumber company, "sometimes in the saw mill, cutting logs for flooring, and sometimes working in the department that made windows and doors." But young Blount wasn't ready to let go of his childhood camping roots, and for twelve summers he returned to Tanager Lodge to teach children how to manage in the wild. Chuck's strong dedication to the camp's preservation ideals led him to become the head staff person under the camp's founder.

After starting a family, the responsibilities of adulthood forced

Chuck to give up his summers at Tanager. He took up employment in the insurance business, working many years as an agent in the Northwestern Mutual Life Insurance Company's Pulaski office. During his leisure time, though, he found a way to return to the woods.

"We often went backpacking in the Adirondacks during the summer," Chuck's daughter, Karen Blount, said of her childhood. "Dad was an Adirondack high peak 46er and he climbed most of those peaks many times. We did many with him." Sounding a great deal like the other children of Pioneers I'd talk to, Karen added, "Dad also taught us all to use a compass, read a map and basic survival skills."

The Blount children got to use those skills during their many camping trips throughout the year. "My parents purchased a tent camper and we travelled around the country in it. We also had a cabin on Raquette Lake which had no road access or electricity. We used a rowboat to get across the lake to our cabin in the summer months and hiked across the iced-over lake in the winter. After school on Friday, we'd head there, arriving after dark. It would often be below zero inside and we each had our jobs: chopping the ice, hauling water up the hill into camp and getting the stove started. We would get up early Saturday morning to make the hike out, drive an hour to Tupper Lake and ski all day. Sundays were the same and then we headed home. This was our winter for years until I went away to college."

Karen sees her father's involvement with the newly-forming search and rescue team in Oswego County as an extension of his love of the outdoors and commitment to teaching wilderness survival skills. That was confirmed when I came across the application Chuck submitted for acceptance into the Pioneers, which along with information about Tanager and the family's camping, also listed his other areas of interest: canoeing, deer hunting and three years as a volunteer fireman. It seemed like a natural fit for Chuck to become a founding Pioneer.

During our phone conversation, Chuck confided in me that he

is showing signs of early onset Alzheimer's, explaining how this has stolen most of his search and rescue memories. But as articles and photos in scrapbooks note, he served a prominent role as the group took shape. At one point, when the Pioneers' number of volunteers grew so big it had to split into two groups, Chuck coordinated the northern Oswego County section. The separate meetings covered business concerns, but the two divisions continued to function as one for trainings. Wayne Dealing, who was invited to join the Pioneers through his acquaintance with Chuck, remembered observing him leading exercises in survival training.

Charles Blount

Though Chuck doesn't recall specific search details or the names of those he served alongside, he clearly remembers what being part of the Pioneers meant and means to him now: "I look back on being a Pioneer with pride. I went on many of the searches and we were able to find a lot of people. When we found someone alive, it was a joy; we were accomplishing something."

Norm Hayden

Strong ties between Oswego County Search and Rescue and the Boy Scouts of America kept showing up in my research of the founding Pioneers' childhoods, which wasn't a big surprise. The link between Scouts and the search team makes sense since both organizations are dedicated to helping people find their way in the outdoors and coming to their rescue if they don't. While I learned that many of the founding Pioneers could trace their wilderness knowhow back to the Boy Scouts, I see the strongest connection between the two groups in team member Norm Hayden.

Norm, a lifelong Fultonian, passed away in 1996, making my research about his Pioneer work challenging. I started with a review of his obituary, which mentioned his involvement with the Boy Scouts, but not in great detail. Fortunately, the Scouts are a close-knit organization, and after mentioning his name to several active troop leaders, I found my way to Earl Lockwood, who served a forty-year term as committee chairman for Troop 761, the Mt. Pleasant troop Norm was involved with. Earl filled in some details about Norm's work and family:

"After serving in the Army's security division, Norm went to work as a purchasing agent for RPM, a papermaking company. He held a second job at Cortini's Shoe Repair, working behind the scenes as a bookkeeper. Norm was also a devoted husband and father to three boys. When they got to be the right age, somewhere in the mid-'60s, Norm's sons joined Troop 761. Soon, he started volunteering on our committee and became a scoutmaster. Over the years, I met a lot of men who were great leaders for the boys, and Norm was one of the best."

Troop 761 was involved with a lot of character-building activities and Norm's contributions would shine when the boys hit the woods. "Our troop often camped in the Adirondacks and other remote places," Earl explained. "Norm was always involved in these and he got to know the wilderness areas really well. Aside from the Scouts, he also took groups of people on the trails in the Adirondacks on his own. If somebody wanted to go on a hike, Norm was glad to lead them."

Earl's description of Norm's personality offered a glimpse of what some of his search and rescue teammates also said about him. "He was the type who, on the first night of a campout, always had a ghost story to tell the boys," Earl continued. "No matter where we were camping, he'd have a story to fit that particular spot. He'd have those kids spellbound with his antics and lessons about the wilderness. Yeah, Norm had something going all the time."

Other Scout leaders agreed. "Norm was about the greatest guy you would ever want to meet," said Dave Rath, who served as his assistant scoutmaster for many years. "He taught me more about scouting than I could ever have learned by myself. He was easy to work with, never getting excited about any situation."

Norm Hayden, left, at a Boy Scout fundraising event.

The same devotion to nature was seen by his family. "Dad was involved with anything outdoorsy," remarked Norm's youngest son Gary. "When he was younger, he was involved in an incident that really made a lasting impression on him. He'd gone hiking with another man in the Adirondacks, and the man had a heart attack and died in the woods. It prompted Dad to learn CPR and then he started teaching it to others. He taught that and first aid for our Scout troop and many of us earned our badges from his classes."

By the time the idea to form a search and rescue team came along, Norm, then age 36, had much to offer the Pioneers. His certification as a Red Cross first-aid instructor helped all the

Pioneers train for emergency medical situations. He'd also become a member of the Brandybrook Sportsman Club, a recreational hunting organization located in the heart of Tug Hill. The 1,700-acre property bordered another 4,500 acres of public land, giving Norm and the other hunters plenty of opportunities to familiarize themselves with woodland environments.

Actually, Hayden didn't have to look farther than his own backyard for wilderness experiences. "Norm's farm on Whitaker Road had been in his wife's family," Earl Lockwood explained. "At one time, it was a working farm with cows, pigs and all, but by the time Norm took it over, it was just the property and a few buildings. It was set on wooded land and dense forest areas, and the Scouts held a lot of their campouts and outdoor living skills exercises there."

Norm's property also served the Pioneers, who found it a perfect setting for practicing rescue techniques. Trainings at his home came with a sweet bonus for those braving its primitive setting, since the Haydens also produced maple syrup on their property. Using an old bus he'd converted into a sap-boiling "shed," Norm went into business, which Gary still operates today. Surely, some of that syrup found its way to the many pancake breakfasts the Scouts held to raise money. And the sap continued flowing into Norm's search and rescue years, when many social get-togethers were held at the Hayden farmhouse. Pioneer Deana Ives still delights in her memories of the tasty maple syrup, and fellow teammate Jim Crombach mentioned how the pancake breakfasts "gave our group a real sense of comradery."

At age 61, Norm passed away. "He'd had health problems," said his longtime friend Earl Lockwood, who saw those problems begin to interfere with his scouting obligations. "Once, when we were camping with the troop out back of his house, Norm took ill and had some kind of seizure. Though physically very sick, he made his way up to the house to find his wife. He later showed me the path he took and I don't know how the hell he got through it, it was so dense. Soon after, he said to me, 'Earl, I'm resigning as scoutmaster. I don't want the kids to see me like that again.' "

Earl told me one final story about Norm, one that speaks of his deep commitment to the Boy Scouts and, to me, illustrates the years of service he devoted to search and rescue: "When Norm passed away, I got a call from Dave Rath who asked if it was okay to put a Boy Scout neckerchief in Norm's casket."

It was a fitting testimony to Norm Hayden, a Pioneer who dedicated himself to the outdoors, and who shared its joys with all who wanted to join in, always assuring their safety along the way.

Ralph Larkin

Deciding to volunteer as a search and rescue team member would have been a logical step for town of Mexico resident Ralph Larkin. Thirty-two years old when the group first formed, Ralph had already logged thousands of volunteer hours for his community by the time he joined the Pioneers. When he wasn't working in the receiving department at Nestlé, Ralph helped a number of organizations, which his application to join the Pioneers showed. One that proved to be invaluable in the team's development was Oswego County REACT.

REACT, Radio Emergency Associated Communications Team, began in the early 1960s as an all-volunteer association which monitored Channel 9, radio's citizen band's emergency channel. Though REACT's primary role started with helping motorists navigate unfamiliar roads, the group eventually offered communication systems after natural disasters and provided support during parades, road races and other community events. Ralph's tenure as a REACT volunteer, which began when he was a young man and included a stint as the group's president, attracted the attention of Bart Bartholomew.

Ralph listed a second volunteer position on his Pioneer application: 14 years with the New Haven Fire Department. His application also covered the array of equipment he could offer the search team. His family's camping gear, snowshoes, binoculars and walkie-talkies were all proof that Ralph knew his way around the out-of-doors. It appeared he was a perfect fit for the Pioneers. However, when he eventually became one of the team's leaders, other members began to see how the passion Ralph had for volunteering could often be offset with his headstrong opinions.

"Ralph had a lot of dreams," Huey Parrow explained in regards to his Pioneer teammate. "He wanted to be an Oswego County sheriff and he wanted to be a DEC forest ranger, but he never got there. It's true that whatever he got involved with, he put everything into it and he was a solid team member, but he had his drawbacks and he didn't always know how to go about things."

"Ralph was very dedicated to his beliefs," Jeannie Parrow recalled, "and he worked hard to do a lot of good things on his own. But he didn't seem to know how to mingle with people. He wanted to do things by the book, but he wanted to do things *he* believed in. From time to time, he'd get upset, and we all learned that was Ralph."

There was a gentler side to Larkin, too, as one of the team members' children, Derek Ives, explained: "When I first started with the team as a teenager, Ralph always had a chocolate bar for me when I showed up for a search. He was that kind of guy, always being nice to me. And he was good at designating leadership, which not everyone can do. Some guys in charge get too full of themselves and want all the attention. Other people know how to lead; they know what they are good at and when to find someone who can do it better. Ralph made sure the right people were in the right place. If you had a big heart and wanted to volunteer, he would take you on the team."

Fortunately, Ralph's commitment to the Pioneers' mission managed to outweigh his often-abrasive personality. When the team celebrated their second anniversary at an August 1973 banquet, he received awards for his communications and public relations, with special note made of his "outstanding dedication." Ralph's excellence in community outreach was evident in the team's archives, where I found a series of search and rescue-related articles, one which garnered a readership beyond Oswego County. In an overview of the Pioneers' success, which Ralph had published in the *Environmental Quality News*, a newsletter distributed by The New York State DEC, he told the compelling story of the group's rapid development into a top quality search and rescue team. Ending it

Ralph Larkin, center, after a search in the city of Oswego. On left, Bart Bartholomew. On right, the Oswego City police chief.

by paying homage to the group's initial motivation, Ralph reminded readers that "Douglas Legg has never been found, but he has not been forgotten."

While serving a term as the team's coordinator in 1975, Ralph received their highest honor, the first "Pioneer of the Year" award. He continued to volunteer with the group until the mid-'90s, when new members brought innovative search and rescue ideas and technologies to the team. These came as a challenge to Ralph's stringent belief in traditional wilderness emergency procedures. Strongly opposing the new members' suggestions on how to modernize search methods, he left the group in anger.

As an ardent volunteer, Ralph's service to community did not end with the Pioneers. He became a member of the Coast Guard Auxiliary and served as a board member of Great Lakes Seaway Trail, a scenic byway dedicated to providing people access to the beauty of northeastern waterways. He also served as a park policeman at Selkirk Shores State Park and a volunteer for Oswego County Cooperative Extension, which utilized his skills in wilderness survival at the Amboy Environmental Center, a rustic campground in northern Oswego County.

When Ralph passed away in August 2013, his accomplishments as a volunteer were clearly a highlight of his life. Twenty-five years of that volunteerism were with the Pioneers, and though his strong opinions proved unsettling for some, his team members focus on the good Ralph brought to the Pioneers, describing him as a caretaker that deeply believed in their mission. Steve Ives pointed out how Ralph's concern sometimes carried the group: "There was a point with our team where there was only one or two regular members and we almost folded, but Ralph kept the Pioneers together."

Robert Halstead

Fultonian Robert Halstead was the only original Pioneer who knew the team's leader prior to its forming. "I lived two blocks from Bart Bartholomew," Robert explained to me in a phone interview from his winter home in Florida. "If I walked across lots and along the creek, I'd be at his house. Over time, we became friends."

Robert was 38 years old when Douglas Legg went missing; already a family man and well-established on the job. "I was employed by General Electric on Electronics Parkway, working on heavy military equipment," he said. Robert pointed out that he had no problem if there was a call for Pioneers to go on a search during his workday. "I was salaried, so I could leave GE if I needed to."

During those busy years with work and family commitments, if time allowed, Robert would be outdoors. "I had hunted most of my life," he said. His son Robert Jr., who I was able to contact through the wonders of Facebook, explained to me how his father inherited this passion for the outdoors and then passed it on to him: "My great-grandfather was also an outdoorsman and I'm sure Dad got his outdoors skills from him. I ended up spending a lot of time hunting, fishing and camping with my father."

The younger Halstead offered a glimpse of his father's personality, suggesting how this may have contributed to the search and rescue team: "Dad is a very friendly people-person. He loves to talk and tell stories of days gone by or what's happened recently. He is a guy you would love to share a duck blind with or a weekend fishing trip. He was not always working overtime as many dads do today; he preferred to spend time with family and friends."

It became clear to me, as we carried on our phone conversation, that Robert, Sr. spent a lot of time in the outdoors. At one point in our talk, while explaining his hobbies and interests, Robert proved how well he understood the deep woods of the Adirondacks and other parts of northern New York.

"I had a camp up near Harrisville, which is about 45 minutes northeast of Watertown," Halstead said. "To this day, it's on a dirt road, and through all those years my family enjoyed the camp, there were only about eight houses on the road. There's no power and no phones. It's pretty much wilderness.

"Recently, my wife and I visited that camp. It's now something my children use and I hadn't been there in years. My son was there with some friends and one of them said to me, 'How the hell did you ever find this place?' I knew what he meant. Unless you'd spent time there, you'd think the whole place was just trees. All the years I spent at that camp with my family, I always thought that a kid could wander away. And it's all woods, basically. That always stayed in my mind."

When Bart Bartholomew contacted Robert to share his concern about the lack of search and rescue operations after Douglas Legg disappeared, the first thing that came to Halstead's mind was the dense forest at his camp up north. "I thought starting the team was a terrific idea because if I ever lost one of my kids, I'd know there would be somebody besides my family to look for them."

Robert Halstead

That's all it took for Robert to agree to help his friend form the Pioneers. Team records indicate he was also proficient in map and compass and served as an assistant to Huey Parrow's instructional programs for new members. Robert also became one of the first team leaders, coordinating search efforts in the field and coaching newer members on how to properly search. To me, though, what made Robert Halstead such a valuable founding Pioneer was his firsthand knowledge and awareness that a friendly campground in the woods can quickly become a frightening place.

C. John LaMay

"John was very concerned about the Douglas Legg disappearance," Brenda LaMay said as an explanation of her late husband's interest in joining the Oswego County Pioneers. "He spent a weekend on that search and talked about what he encountered when he got there: the thick brush which made it almost impossible to navigate and the heavy rains that made it even harder to search."

Brenda, who met me at the Fulton Library for our interview, arrived there with a notepad and pen. She admitted she hadn't thought about John's involvement with the group in a long time and promised to jot down my questions, research them, and get back to me. She followed through on her promise, beginning with finding out how John first heard about the meeting at Bart Bartholomew's home.

"I'm pretty sure his interest came from knowing Ralph Larkin." Brenda explained. "Ralph lived next door to John's grandparents in New Haven. Over time, John also became friends with Bart, and the two of them would get together a lot for coffee. With both men, John was always discussing situations like the Legg boy's search and the theories behind his never being found. I remember that all the men in the original group were very driven to make the team succeed."

John's childhood was filled with activities which prepared him for the rigors of creating a search and rescue team. Brenda told me that her husband was born and raised in Fulton, and like other Pioneers, his youth revolved around scouting. "He was the sort of Boy Scout who paid special attention to outdoor survival skills like knot-tying and compass use," she said. "John got to use those skills during many summers when his family attended the Dempster Grove Campground, a Christian camp in New Haven, New York. The Grove offered an annual weeklong family camp experience and his family would often go on hikes. John always used his compass to find his way back."

When he graduated from Fulton High School in 1960, John enlisted in the Army as a paratrooper. "He didn't have a very glorified job while in the service," Brenda shared. "During his four years, his job was to bag the bodies of soldiers who had died in service. When he came back to the United States after his tour of duty, his mom said that he was much more mature. His priorities had changed; he liked to do things for people and help others."

John, who was 29 when the Oswego County Pioneers formed, worked for many years at Crucible Steel and he was assistant circulation manager for *The Palladium-Times*. "After that," Brenda explained, "we owned a small part of Oswego County Mutual, a homeowners insurance company located in Parish, and he was also an independent broker for other insurance companies. But John loved to be outside, so he golfed, did a little hunting and, of course, there was the search and rescue team."

I mentioned to Brenda that John's name appeared quite often in Pioneer archives as a group leader. "John wasn't afraid of things," Brenda responded. "So, it would have been natural for him to take a lead in such activities. I remember there being a lot of phone calls when the team started up. The leaders took turns trying to get team members to go out on the searches. There was also a lot of training on search and survival techniques."

Brenda remembered that, as the team became more organized, the original inertia calmed down. "But from time to time," she added, "there would be a resurgence and the men would get back together. John was also involved with trying to get other teams started throughout New York State when the men realized there was a lot of the Adirondacks to cover."

Brenda couldn't pinpoint the exact date that John stepped down from the Pioneers, but she thinks he was involved for about five years. As an Army veteran, he became active with the Veteran's Association, and Brenda remarked that "he travelled throughout New York State to talk with other veterans, some who had been wounded in the war or who were having trouble getting a job after leaving the military." Later in life, John spent a lot of time with his son; the two shared a baseball card business. "And we always did a lot of camping," Brenda said about their later years together. "We rented a site at

THE PALLADIUM-TIMES M

John LaMay during his years at The Palladium-Times newspaper.

Brennan's Beach on Lake Ontario and we'd often take day trips into the Adirondacks."

I imagined those trips to the Adirondack Mountains would have served as reminders of John's contributions to Oswego County Search and Rescue and his participation on the search for Douglas Legg. Brenda informed me that John had been battling cancer for ten years when he passed away on July 10, 2011. It took me a moment to note the significance of that date: Pioneer John LaMay died exactly 40 years from the day Douglas Legg disappeared.

John Knaizuk

Even with the far-reaching abilities of today's internet search engines and social media, tracking down the stories of the ten people who formed the Pioneers 45 years ago can be a difficult task. That was the case with John Knaizuk, Jr. Details of his life, garnered from interviews with his fellow team members and Pioneer paperwork, are sketchy at best. I tried all the "sure bets" on the internet: Ancestry.com, Geneaology.com and Facebook friend searches, but according to my disappointing results, John seems to have disappeared.

I used Knaizuk's application to join the Pioneers as a starting point for his bio. It lists his birth date as October 30, 1938, making him 33 years old when the team began. John originated from the New York City area and lived in Fulton during the 1970s, when he volunteered for the Pioneers and was a professor in SUNY Oswego's computer science department. On his Pioneer application, he listed "nature study" under skills and hobbies. This seemed to concur with something I learned about John's involvement with extracurricular activities at the Oswego college.

Dick Kaulfuss, a SUNY Oswego student who participated in the Douglas Legg search, informed me that John was an advisor for the campus's outing club, of which Kaulfuss was a member. John most certainly would have heard about the Legg search's disorganization and the subsequent decision to form a professional rescue team in the Oswego area. That may have prompted him to contact Bart Bartholomew and offer his help in forming the team.

The combination of John's interest in nature with the outing club and his mastery of computer skills through his professorship proved a bonus for the Pioneers. Jeannie Parrow remembered Knaizuk as a whiz with numbers and statistics. "At our meetings, when we came to the financial report, our treasurer would list the dollar amounts that had come in or gone out, and before the new balance was announced, John would have it calculated out to the penny in his head."

John Knaizuk, right, preparing for a ropes training class with Ralph Larkin (left) and Steve Ives.

There were also ways in which John's aptitude with details contributed to the Pioneers' paperwork. The team's archives indicate he served as their first review board officer, a position which involved keeping track of each member's credentials, search and training participation, etc. Wayne Dealing, an early Pioneer, said that "John was good at putting things together, including classes in the outdoors. Huey Parrow and the other team organizers relied on John a lot, making him one of the team leaders."

Huey filled in a few more details of John's life that suggest why his whereabouts and well-being are hard to track down. Parrow remembered that after leaving Oswego John and his family moved to Albany. Further complicating things, as Huey noted, "at some point after the Pioneers were formed, his wife joined the Mormon Church. The rest of the family, including John, followed her into the religion. There was talk that they moved to the Utah area."

Even with Huey's keen ability to track down Pioneer members and other important details about the group's history, I could not get the full story of John Knaizuk. That makes him the founding Pioneer whose life and contributions to the group remain, like the whereabouts of many a missing person, a mystery.

George McCulloch

At first glance, George McCulloch seemed like the exception to the rule when considering the necessary credentials for a Pioneer Search and Rescue founder. For starters, George was 66 years of age when he joined the team, a good three decades older than the other men who showed up at Bart Bartholomew's house. George had been a longtime resident of Syracuse when he heard about the plans to form the team, making him the only non-Oswego County member to sign on as a founder. But the typical Pioneer characteristic most lacking in George was that he was not a hunter, nor would anyone have called him an outdoorsman – unless you consider skydiving outdoorsy.

Already one of the most celebrated skydivers in Central New York by the time he inquired about becoming a Pioneer, George made sure to note on his application that he had successfully completed 525 jumps. He may have included this achievement in hopes of balancing what most certainly would have seemed like the deficit of his advanced age. But anyone walking side-by-side with George in those first wilderness trainings would have had no doubt in his ability to withstand the demanding realities of search and rescue.

"That man was fit as a fiddle and his mind was sharp," Wayne Dealing shared. Robert Halstead agreed, adding that "when George joined, I was terrified of him. We were all young and here was this old man. I didn't think he belonged on our team, but by God, he was just as good as anybody who went out on those searches. He was in good shape and could outlast the group at times."

How did someone born in South Dakota with a long and successful career in Syracuse end up joining the Pioneer team? A small note in George's obituary gave me a clue to his Oswego County ties: During his teen years, his father, a reverend, was assigned a Bundyville church and the family moved to Minetto, New York. Around the same time, George had already discovered his love of newspaper reporting, and before he graduated high school he was already on staff for *The Oswego Times*, a precursor to *The Palladium-Times*. From there, George advanced to Syracuse's *Post-Standard*, where he worked 16 years as a city hall reporter. World War II ended that career for George, when he voluntarily resigned from his job to enlist in the Merchant Marines and then the Air Force. Upon the completion of his tour, he returned to Syracuse and worked for city government as an urban renewal planner.

I discovered one other link to George's interest in the formation of a search and rescue team. In a Syracuse newspaper article released shortly after his death, it was noted that, in 1961, George had participated in the search for a Raleigh, North Carolina boy lost in the Catskill Mountains. I imagine that once a person experiences the harsh realities of searching for someone missing, it's hard to forget.

George's wife, Harriet McCulloch, would have been an advocate for her husband's volunteerism in the important work of search and rescue. The McCullochs met while attending the same college, joined the service together and then furthered their education on the GI Bill. Later in life, the McCullochs became involved in many civic organizations and social clubs, and at 54 years old, George took his first skydive jump. Harriet joined him several times and the two became known as "The McCulloch Team."

George had a particular twist with his aerial hobby: on each birthday he would enjoy a skydive, adding one second of the free-fall portion of the jump for each year he'd lived. As those years added up, his freefalls got more exciting and crowds would form to watch. Robert Halstead recalled some of the drama involved with George's daring feats:

"One year, a bunch of the search and rescue team went to see him jump at the Fulton Airport. After the plane took off, it went so high you couldn't even see it. There was a guy that jumped with George – a jump master, maybe – and after their stunt, the guy said, 'I'm froze! I ain't never going to jump any higher!' Yes, George was something else again."

In 1970, George retired, and a year later, when the Pioneers formed, he became a founding member. Harriet joined shortly after. Several Pioneers have reflections about the McCullochs' unique contributions to the team. Jim Crombach described George as "happy-go-lucky. He wasn't a take-charge guy, but always willing to help." Wayne Dealing offered that "George had an absolutely positive attitude; Harriet, too. They were always willing to step in and promote the team." Jeannie Parrow added this thought about how the McCullochs' age influenced the Pioneers: "They were the kind of people that everyone would want to have as a mother and father."

The McCullochs stayed active with the group until September 1982. In a letter accompanying George's formal resignation, he listed a persistent eye infection, aggravated by a search in extremely cold weather. His doctor warned that extended periods of time in fluctuating weather conditions could lead to permanent eye damage. Since the McCullouchs lived in Syracuse, it seemed impractical for Harriet to attend meetings and searches in Oswego County on her own, so she also resigned.

George McCulloch

On his 74th birthday, George took his one thousandth skydive, which gave him entry into the U.S. Parachute Association's Gold Wings Club. By 1982, George took his last dive at age 77, and three years later, in February 1985, he passed away. His obituary listed him as one of the country's oldest skydivers. Many tributes to George were offered, both for his aerial prowess and his years as an ace newspaper reporter, and perhaps this one, from fellow *Post-Standard* staff person Mario Rossi, gives a hint as to why he became such a valuable member of the Oswego County team:

"I've known George for many years...He was a top reporter, motivated by a deep and dedicated search for the truth."

Steve Ives

Steve Ives was the first Search and Rescue Pioneer I met, having worked with him on the memoir he wrote for the Fulton Public library. His memoir offered an informative overview of the team's formation, and after I decided to write the Pioneers' full story, I interviewed Steve several times. One interview took place at a Fulton restaurant, and while sharing a cup of coffee on a particularly wintry day, he told me about an early life experience that was a catalyst for his attending the first search and rescue meeting at Bart Bartholomew's house.

"There are 50 acres of woods on County Route 6 that my grandfather owned, and when I was about eight years old, I wanted to take a 'maiden solo voyage' on my bicycle. I knew that area like the back of my hand, so I asked my dad if he would let me go alone in the woods. 'I'll just do this,' I said to him, 'and I'll meet you on the other side.'

"When I was in the middle of those 50 acres, I got lost and started to panic. Every branch that I walked through seemed to reach out for me and it scared me to death. At first, I dragged my bicycle through the brush because I didn't want to lose it and I didn't want anyone to know that I was lost. But, after a while, I couldn't pull it anymore, so I just left it behind. I never found the bike, even though I later searched that whole area more times than you could imagine.

"Finally, I got ahold of myself and spotted the back of a house which faced County Route 6 and realized where I was. I skirted the road all the way down to where I knew my dad would be, and there he was, along with my sister, brother and some cousins. They were all looking for me – searching for me. I told them that I wasn't lost, but my face, all puffed up from crying, told otherwise.

"When I first heard about the Douglas Legg search, the eight-year-old me came back. That poor kid, I thought about Douglas. He probably panicked like I did and I didn't want anyone to have to go through that. It was a very important piece of why I joined search and rescue, along with the fact that if that had been my son, I wouldn't have been able to pay someone to search for him."

There was one more important reason why Steve sought out the Pioneers. Early in life, he had learned from his parents how to be a responsible adult. "They were people that would just naturally help others," Steve pointed out. "When I became an adult, I wanted to find some way I could help and thought about the Volney Fire Department, which was a logical place to volunteer, but I held off. When search and rescue came along, I thought I would do that."

Eventually, Steve found his niche with the Pioneers. Unlike Huey Parrow's mapping skills or Bart's abilities as a leader, Steve's strength centered on bringing people together. "When the group first formed, there were differences of opinion, and people often said that I brought those differences together so that we'd walk away thinking 'Okay, we have a plan.' I was born with those skills; they came with this package of who I am. I actually first noticed it as a kid when I would be playing sandlot football or baseball. I was the one who tried to calm down kids who were looking for a fight, getting in the middle to say knock it off. Most of the time when I was kid, it didn't work very well, but in the adult world, it has."

This ability to find compromise didn't come easily for Steve, who initially hadn't considered himself as a leader. "I remember at one point saying to Huey, 'I can't do this.' But he kept encouraging me, and somehow, I learned I could do it. I think it was the people under me that were allowing that part of me to come out; it's like they were holding me up."

Others who served alongside Steve acknowledged his contributions. Jim Crombach, who ended up not only being a team member of Ives, but also a close friend, summed up how he saw him: "Steve has always been involved with helping people, especially the downtrodden. It's the type of person he is."

Richard Bartholomew agreed that Steve's talents were important, noting that "when we were on a search, everyone would line up and Steve would be right in the middle of it, talk-

Steve Ives, carrying a mannequin out of the woods after a Pioneer training.

ing and trying to keep people paying attention as they went along." Richard added a vibrant visual of Steve in action: "He was like the Grizzly Adams of our team, with his burly beard and ruggedness. He was a typical woodsman, but he had a persona about him; he was in his element."

Richard is right; Steve *was* in his element and still is. As the longest-running member of the Pioneers, he's been a part of every important event the team has experienced. Steve only stepped away from the Pioneers once, after a search took an enormous emotional toll on him. But he returned, and today he's still on the active call list, listening to the details of each new search, trying to figure out how he can best help.

With the ten founding Pioneers in place, the team could turn their attention to achieving their goal of creating the best search and rescue team they could. As I reviewed the group's history, reading the names of hundreds of other people who would pledge their commitment to the team, I kept reflecting on the men who started the Pioneer's journey to success. I've come to think of these founders as one unit, but as Steve Ives frequently reminded me, "We all had our personalities and idiosyncrasies. However, when we formed the Pioneers, we put those uniquenesses together and somehow made it work."

Chapter Five

Blazing a Trail Into the Unknown

How did Bart Bartholomew and the founding Pioneers form their search and rescue team without any guidance from a preexisting organization of its type? How were they able to turn their own wilderness experiences into legitimate trainings? How did they address the material needs of a professional emergency services group, first acquiring the essential equipment and supplies, and then finding a way to transport it to the dangerous environments they'd be searching? And how would the Oswego County team even begin to meet these challenges without a working budget?

The Pioneers' attempt to answer these questions began like any other such endeavor in pre-internet 1971: with family, friends and neighbors. Across backyard fences, in line at the grocery store, after church services or during coffee breaks, team members talked up their new project. People were supportive and encouraging, but no one had a solid lead on where to begin. In the meantime, Bart and others on the team were contacting government agencies and volunteer groups to see if anyone had heard of such a thing as a search and rescue team? The result of these inquiries was disturbing: not only were there no such teams in Central New York, but Pioneers had not been able to identify a single one throughout New York State.

My research of how and when professional search and rescue teams first formed concurred with what the Pioneers had learned. While the concept of organized searches for missing people had started on the west coast in the early 1950s, New York State had not recognized such a need until two decades later. In October 1970, the state's Department of Environmental Conservation was established and the organization was just beginning to develop its list of priorities. Nine months later, Douglas Legg disappeared, and the need for search and rescue expertise shot to the top of the list.

Soon after, the DEC announced their intention of creating three specially-trained search and rescue teams, aptly christened with wilderness-appropriate names: The Blue Fox, which would cover the western Adirondacks; The Red Eagle, overseeing the eastern portion of the Park; and Grey Hawk, responsible for the Catskills. Those teams would not even be in their formative stages until well after the Pioneers began their work, and though conversations between the two fledgling programs showed DEC support for Oswego County, the state had little in terms of resources to offer.

Without any local assistance to count on, Bart Bartholomew resorted to what seemed like a plausible plan B. Through his keen attention to the details of the Douglas Legg search, Bart had read about the Sierra Madre Search and Rescue Team from California. If no one close to home could help his team get off the ground, why not reach out to those who could on the other side of the country?

"Bart sent a letter to that group," Steve Ives explained. "From them, he found out about a Boy Scout Explorer Post which had shared their wilderness training program when search and rescue teams were forming on the west coast. Bart contacted the Scouts and they replied with a handbook covering how to search and the different kinds of searches. That was the first real information we got."

While the Pioneers carefully studied the Scout handbook, Bart prepared a long list of details to be addressed at their next meeting, held five days after the backyard gathering. Topping the list was creating and assigning leadership roles, which Barbara Bartholomew noted in her July 29 press release: "Bart Bartholomew was elected as the group's chairman coordinator, Ralph Larkin as vice chairman and John LaMay as secretary." A treasurer would eventually be appointed, although, without any financial resources readily available to the Pioneers, creating the position was merely a formality.

Along with these more traditional committee roles, the team added a few specific to search and rescue. A search coordinator would be a senior Pioneer member who oversaw all operations once the team arrived at the search site. The person in this role discussed details of the missing person with the lead law enforcement agency and relayed it to the rest of the team. A communications team was responsible for manning radios and transmitting information between searchers in the field and the coordinator.

The all-important work of searching for a lost person would be overseen by a field officer, who also served as the team's instructor. "The Pioneer leaders wanted everyone on the same page regarding compass and map-reading skills," Huey pointed out, "and our members' skill levels were all over the board. Since map and compass would be the 'bread and butter' of the team's search strategy, it was one of the first procedures that members were taught. I knew how to teach the skill, so I was elected to be our first field officer."

Steve Ives added one more important duty of a field officer: "He assigned leaders for each team of searchers." Team leaders would be responsible for the volunteers who carried out Pioneer search strategies. It was here, under a team leader's direction, where the actual search for a missing person happened. It's "where the rubber meets the road," so to speak, or perhaps "where the hiking boot meets the trail." Leaders kept the teams in line and on task and they stayed out in the field until the lost person was found or until those in command ended the search.

Not all key Pioneer positions took place in the wilderness. Another important role the founders created was that of a review board, whose job it was to oversee search-related paperwork, including sign-in sheets of search volunteers; tally sheets, also known as "incident hours," which compiled the time each volunteer contributed; and records of each searcher's actions in the field. Daily, an "incident packet" was compiled, summarizing the key accomplishments of each day's search efforts. But perhaps most importantly, the packet also kept track of everyone who'd showed up to search and made sure they were accounted for at the day's end.

Throughout its 45-year history, with minor changes in a few job titles, the Pioneers' chain of command remained essentially the same.

Included in her July 29 press release, Barbara Bartholomew made sure to note the positive direction Pioneers were heading, pointing out that the group size had now grown to 21. She also described the widespread Central New York area represented by team members. From Oswego County, Pioneers came from Central Square, Mexico, Hannibal, Oswego, Fairdale, Scriba and Volney. From nearby Onondaga County, volunteers came from Brewerton and Syracuse. And for the first time, the team's name proudly appeared in print: The Oswego County Pioneer Land Search and Rescue Team. (In 2007, the team would drop the word "Land," since they also were conducting aquatic searches in rivers, lakes and ponds.)

Offering a glimmer of hope regarding the group's desire to discuss search and rescue goals with like-minded individuals, Barbara reported "a special meeting on Monday, August 2, with Robert Gagnon, a Liverpool man who was currently setting up the Onondaga County Federation of Sportsmen's Club Rescue Team." Pioneers leaders were looking forward to the discussion with Mr. Gagnon, but they also had something more immediate on their minds: the California Boy Scout manual spelled out how to effectively carry out a land search, and no amount of discussion would teach this. The Pioneers needed to head into the woods.

Because Douglas Legg went missing in the Adirondacks, the

team's leaders considered that wilderness area as their idea training site. But travelling nearly three hours seemed liked a long way to go for deep woods. Since the group had pledged to run drills regularly – Barbara remembered them training *every* Monday – it didn't take long for the group to determine that there were ideal conditions right in their backyard. Nearly two-thirds of Oswego County's 1,300 square miles is forested and the team understood how a person could just as easily get lost in them as they could in the Adirondacks. Better to train close to home, Pioneers reasoned, where every precious hour could be spent practicing.

In early August, the team gathered at the North Hannibal home of member Robert Ingersoll for several hours of "feet on the ground" searching. Leaders assumed their roles: Bart Bartholomew provided focus for the group with an overview of the day's goals. Search area boundaries were marked off with string and fluorescent tape by Huey Parrow, who also gave the 16 members in attendance a quick map and compass review. Steve Ives and a teammate manned the Pioneers' command center – a car parked on a road bordering the area to be covered – where orchestration of the search would take place. Steve also divided the rest of the group into two seven-man teams and told them who their "lost person" was: a dummy hidden somewhere in the swampland. A single compass reading was the group's only clue.

A modern-day version of the "dummy" used for search and rescue trainings. Pioneer member Burnetta Bennett explained that "we took some old clothes, stuffed them with plastic bags and attached a cosmetology head to it."

The searchers headed into the thick cover of trees, each team leader equipped with a compass, map and walkie-talkie. Everything appeared ideal for a productive first training – well, everything but the weather. Heavy rain fell throughout the exercise, exasperating the already swampy conditions behind Ingersoll's home. In retrospect, longtime Pioneer members who described that first training to me believe the poor weather was an important omen for the team: People don't always get lost on a sunny afternoon, they assured me. The teams trudged on.

An early Pioneer team photo after a search and rescue training.

By late afternoon, the "subject" was found. Simulated first aid was offered and a stretcher constructed from tree limbs and team members' jackets transported the "injured" to the main road. The first training of the Pioneers was deemed a success and their satisfaction gave the group a measure of confidence. They were ready to head home and await their first search callout. But before the team was released from their training, Bart requested they conduct a business meeting. Though exhausted from their push through swamp and rain, the members convened in Ingersoll's home.

First up on Bart's agenda was a vote on the Pioneers' official constitution and by-laws, drafted in a special committee headed by John LaMay. It successfully passed. Robert Halstead, the team's review board chairman, collected information from the group's growing number of members. Hastily written on loose-leaf paper and notepads, these makeshift résumés, found in the Pioneers' archives, provide a glimpse of the newer recruits. Along with basic information on each aspiring member, applicants also shared important details about their interest in joining:

"I was a star Boy Scout," offered Granby resident Gary Frost, "and I also raise and train dogs, including quality breeds such as bloodhounds." "I own most everything having to do with the out-of-doors," Ron Utley explained, including "an 18-foot canoe, four tents, hunting equipment, goodies and various junk." George Sedner, of Phoenix, felt compelled to express his sincere support for the Pioneers' goals by adding this note: "As a family man, I can appreciate the offered efforts of such an organization you have proposed. An undertaking of such magnitude is surely to be met with great enthusiasm in our locality and, indeed, our state."

As the Pioneers became more organized, an application form to join the team was created. On a single sheet with what appears to be the first Pioneer letterhead, applicants were asked to fill out five sections: name, address (including a road name was required), phone number, directions to their home, and a list of any equipment they might have. Red Creek resident Thomas Lytle's application stood out with his list of available supplies including CB equipment and Adirondack topographical maps.

Items such as Lytle's were included on the group's first comprehensive list of equipment available for searches. Copies of the four-page document were printed and given to each Pioneer leader. Separated into categories, there were "big ticket items" such as boats, four-wheel drives (and whether they were for off-road use only), trucks and campers. The next section included supplies such as steel cables, tarps, umbrella tents, wall tents, hooks and bars. Scuba gear, canoes, camp stoves and chainsaws were grouped together, and a special section on winter search essentials included snowmobiles, ice ropes, snowshoes, a snow trailer and rescue sled. No matter the season, the Pioneers pledged to be ready for their first search callout.

Meetings and trainings continued. There were search techniques to be perfected, including a three-month intensive first-aid program that was required of all team members. In one of Barbara Bartholomew's press releases, she noted that "by November of our first year, Ernie Ladd of Central Square, chief instructor for the team, had issued 27 certificates to Pioneers for successfully completing 36 hours of classes in American Red Cross Advanced First Aid." (Huey Parrow also credited Janet Lewis, of the American Red Cross, as being instrumental in the Pioneers' early emergency medical training.) The article also mentioned several Pioneers furthering their medical proficiency by becoming EMTs. Course fees for all this training, Barbara noted, were covered by participating team members.

All of the Pioneers' press releases ended with a call for new volunteers, and within a few months of the group's formation, people enthusiastically responded. As word spread about this exciting new concept of emergency service, the team ballooned to 50 members. On paper, the membership roster looked impressive, but "there would be nights where there was only two or three of us at a meeting," Steve Ives remarked. "At one point, the group almost folded, but then a high-profile search would occur, and with it, more interest." Huey Parrow commented about the fluctuating numbers during those first few years: "Some stayed a little while and then left. Nothing against those people; they heard about it and thought it sounded good, but it wasn't what they were looking for."

Steve mentioned another reason why some members didn't remain with the Pioneers: "From time to time, we'd get people who joined the team that didn't want to go along with our guidelines and did unsafe things. One guy thought that it was okay to have a machete in the woods to cut down tall grass and brush, not really considering the safety of others searching right next to him. Quickly, we developed a code of conduct for searchers."

Pioneer Dale Currier, who joined the Pioneers a few years

after they formed, pointed out one more problem associated with volunteer groups: "There are people who are joiners, but often this is so they can say 'I belong to this group and this group.' But those people don't participate a lot. They come for the fun stuff, the easy stuff. For the original Pioneers, though, right from the get go, it was personal to them. They believed with their heart and soul that they never wanted anything like Douglas Legg's disappearance to happen again. The team was primary for them, and if they weren't at work, they were Pioneers."

One of the first people to join the search team after it was founded was Wayne Dealing, who invited me to his home to discuss how he'd found his way to the team. "My first wife Sandra and I had just moved to the Central New York area and were looking for ways to do our civic duty. NOCA, Northern Oswego County Ambulance, was just developing and needed its members to be EMT-trained. Sandra and I enrolled in a class at SUNY Oswego and one of the people in attendance was Chuck Blount, who invited us to a Pioneer meeting. At the end of the evening, we signed up to be a part of it."

Wayne's phrase "signed up" made me curious if joining the Pioneers was really as simple as that. Jim Crombach confirmed that it was: "There wasn't really any period of being a trainee or an apprentice. If you were interested in joining, you were in. During the time when the team was relatively new, a lot of people were joining at once, so several trainings were offered. If anyone was interested, Steve, Bart and Huey were more than glad to give instruction for those anxious to get started."

As the Pioneers began to clarify what was expected of volunteers, their news articles became more specific. An August 1971 release stated it like this: "Needed are persons with background experience as woodsmen. Desired skills would include first aid, map and compass, hiking, survival training and forms of rescue training." Finally, the minimum age of 18 was indicated as necessary for inclusion in the group, along with this stipulation: those interested would preferably be men.

I was confused by this last requirement, having already interviewed several women who were early members of the Pioneer team, so I checked back with them and others on the question of gender. "When women joined the Pioneer team, they were full members," said Jim Crombach. "It wasn't anything like a women's auxiliary; everyone could participate in any facet of the organization."

Jim said that when his wife Nancy joined the team, she found it to be unlike other volunteer groups where women supported the men's efforts by cooking meals and setting up celebratory events. Still, while reviewing the Pioneers' scrapbooks, I did locate one photo with the caption, "Pioneer Women's Auxiliary Group Meets." I asked Jeannie Parrow and Steve Ives why, if women were full members of the Pioneers, such a phrase would have been used.

"At that time, it might have been seen as politically correct to use a term like 'women's auxiliary,' " Steve remarked. "But that phrase didn't last long, because the women who were drawn to search and rescue were not only outdoor oriented, but also independent." "Back then," Jeannie added, "some people felt that women shouldn't work or be involved in certain fields. In fact, you still see that today. But, we women were there to support the team wherever we were needed."

Along with Jim, Steve and Jeannie's explanations, a review of later Pioneer press releases set my mind at ease. The August 1971 news article was the last time the preference of male applicants would be mentioned.

Another indication of the Pioneers' interest in welcoming all to their group had to do with the age of its members. The team had already stretched its upper age "limit" by including Harriet and George McCulloch, who were in their sixties. But the Pioneers also welcomed those on the other side of the age spectrum. Yes, Richard Bartholomew was the son of the group's founder, but when he became a Pioneer at age 15, it wasn't just because of his dad.

"I was twelve years old when the team started and I used to go on searches as a young kid," Richard explained. "The meetings and trainings always fascinated me. People would be practicing with their compasses, working on emergency techniques for first aid and memorizing terminology for CBs. I ended up learning all that, too."

"It was a great group of people to grow up around," Robert Halstead, Jr. said of the adult Pioneers. "I was fourteen at the time, and as a junior member, I went to meetings and trainings. I even went on searches with the rescue team. While all this was going on, I was really hoping to help the people who were lost and in need."

The Pioneers found other ways for their children to help, especially during trainings. In place of the dummy used in the first mock searches, the team started hiding youngsters in the woods as live "subjects." *The Palladium-Times* Sept. 29, 1971 issue described one such training which created the scenario of "an injured 10-year-old boy (lost in) a densely-wooded area at Nestlé Park, outside Fulton." The subject, Huey Parrow's son Robert, was well-hidden for several hours. Searchers eventually found the boy, who had crawled under heavy underbrush for shelter after "fracturing his left leg" and consequently "going into shock." Simulated first aid was administered, Robert's leg was splinted and he was carried out of the woods on a stretcher.

Some of Steve Ives' children also took part in trainings. His 17-year-old daughter Mariah did a believable job of portraying the type of troubled people Pioneers might encounter on a search.

"Mariah was playing a person who was suicidal and the team had to try to talk her down," Steve recalled. "Before we started, I coached her to remain hysterical until someone asked if she had family problems. At that point, she was to let them talk her down. After about half an hour, someone finally asked her about those family problems."

Another of Steve Ives' children remembered his time with the Pioneers as a rare opportunity for a young person. Derek Ives had been aware of his father's commitment to search and rescue from an early age and couldn't wait until he could be involved with the team. "By the time I was 13, I'd pestered my dad enough that he finally caved and said I could go on one of the searches in the Adirondacks," Derek said. "By the time I was 16, I was the guy in the boat with search dogs on lakes and rivers. I was seen as an actual search member, not some kid hanging around. This did a lot for my confidence, to be part of the learning, searching and figuring out what the team was going to do."

"Using young people as live subjects could have its challenges," Pioneer Howard Bennett admitted, as he explained a search training held in conjunction with New York State forest rangers and local fire departments: "I recruited my nephew and his friend to be our subjects and we had planted them in the woods about 200 yards apart from each other so they'd have company. We instructed them to stay in place, assuring the two teens that if searchers didn't find them, someone would retrieve them."

Within minutes of the search training's start, one of the boys panicked and came charging out of the woods almost a mile from where he had been positioned. Shortly after the boy was located along the roadway, the forest rangers received a call for their assistance at a crime scene in Cortland County. They left, and in the interest of safety, a decision was made to end the training and retrieve the other boy. But, when team members went back to the location where they'd left him, he wasn't to be found.

"After searching the area with no luck, it was starting to get dark," Howard continued, "so a formal search operation was initiated. Another team member went back to the boys' original location with a few firemen and called out one more time. From high up in a tree, the boy answered our call. When asked why he didn't respond the first time, he said, 'You told me not to say anything if people came around.' We learned not to be too literal with live subjects."

These diverse trainings illustrate the commitment Pioneers had to thoroughly cover all aspects of a search. "It was our goal to prepare ourselves as much as we could for any situation we might find ourselves in," Steve Ives explained. "Then, after each training, we'd critique it and discuss what could have been done better."

Whatever search and rescue techniques the trainings covered, Pioneer founders insisted on accuracy. "Our team leaders were very strict," Huey Parrow stressed. "From time to time, if I was assigned to the command center, I'd go out and see how the teams were doing. If they weren't following regulations and were getting sloppy, I'd chew them out. Everyone was expected to give 100 percent, and if a team member wasn't searching to the specifics, they'd be putting our name on the line."

A few people with less than good intentions found their way to the Pioneers and "had to be called down," Huey noted, mentioning one instance when new members tried to take over the team. "We had a meeting and these new guys started telling us what was going to be done. I raised my voice and said, 'No, this isn't how it's done. The team is a team. If you have an idea of how you want things to go, come to a meeting and we'll discuss it.' This shocked the group because raising my voice wasn't my style. But I saw that some people wanted to destroy the team."

The Pioneers' strong control and adherence to strict

guidelines was a sign of their professionalism during searches. At times, though, a search could draw large numbers of volunteers, many who were untrained. "If the law enforcement agency in charge didn't have enough trained leaders, they would assign a couple of our team to do so," Huey noted. "We'd make sure rules were explained at the very beginning and then were followed."

Big searches could also mean Pioneers might end up on another team, which happened when Deana Ives participated in the search for Heidi Allen, the 18-year-old Oswego County resident who went missing in 1994, and despite a widespread rescue effort, was never found. Deana recalled what it was like when she was placed on a team without her fellow Pioneers. "I saw how unprofessional some volunteers were acting. They were arguing and almost getting lost themselves. I couldn't wait to get back to my team."

Deana and Steve Ives's son Derek was also on the search for Heidi. "I was taking a Criminal Justice class in high school at that time. Our teacher offered the class a chance to volunteer on the search for Heidi, and Huey offered to come in and talk with us about what we could expect and what he expected of us. He looked us all in the eye and said, 'If any of you aren't serious about this, I don't want you on the team. If I see anyone not following directions, we're done. This isn't some high school field trip; this is the real deal.' "

Since searches took place all over New York State and beyond, spending extended periods of time away from home were common. The Pioneers slept where they could; sometimes that meant a warm church basement or with the missing person's family. But it also could be in their car, a barn or in the middle of the woods.

New members also had to consider the harsh environments in

Pioneer team members
setting up lodging in an
Adirondack shelter.

which they were expected to function. There were real risks for personal injury, which could sometimes be life-threatening and other times, as was the case for Steve Ives, perplexing: "After being with the Pioneers for a while, I noticed something on my back. At first, I thought it was a pimple and I had my doctor look at it. He kept his eye on it, measuring it to see if it grew, but for almost 20 years, we couldn't figure out what it was. Then puss started coming out of it, and along with it came a piece of thorn. It started hurting more, so my doctor cut it open and pulled out a second section of thorn. Eventually, the team started using heavier jackets for extra protection in those areas that had prickers and such. You never knew what kind of terrain you were going to end up being in."

Along with the growing success of their simulated search trainings, the Pioneers began making inroads toward their goal of acquiring the latest emergency rescue information. The founding members were able to obtain training manuals related to search and rescue from Washington, D.C.'s Superintendent of Documents and the Air Force's Library. Topographical maps were made available from the United States Department of the Interior. Locally, contact was made with several organizations that could assist the team. Found among early Pioneer files was a handwritten list of groups willing to contribute to their development as a professional search and rescue team:

> ➢ The Onondaga County Sheriff's Department offered night search training and mapping skills. Its special tactics group provided helicopter rescue training.
> ➢ Niagara Mohawk contributed guidance on how to approach utility emergencies.
> ➢ The United States Coast Guard Auxiliary introduced maritime search plans to the group.
> ➢ The Syracuse Fire Department opened up their trainings in hazardous materials, rescue squad formation and reenactments of fires. (Here, the Pioneers learned how to use air masks, which they might need when searching caves, tunnels and mines.)
> ➢ The College of Environmental Science and Forestry loaned their library of films on wilderness survival.
> ➢ Oswego County's Conservation Officer provided a map and overview of the wilderness portions of the county.
> ➢ The DEC, who were finally getting their three search and rescue teams up and running, agreed to started training with the Pioneers. "They were in the same boat as we were," Steve Ives explained: "What exactly does a search and rescue team do?"

In time, the Pioneers began answering that question, addressing not only the nuts and bolts of creating a search team, but also the underlying philosophy that drove it. Early on, Pioneer leaders began to comprehend how difficult it could be for their members to conduct a search for someone who might not ever be found. They knew the importance of keeping morale high, as shown in a March 1972 letter from Bart Bartholomew to his team:

"It is my feeling that on our recent training, the Oswego County Pioneer Land Search and Rescue Team did an excellent job in their part of a coordinated rescue effort. But as we all know, each time we go into the field we learn of not only our strengths, but also our weaknesses. This is one of the primary reasons for having such training exercises. If we accept our errors and mistakes as a learning agent, this can only improve the total effort.

"This was the first time we had even tried to negotiate (specific search) types. We could not be expected to accomplish this without a few flaws. I know that in the future we will perfect the(se) search patterns. We all put in a long day; some from seven a.m. until three-thirty p.m. I feel that our team proved one vital point: at the end of a long day, we were still an effective search team.

"Let us all learn as we grow, and out of this will come the best team in New York State...this is my hope and yours, too. I'm confident that, as a result of these training exercises and programs, when a real search occurs, we will be prepared!"

All the efforts to properly train for searches *did* begin producing results for the Pioneers, giving their leaders a chance to address less critical, but essential aspects of the group. First up was the question of uniforms. Without financial resources to speak of, team members were expected to provide their own search gear: hip boots, sweatshirts, windbreakers, rain gear and gloves, and for cold northeastern winters, parkas and heavy jackets. One item I noted on the Pioneers' list of suggested clothing, however, stood out as unusual for a group heading into the woods: hardhats.

When I inquired about this uniform requirement, Steve Ives explained that "one of the original Pioneers worked at the Oswego Industrial Supply Company, so part of our official uniform was a bright orange construction hardhat. Some of them were donated, but the rest were purchased. These would protect us from falling tree limbs and rocks, and they also helped our visibility, especially when planes were brought in for overhead searches."

"When the team was in its second year, we voted to get search and rescue T-shirts," said Huey Parrow. "Those who were willing and could afford it also purchased long-sleeved tan work shirts and green pants."

Top: The Pioneer team's fluorescent orange shirts and jackets became part of their uniform. Right: The first official Pioneer patch, created by team members Jackie Richards and Carla Ives in 1971.

Chapter Six

It's Not Just a Walk in the Woods

A frantic call comes in to the 911 Center: "My son is missing!" As the parent struggles to explain whatever details are known, the trained dispatcher initiates Oswego County's 911 emergency dispatch system. Using a set of protocols for determining the urgency of the incident, within minutes, the dispatcher simultaneously notifies law enforcement and the Pioneers. Dispatch information is provided to search and rescue members directly through county pagers and a sophisticated smartphone app. Instantly, all team members have the incident information, and as they head to the site where the boy was last seen, they use the county's radio system to coordinate their response while communicating with law enforcement units. Once on the scene, they meet with the law enforcement agency in charge, set up their command center, formulate an initial search plan with team leaders, and send volunteers into the woods. A 2016 search and rescue effort has been activated.

Emergency rescue procedures would have looked a lot different had that boy gone missing in the 1970s, when the Pioneers were just beginning. Without timesaving communication equipment to alert the team of a callout, an old-fashioned phone tree would have gradually spread the word to its members, that is, if the team had even been contacted. When the Pioneers first formed, being included in lost-person situations had less to do with their professional search procedures and more with who they knew and who knew them. Here's how Roger Fox, who joined the team in 1994, explained if and when they would have been contacted in its early years should there have been a search for a missing person:

"If a Pioneer team member's uncle went missing while hunting, the team would have been involved on the search. But if there was a missing two-year-old and it had been reported to authorities, we might have never been notified. Back then, when law enforcement thought of search and rescue teams, they'd say, 'Oh, yeah, they go looking for people in the Adirondacks.' To them, search and rescue was an isolated specialty."

One reason for the Pioneers' exclusion from search and rescue proceedings was the change many emergency agencies were undergoing in the 1970s. There were a number of organizations – state troopers, forest rangers, police and fire departments, ambulance corps – all trying to establish their role in the emergency services hierarchy. Some delineations were clear: A house fire was the fire department's territory. In a domestic dispute on a city street, police took charge. But if a person with suicidal tendencies went missing in their hometown and eyewitnesses saw them heading into state-owned forest, who should have led that search?

The decision of which agency should take the lead became muddied with searches such as the one for Douglas Legg, when numerous agencies sent personnel to help. In the aftermath of the confusion, directors of emergency agencies, government department heads and politicians discussed who had authority and where. After much debate, areas were designated: in a municipal entity with a law enforcement agency, its police department was responsible. Outside those boundaries, state troopers were in control, with the exception of state-owned lands such as the Adirondacks, where forest rangers took the lead. In a missing person case, all other agencies – including search and rescue teams – would take direction from the designated law enforcement officers.

Pioneers told me that, while this ruling looked official on paper, it would be decades before all participating agencies followed it. Knowing the team's commitment to well-executed search methods, I wondered how having to wait to be told they could begin had affected their work. "We were there for support and we knew it," Huey Parrow stated. "In my role as field officer, I would go into meetings with whoever was in command, they would give me a map of the area, a ball of string and ribbons for the lines and send me on my way." I could hear the frustration in Huey's voice as he continued. "There were things done on searches by state troopers, forest rangers or police that were considered none of our business."

Under the constraints of this law enforcement ruling, the Pioneers had trouble starting to make others aware of their search abilities. "Once we were established," Steve Ives explained, "we began pushing into territories of other agencies. We'd show up and be seen as just a bunch of untrained volunteers: 'Here's a new group that wants to invade our territory.' We had to make ourselves known as a serious commodity."

Being acknowledged as a professional search team would eventually come, with Bart Bartholomew making the first inroads through his work with the city of Fulton's Civil Defense Department, which he oversaw. The team's first set of by-laws noted that the Pioneers were affiliated with Civil Defense "to be available for emergency service whenever requested by the director of that office."

Founding Pioneers remembered other early supporters. Steve Ives mentioned how Don Gardner, a Fulton police officer and fireman, "would let us know if there were search situations in the city." Huey Parrow listed several others: "Del Slocomb of the state police at the Fulton Barracks was someone we worked with a lot. And, we were fortunate to have Major Charland from Troop D out of the Oneida barracks become one of our big backers. He volunteered to introduce us to different emergency agencies around the state. At one meeting, a guy from one of those agencies said, 'There's nobody in the area who is as good as our men.' Major Charland stood up, pointed to us and said, 'This young team is far more experienced than your group will ever be.' The guy got real quiet."

Huey's list also included DEC forest rangers, who he can still name from memory: "Robert Bailey, District Forest Ranger in the Lowville area; Ranger Wilber Peters, Homer, New York; Ranger Edmund Pizon, Syracuse; and Ranger Robert Hendrickson, Lewis County." The list is impressive, but I try not to think of these men as simply names on a list. One by one, with each search, the Pioneers had to introduce themselves, explain their methods and prove their qualifications to these professionals and their organizations.

As I listened to the founders tell me about their setbacks and successes, I could picture the group moving forward year after year, and in time, the Pioneers were being called out whenever a person went missing, ready to put into action their "three-search strategy."

Founding Pioneers don't remember exactly where the model for their three search methods originated, but Steve Ives thinks it may have been part of the information the team received from the California Boy Scouts. Carefully studying the Scouts' techniques for finding a missing person, the Pioneers developed them into three distinct types of searches, then trained extensively and became proficient in them. Today, with a few minor changes, the team still uses the same strategies. Here's how Steve Ives explained the three search types and how the search coordinator decided which to use:

"Let's say we'd gotten a call from law enforcement about a three-year-old boy who'd been missing for a couple hours. Maybe he was mad at his parents and took off. We'd arrive at the scene – maybe it was a farmhouse surrounded by woods – and set up our command center, where our team's search coordinator worked with the law enforcement agency in charge to develop a plan. Radio operators set up communications to stay in touch with team leaders in the field. A first-aider was on hand in case of injury to the lost person or team members, and a 'right-hand man' was in charge of equipment and supplies needed on the search. After talking with the family, we'd theorized the little guy might have gone to one of the ponds near his house to throw rocks. A Type I search was determined best."

An early Pioneer training manual explained a Type I search as "ridge running, trail and drainage investigation, and structure inspection." It was used if the team arrived at the scene shortly after the subject was reported missing. Team leaders were quickly briefed by the search coordinator and teams were dispatched to check nearby terrain, trails, bodies of water and structures like abandoned cabins and sheds. If the search began early enough, this quick check of easy-to-reach, easy-to-search areas sometimes located the lost person before too much time had passed.

Back to Steve Ives' scenario: "Teams of one or two people went to locations like the ponds, checked them and reported back. At the same time, other two-person teams were checking the most dangerous areas around the house: wells and such; anyplace the boy might get hurt."

Though Type I worked for situations where a missing person was still in the general vicinity of where they were last seen, it wasn't often used. "Especially in the early days of search and rescue," Steve continued, "our team wasn't contacted until several hours, or sometimes days after the person went missing. Families often waited before calling for help; they'd be confident they would find their loved one or were embarrassed by having to explain the situation."

Additionally, since the Pioneers weren't always recognized as a viable search and rescue alternative for the lead law enforcement agency, they may have been called in late to an active search. When the team finally showed up at the site, precious time had passed and a Type II search was deemed the best choice.

The Pioneer instruction manual explained Type II's objective was "to cover geographic areas rapidly and efficiently." It assumed that the lost person was alive and responsive. Steve Ives continued explaining the search for the lost three-year-old: "Our leaders would figure out how far the child could have travelled in two hours and then put people at the edges of those perimeters to box the area in and make sure he couldn't get any further. Then, the coordinator set up the grids."

Pioneers explained that grids divide the search area by breaking it into sections.* When drawn on a map of the area to be searched, these sections might look like huge squares. Roads, trails, streams, power lines or prominent ridges served as the squares' borders. Areas where these visual landmarks didn't exist were bordered with string and brightly-colored ribbon. Each of these squares would become a search area for teams.

The Pioneers line up, preparing to search for a missing person in an area sectioned off into grids.

Search teams of six to ten people were then formed, depending on the number of volunteers available. Team leaders organized searchers in a straight line, quite a distance apart, keeping in mind each searcher's experience and the search area's terrain. As the team headed out, in Steve Ives' search scenario of

---

* Huey Parrow noted that law enforcement often already had the outer perimeter of a search area designated for the team. From that, the Pioneers' field officer would work out grid areas to be searched.

the young boy, they would occasionally receive "voice commands, which were passed down the line. Team members would stop, call out the boy's name and wait 30 seconds to hear if he answered."

If the team failed to find the lost person when it completed its first sweep, the manual instructed the entire line to shift sideways in file order and search the area parallel to the first one. The same procedures were repeated until the entire search area was covered. The teams then returned to command center, where further instructions were given. If Type II failed to bring closure to the search, a call was made to activate Type III.

The Pioneers' training manual included a list of search situations where Type III would be activated: when a small child or elderly person was incapable of travelling far; adverse weather conditions; if there was an assumption that the subject was injured, ill, exhausted from exposure, incapable of moving or answering a searcher's shout; if the subject was presumed dead. Steve applied Type III's protocol to his case of the lost boy:

"Now, team members were almost shoulder to shoulder and nothing was going to get by us: something dropped, an overturned leaf, any indication of this boy. Every inch of terrain was inspected.* This," Steve assured me, "was very time consuming, but once we'd finished a Type III, law enforcement knew the area could be cleared as properly searched."

The training manual concludes its search section by spelling out what every Pioneer member had to keep in mind: Type III searches ended only when the subject was found or the law enforcement officer leading the search determined all avenues to

---

* Pioneers weren't just looking down. On searches where it was believed the victim had died, they also checked above them. "We looked for vultures circling overhead," said Jeannie Parrow. "If we saw them gathered over a certain area, we headed there to do a land search."

find the person had been thoroughly examined. That may only have happened after many hours, days, weeks or months. There are some missing person cases, as I learned from the Douglas Legg search, which have never officially ended. Steve Ives concluded his story of the lost boy without mentioning a resolution. After 45 years, he is well aware of what my review of Pioneer search files has shown me: the end result for a missing person can be anywhere from joyous to devastating.

As I learned how searches were carried out in the Pioneers' early years, I initially focused my research on understanding their role at a search site. But knowing that Pioneers had families and work obligations, I began to question how they managed to actually respond to the calls for assistance. After all, people don't conveniently get lost on a Saturday or Sunday afternoon. And they aren't always found in a couple hours. How did Pioneers fit volunteering for an organization which had no set schedule into their already full lives? How did their families at home cope?

In terms of the Pioneers' jobs, I found out that their ability to fulfill search and rescue duties during work hours depended on where they were employed. For some, work commitments weren't a problem. As we saw with Robert Halstead, who was a salaried worker at General Electric in Syracuse, some employers supported the Pioneers' volunteer work. It was a similar situation for Wayne Dealing, who held a job with a telephone company:

"At that time, telephone companies didn't have any restrictions on getting time off work," Wayne told me. "In fact, what you could do for your community was recognized as public assistance and they actually smiled on that. As long as I called and let the supervisor know that the team had been activated and we were on a search, it was fine. But there was a one-day restriction on that. The next day, you were back to work."

Not every company was as understanding. "It depended on their attitude," Huey Parrow pointed out. "My first boss let me go on searches and even paid me on those days. But when I switched jobs, my second boss said 'Why the hell do you want to go and search for those people, anyway?' "

A switch in employment could also mean the end of a person's association with the Pioneers, as happened to Jim Crombach: "When I joined the team, I worked a straight day job at Dilt's in Fulton. In the summer of 1977, I went to work for Owens Illinois with the crazy, God-awful swing shift they had. I started to lose touch with the team because my life got out of sorts, so I stepped down." *

For those with jobs that wouldn't excuse employees for a search, joining the team at the end of the workday was challenging. "I used to work for a company which required my working in a very cold setting," said Steve Ives. "Some nights, I'd come home after a full day's work, get warm, have a nice meal and spend time with my family. I'd go to bed and the phone would ring: Somebody's lost over in Hannibal. I'd say okay, get up and do what I had to do. Maybe it's pouring rain, but it's back out into the cold while I tried to be at my peek condition for the person who is lost and their family."

Some Pioneers took steps in order to be ready when the call came. Resources needed for the wilderness environments they were heading into would have already been collected into a good-sized backpack. At an interview with Howard Bennett, he showed up with his backpack and carefully removed each item to show me what was important for a searcher to have on hand: compass, rope, knife, tarp, flagging tape to mark locations, a whistle to

---

* Jim would rejoin the team in the 1990s, after changes in his job allowed him time to again volunteer with the Pioneers.

blow if radio communications failed, ear plugs for deep-swamp searches and hand warmers for frigid winter callouts. Digging deeper into the backpack, Howard pulled out his fire-starting kit, raingear, gloves, spare clothing, quick-energy food items like candy bars, and canteens of water.

Some rescuers, I learned, actually kept two backpacks ready to go: a lighter pack for summer searches when there's no need to worry about temperature or snowfall, and a second, more complete pack that added in cold-weather items or for anticipating a longer search time. Many rescue team members kept the packs right in their vehicles – one less thing to think about when that call woke them from a deep sleep.

Eventually, Pioneers arrived on the scene, ready to begin their search. But, as Steve Ives explained, "there's a certain amount of planning that has to happen before we can start. I often would think that we were just standing around while there was a person out there who needed us. I knew we had to be thorough and we had to do searches properly, but I was anxious to get started." Pioneers have a phrase they use to describe this unavoidable part of their duty: "Hurry up and wait."

An exception to those waiting would have been the Pioneers' communication team, which, in most of their early searches, was run by Jeannie Parrow and Harriet McCulloch. During searches, the two were required to interact with all personnel, including law enforcement, and in the early 1970s, this type of work was still primarily being performed by men. But that didn't stop the two women, both of whom had already lived full and nontraditional lives: For Jeannie, her self-described tomboy youth included time spent in the Adirondacks on snowmobile. "I also rode motorcycle and drove a race car," she pointed out. "Once, I won the Ladies Powder Puff race at the Fulton Speedway." Harriet, who was born in the early 1900s, became a pioneer of her own as a professional businesswoman. The McCullochs never had children and Harriet devoted her life to working outside the home. Looking for a way to help the civilian efforts during World War II, she led various radio communication classes for young Army recruits at the Oswego State University. This experience would lend itself to her work with Jeannie when they became the Pioneers' communication team.

From their command center, "which would often be a card table at trail head, or in a car along a country road," Jeannie explained, the women set up their radios. Connections between the communication team and those on the search were critical, and with teams often searching several square miles of an area, the Pioneers relied on their radio system. Founding members covered the cost of their first communication equipment – handheld walkie-talkies – which worked a lot like the original CB radios that truckers mounted in their vehicles. They were effective when they worked.

"They could only be used between very short distances," Huey Parrow recalled. In those cases, Steve Ives added, "you'd have to put an additional radio unit out between the team leaders in the field and the command center. The additional person would radio info back and forth. They were known as 'repeaters,' and at the time, it was the best you could get. Then again, up in the Adirondacks, you'd have even worse communications."

Steve was talking about dead zones, areas where early versions of communication radios did not work at all. "There were times the Adirondack terrain would interfere with our transmissions," Howard Bennett explained. "If a team was searching a mile away from the command center, the radio signals would hopefully bounce off a mountain. If this failed, we would just plug along until communications were reestablished."

When the system worked, it was an essential part of the search procedures. Steve explained how radioing back to the command center could help a team: "We'd be out in the field and radio in 'I'm at this location on the map and we found this piece of evidence.' Command center took that information and tried to place it on their map. They might find a mistake and radio back: 'If your calculations are correct, you should be over here on the map. Are you sure you've got that right?' And it would go back and forth."

Jeannie and Harriet were not only relaying information to Pioneer coordinators and team leaders, but also to law enforcement in charge of the search. "We were often housed in the same area where state police or forest rangers were," Jeannie Parrow explained. With their close proximity to the lead agency, the two were privy to important decisions being made about the search. "It wasn't like we chatted back and forth with them," Jeannie noted, "but we could listen to their radios; it was a way for us to monitor what was going on."

Through all this, as important details of a search were transpiring, someone needed to record them for future reference. "Normally, I'd be on the radio and Harriet would take notes," Jeannie said. "She could hear everything team leaders in the field were saying to me and my responses, and she would write them all down." The Pioneer search reports I found in files indicate

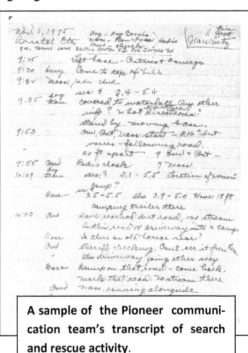

A sample of the Pioneer communication team's transcript of search and rescue activity.

the enormity of Harriet's task. Each report needed to capture the evolving search, and at times, details came quickly and from multiple sources. Noting the time of each event, Harriet would write down the people involved, their location and a description of items significant to the search. A piece of clothing, a footprint, a drop of blood; each were logged, carefully scribed in longhand.

There was one more issue concerning the Pioneers' walkie-talkies: By the 1970s, these communication devices had become fairly inexpensive and were seen as a household "toy" for many. "Radio frequencies are transmitted through the air, and anyone could listen to what was being said if they had a scanner," Jeannie explained. "People who knew the search was going on would listen in, getting information about the missing person, sometimes before the family."

Along with the communications team, the search coordinator also worked with team leaders and volunteers heading out into the woods. Whenever possible, the coordinator supplied them with maps of the search area with hand-drawn grids. In the early days, these were simply sections of New York State or county maps reproduced on a copy machine. In time, Pioneers began using topographic maps, which featured graphic detail of an area's terrain, waterways and elevation. With over 200 topo maps covering wilderness sections of New York, this was an expensive inventory for Pioneers to keep. Copies of the maps were made and when a search area was determined, they were pulled out and given to the communication team and each team leader.

When all plans were in place, the search teams headed out with their maps and compasses. Properly trained, searchers could depend on their compasses to keep them on track – unless they happened to be searching in the mountains. "There are still places in the Adirondacks that will give you a false reading on your compass," Jeannie pointed out. It's because of the magnetic fields up there." Huey Parrow added: "Due to the amount of iron in that area, compasses can go totally haywire. When that happened, we'd put the compasses aside and rely on maps and landmarks for a clue of where we were."

Once the Pioneers were out in the field, all their training was put to the test. Simulated searches, with homemade dummies and people pretending to be injured, could only go so far to prepare a person. When someone's life is actually at risk and there's dense forests to navigate, things suddenly get real. With each Pioneer I interviewed, I made sure to ask what I considered a key question: What's it like to be out on a search?

Steve Ives started off addressing my question by talking about what often went on in his mind as a team leader: "I've got to make sure the search is done right. I've got to think about who I have on the team and what their credentials are. I'll need to make sure that everybody is walking in a uniform line, so I'm watching that. Then, if we find the missing person, I'm thinking about who I'm going to use in what way. I'll want the best volunteers there when we find the person."

Pioneer Joe Homola, who's been with the team since 2006, explained what everyone else on the search team should be thinking: "When you're out on a search, you are there to focus on what's going on around you. You're going through woods and trying to keep yourself safe, keep your eyes open and be aware of the people around you. You're putting all your senses and abilities into

Steve Ives (left) and Pioneer team member searching for evidence.

hopefully finding clues. To maintain that kind of concentration for a long time is a job. You take your mental breaks when you can, have some water, rest up, and then you are up and back at it. It's not just a walk in the woods; it's a focused walk and your mind set has to be on that."

The unique physical environment where a person often goes missing requires special attention from searchers. The same conditions which may have caused a person to get lost could mean trouble for the searcher as well. The terrain of the Adirondack Park and other areas in New York State were something Pioneers needed to prepare for. In the team's paperwork on a search for a hiker lost in the Park's Mt. Marcy area, I found a handout attached titled "Search Guidelines," which covered some of these precautions:

"While searching, move very slowly – try to keep your hands on tree branches at all times. The terrain you will be in is extremely dangerous. It is very steep; there are many boulders covered by rotting logs which makes for treacherous footing. Thick vegetation usually prevents you from being able to see the ground and where to put your feet. Be sure you have your feet on firm ground before placing your entire weight down."

Add in the element of long winters in northern New York State and those same areas can become more dangerous. The heavy snowfall the area experiences (several inches per hour is not unusual) can wreak havoc with searches. Typical signs that a person leaves when walking through the woods – footprints, leaves and brush trampled, twigs broken – can be covered over in a matter of minutes. By the time a team arrives to search an area, any indication of a person being there may be snow-covered. Deep drifts can prevent searchers from even moving through an area. But that didn't mean the Pioneers avoided such pitfalls, no matter the season.

"We didn't go around swamps," Steve Ives stressed, "we went through them in order to check what might have been in there." Jim Crombach agreed: "It's not normal to walk through a thicket of pricker bushes; it's normal to walk around them. But our training stressed that we go through briar patches or through swamps, so we did."

Exceptions to the mandatory "walking through the swamp"

rule were rare, but sometimes necessary. Huey Parrow, who told me about searching in swamps up to his waist, said that "it all depends on the weather. If it was brutally cold, we'd make exceptions. But we didn't just ignore a swamp, we'd thoroughly look it over. Were there cracks in the ice? Had things been disturbed? We'd make sure to log any information in our report: This particular swamp, because of the weather, wasn't searched."

The time of day – or night – that Pioneers headed out into the woods was also a factor on searches. Early on, the team determined that night searches would be executed only when absolutely necessary. "As long as there was daylight, we searched," Jeannie Parrow explained. "But if it wasn't a life-or-death situation, the search was called at dusk, because at night the volunteers' lives were in jeopardy, too. You could come up on a mountain ridge with a drop-off and you could walk right off a mountain. If necessary, we'd pick up the search the next day."

Wildlife living in areas that volunteers are meticulously searching is another challenge. Bear in the Adirondacks and the northern parts of Oswego County were an obvious concern, but I wasn't expecting Pioneers to tell me about a search that involved poisonous snakes.

"We were called to Bergen Swamp in Rochester to help look for a photographer who had gone out to take pictures of wildlife and didn't return," Steve Ives said. "This swamp had Massasauga rattlers, which are a type of pit viper and very aggressive. We were down on our hands and knees searching, and had we been told ahead of time that poisonous snakes were in the area, I would have worn something to protect myself.

"While we were on the search, our team heard three gunshots. At first, we thought it was a warning or distress signal, or maybe that they had discovered the missing man. But it turned out the shots came from a state trooper who stepped in the wrong place. When the snake didn't have any place to retreat, it attacked the officer, so he had to shoot it.

"Eventually, they recovered the photographer's body. He only had moccasins on his feet and a regular pair of pants. After the autopsy, it was determined that he had died from a snake bite."

Considering the mental focus required and the environmental extremes in which they needed to search, Pioneers could be under a lot of pressure. There wasn't time for idle chatter. "Talking during searches would be minimal," explained Jim Crombach. "If there was talk, it would be a discussion on what we were seeing. Many times, if we had enough people for all search roles, a team leader would bring up the rear. This gave him a chance to see if those in line were searching properly, and if he needed to say something, there couldn't be a lot of chatter going on."

Step by step, searchers moved toward their goal of finding the missing person. Should that goal be met, it oftentimes only came after first finding evidence that the subject had been in a search area. The procedure when discovering something connected to the person was straightforward: Pioneers were to take care not to compromise the condition of the article – say a shoe – with their hands. Instead, they radioed the communications team, described their find and awaited instructions. If the direction was to continue on, searchers carefully put the shoe in a plastic bag and placed it in their backpack. Notation of where it was found went on the map, and upon returning to command center, the evidence was turned over to law enforcement.

Locating clues gave the team some much-needed hope as they carried on. Pioneers told me about how important it was to a search when that happened. They mentioned other milestones, as well, such as thoroughly covering a search area, working through an unexpected turn of events in their rescue plan, or making a decision that favorably changed the outcome of a search. Those pivotal moments were often what Pioneers most wanted to talk about, which is understandable. They are often the most dramatic parts of their story and hearing about the dangerous and unpredictable conditions the team encountered *was* fascinating.

I also knew there were other details of each search that I needed to learn about in order to more fully understand them. To cover those aspects, I found it useful to read the paperwork Pioneers compiled about the searches they were discussing with me. For example, here are excerpts from a report I reviewed after hearing several Pioneers tell me their recollections of a particularly emotional search:

Paper-clipped together, the report, dated November 1, 1975, began with a one-page data collection form titled "Oswego County Pioneer Land Search and Rescue Team Information Sheet." This covered basic facts about the missing person: name, address, sex, race, age, height and weight, hair and eye color. Employment, if applicable, was noted. Also listed were medications the person took, the clothing and footgear they were last seen in, any items they may have been carrying, and the name and their relationship to the last person who saw them. The final line included a space for additional notes. In this particular case, the reader is referred to the Pioneers' summary of the search.

The typed summary began with information the Pioneers would have received when they began the search: "Mrs. Shirley Lauroesch, age 51, was last seen by her husband, Mr. Lauroesch, on Monday, October 27, 1975, at their home in Webster, New York. Mr. Lauroesch stated that Mrs. Lauroesch was very depressed because of a cancer operation on her breast and loss of sight in one eye which her doctor feels may also be due to cancer.

"On October 26, 1975, Mr. and Mrs. Lauroesch went to church. The sermon was "Life After Death," which upset her greatly. After church, Mrs. Lauroesch asked her minister to meet with her on Tuesday, October 28, 1975. She never met with him.

"Further investigation revealed that Mr. and Mrs. Lauroesch have a camp in the town of Bristol off South Hill Road, and that Mrs. Lauroesch had loved to be there. She also loved to walk to the waterfall on one side of the creek near the camp.

"Checking with Mrs. Lauroesch's doctor and pharmacist revealed that she had filled a prescription of Elavil (50 tablets) on October 27, 1975. (20 could be fatal.)"

The summary goes on to cover other key developments in the case, such as the location of where Lauroesch's car was found and what areas the sheriff's department initially searched. From the point when the Pioneers were called in, on November 1, a log of every search detail, along with the time it occurred, was maintained. Information included who conducted the searches, what areas were covered, when reports were given and when mutual aid (such as support from other search teams) was called in. Some of these notations are mere minutes apart.

The log note for 11:26 a.m. indicated the Massasauga Search and Rescue Team reported a "10-55," the code number that means the subject had been located and was presumed dead. 11:27 a.m.'s log showed the sheriff's department being notified. The 12 noon log, the summary's final listing, stated that all search and rescue teams were out of the field and dismissed.

The next page of the report listed all emergency agencies involved: three search and rescue teams, the command center staff, Ontario County Sheriff, New York State Police and four fire departments. Total manpower was 75 searchers. Stapled to the typed report are the handwritten notes taken by the communication team, a road map of the search area and a topographic map of the location where Mrs. Lauroesch was found.

A final paragraph described the area where the subject chose to end her life: "A small knoll with evergreen trees on top. Just off left side of trail leading toward her camp. A blanket was laid neatly on west side of knoll near a small evergreen tree. Her purse was on the blanket along with pill bottle and wine bottle. Subject had rolled or fell from blanket. She was about 150 yards from where she had parked the car."

I questioned the significance of those final notes, unsure why such personal details needed to be included in the report. An addendum labeled "Important Note" put some of my question to rest and also illustrated why the Pioneers carefully considered every factor of a search. The note read, "Consider for future suicide searches: To do what subject thought she must do, she prepared an area facing the sun or sunset where it was warm. She also went up a knoll – maybe to an open area, so as to be found, or, being a religious person, maybe to be nearer her God."

Not every search the Pioneers undertook ended so tragically, but as I began to comprehend the full spectrum of their work, I realized there is another dimension to search and rescue. Beyond the physical and intellectual challenges Pioneers face – walking into the unknown, combing every inch of an inhabitable area, discovering important evidence and then, hopefully, finding the missing person – professional search and rescuers must also contend with the often-conflicting range of emotions inside them.

Chapter Seven

At the Heart of Every Search

"It's crazy when it all happens at once. Your phone is going off. You turn on your radio and someone is asking 'Are you going to get the truck and trailer?' and you start thinking of all these logistical things: What kind of equipment do we need? Who can get it there? You look at the "I Am Responding" app to see who has responded to the callout."

This is how Pioneer Aaron Albrecht began answering my question of what's it like to be out on a search. I met with Aaron, the current Pioneer team's assistant coordinator, on a cold February afternoon at Camp Hollis on Lake Ontario. The Pioneers were part of a county-wide winter camping program and I'd watched them conduct a winter survival workshop. Following the presentation, Aaron and I met in the Pioneers' mobile command center, a custom-built trailer that carries everything modern Pioneers need, including, thankfully, a heat source. Before I asked Aaron to tell me more about what it's like for him on a search, I needed to understand the "I Am Responding" app.

"It's an app for our phones that is linked directly to the 911 Center. We use it to learn details of the search, find out who's able to make the call and report our status on participating. It allows anyone on the team with the app to see who else is responding, who might want to car pool for searches outside Oswego County, and also informs leaders if they need to call other teams for more help." As one of the Pioneer team's coordinators, Aaron uses the app to begin planning for the search: "I can start thinking about what kind of role I'm going to play. Are there more experienced people than me or am I going to have to facilitate? Sometimes it's two in the morning, I'm not even fully awake and I'm trying to decipher all this."

Founding Pioneers didn't have modern devices like response apps, but they still grappled with the kinds of questions Aaron described, which he elaborated on during our talk: "You wonder about possible scenarios. The age of the person? Their abilities? Why is the lost person where they're at?   Has the person just recently gone missing? Is this going to be a live rescue or a recovery search (searching for a deceased person's body)? Is there a storm starting to roll in? With all these things, I am thinking: Where does this rate in terms of urgency?"

As Aaron prepares to go on a search, he does one last thing: "Before I even get in my car and put it in drive, I say a quick prayer. I pray that we can find this person quickly, that all the searchers stay safe, and whatever the lost person is going through, I pray that it will work out for the best."

At the search site, as the team sets up the command center, pulls out equipment and gets ready to head out, each Pioneer is also experiencing his or her own thoughts and emotions. Here's how Scott Morehouse, the Pioneers' current coordinator, explained that aspect of a search: "My adrenaline gets pumping as soon as I get the initial call for the search. When I arrive at the scene, which could be at the local fire department, town hall or sometimes it's the home of the missing person, I'm being drawn into the meeting, into this group of people dedicated to finding the missing person."

I met with Scott before the start of one of the team's monthly meetings, and before he has to attend to the business side of leading today's Pioneers, I asked him to tell me more about what pulls at his emotions as his team moves into operational mode. Scott quickly identified the one variable that comes with nearly every search case: the family of the missing person.

"You encounter the family face-to-face as you start the search," Scott explained. "You don't know if you are going to be there one day or five days, and you have no idea how this search is going to turn out. You are the family's only hope. At the end of the day, you'll see these same people when you come out of the woods. And the look on their face is 'What can you tell us? What are you bringing back to us?' "

Family being at the search site is something Pioneers have learned to work with, and their presence certainly made sense to me. Family wants to be there when word of their loved one comes in. But just waiting the long hours or days can be as difficult as the not knowing, and many relatives of the lost person also want to help, to be part of the solution. This adds a challenging aspect to the Pioneers' work, since most people are not trained in search and rescue.

Aaron Albrecht explained how team leaders have handled inexperienced volunteers such as the subject's family: "If a family member wants to be in the middle of the search, I often do what was done for me on my first search: put that person in the middle of a grid line where we can watch and guide them."

Burnetta Bennett also talked about the concerns when working with family members: "Our team leader had to be careful that these untrained volunteers didn't mess up any areas where there might be footprints of the missing person. Finding their tracks could show us which direction they were headed, and if everyone is tromping over the area, it's hard to distinguish whether footprints belong to the subject or a searcher."

Back at the command center, the communication team also deals with family. "If we were radioing in the open, relatives, friends and community members would know we were talking with teams in the field," Jeannie Parrow noted. "They'd huddle around to listen for reports. So, if something happened – the team found the person or an article of their clothing – I'd excuse myself from the area and go somewhere private. Or we developed a code to relay information that those who weren't involved with the search wouldn't understand."

Interacting with family could also be of benefit to the Pioneer coordinators as they worked out search plans. Sometimes asking a family member the right question could provide great insight into the missing person's life. Was the subject upset about something? Had they gotten into an argument with someone? Who were the person's best friends? Did they have a favorite place to go when something was on their mind?

Hugh Parrow, Jr., remembered his mother and father talking with family members or friends of the missing person: "They wanted to know everything about them. What was their personality like, were they healthy at the time, were they used to being outdoors or in the woods? They'd collect as much information as they could, review their efforts and head back out to search more."

Huey, Sr. shared an example of how connecting with the family of a lost person can be helpful during a Pioneer search. A recently-discharged Vietnam War vet had gone missing near his home and the search had gone on for some time without success. When the forest ranger in charge failed to make inroads with the man's family, Huey offered to help.

"I suggested that the ranger slip a coat over his uniform and the two of us go visit the missing man's wife," Huey said. "When we got there, I asked the woman if I could have a chat with her about her husband. She didn't know me, but I told her I wasn't from law enforcement and that I was part of a search and rescue team looking for some help to find her husband. She seemed to confide in me and told me all sorts of things she would have never told the authorities, including the fact that her husband had been using drugs since he got home from the war."

It's beneficial when family members are cooperative and supportive, but this isn't always the case. At times, Pioneers have to cope with family members who don't comprehend the complexity of the search for their loved one. "A child had been missing for two days," Steve Ives explained. "We started searching along a river on a Sunday afternoon while the family of this missing child was having a party on their back porch overlooking the waterway. Eventually, the child was found having drowned under a dock while this party is going on.

"I had to swallow that," Steve admitted. "I wanted to go up and smack some of those people partying. But somehow you deal with it. You have to focus on the conclusions that you hopefully bring to the family; the closure. At times like that, I'd look into myself and say, 'What am I made up of?' You have to keep things in perspective in order to keep going."

Though the circumstances of each search for a missing person make it unique, there's one variable they all have in common: The question of how the search will end. From the moment they are called out, Pioneers begin to envision a search's conclusion. As the hours or days of the search stretch on and new details of the missing person are revealed, the team members' imagined ending shifts. In some cases, this shifting can swing back and forth several times, but Pioneers hold on to hope as long as they can. When a search ends with finding their missing person alive, the trials they'd endured pale in comparison to what a searcher feels.

"It's hard to understand if you've never been on a search," said Roger Fox, "but when you get your first find of a person who is alive, you are so high that you are hooked. There have been many occasions when I've been lucky enough to be one of the people who found the missing person, which is somewhat rare."

Jeannie Parrow also feels fortunate to have participated in some live finds, and in reflecting on her years with search and rescue, those are some of her most vibrant memories: "There was a mentally-impaired child lost for quite some time in the Redwood, New York area and several teams were looking for him. When he was found alive and we saw the helicopter take him out of the woods, it was such a feeling. We waved and hollered. That was our reward."

Scott Morehouse explained the extraordinary feeling he experienced when the Pioneers found a missing person alive who had been presumed dead: "In the summer of 2015, a fire chief in Avon, New York went out for a hike and didn't return. The fire and police departments were looking for him, and after seven days, they all thought there was no way, in the middle of a hot summer, this guy could still be alive. But the agencies felt they owed it to his family to keep looking and we found him on the seventh day. He'd slipped into a ravine and couldn't get out, but because he was able to drink the dew off leaves on the side of the ravine, he survived."

Among the joys of a live find is witnessing the reaction of a missing person when they first encounter their rescuers. "We'd gotten called down to Auburn where an older gentleman had gotten lost," Steve Ives said. "We drove down from Fulton, and just as we got there, the sheriff was bringing the gentleman out of the woods. They sat him down at a table in his house and he looked out the window at everyone who'd gathered for the search. 'Were all these people out there for me?' he asked. He began to weep because there were so many who wanted to help him."

In that situation, Steve and the Pioneers hadn't actually participated in the search, but it doesn't mean they should feel they weren't part of the live find; an attempt to help had been made. On bigger searches there can be hundreds of volunteers, and if the person is found alive, no one knows who will make the find. A person new to search and rescue who has volunteered for hours or days but isn't at the site of the find, may feel they've come up "empty-handed." Roger Fox remembered talking about this with a DEC ranger who'd been on hundreds of searches. "You know how many people I've found?" the man asked Roger. "None. I've never been the person to find somebody. Not everyone gets to experience that."

Family members of a missing person sometimes have an awareness of the effort made by all who participated on a search:

"We put a lot of emphasis on the guy who found him," mentioned Pat Wilson in a letter to the Pioneers after their four-day search and eventual rescue of her grandfather. "But everybody had the same chance of finding him and it was everybody's effort that did. So, in a sense, everybody found him."

Aaron Albrecht, who starts each search with a prayer, described a particularly joyous occasion when his prayers were answered: "This was one of my first searches, which was for an elderly man with dementia. We got the call about one a.m. and I got to the search site about two, so, of course, it was real dark. As the troopers were talking to our search coordinator, I could feel my knees knocking. I was nervous because it was a big situation and I was part of it.

"We broke off into groups and searched behind the subject's house. At about six a.m., I was about ready to leave for work, but I heard on our radios that they had found him. He was okay, but he couldn't walk very well, and because it had been raining all night, he wasn't able to get back home on his own. If we weren't there to find him, I don't think he would have survived much longer. It hit me on that search: We made a difference; we brought him out of the woods."

In some cases, a search ending with a live find might not resolve itself as smoothly as those described in the last few scenarios. There are times when a search team comes upon their missing person and it isn't clear if they are dead or alive. If the person has been missing for a long period of time, they may be unconscious or suffering from extreme hypothermia. They may be in shock. Or they may simply be sleeping. Even though finding their subject alive can be exhilarating, as their earliest searches taught them, the Pioneers learned to approach each live find with caution.

There are good reasons the team emphasized during their trainings how to handle finding someone who had been lost.

Recent studies of a person's brain activity while in crisis explain what the Pioneers have come to understand: a debilitating transformation in brain chemistry takes place when a person finds themselves in trouble; in our case, when they are lost. To make matters worse, the missing person's change in brain function intensifies when they *admit* they are in crisis, as if they send a message to their brain that they cannot process information correctly. As Pioneers told me, the single most important way a lost person can help themselves is to keep their wits about them. But what happens if they don't? What's it feel like to be lost?

My friend, Adirondack hiker Vince Markowsky, had plenty to say about this phenomenon. Vince has been lost a few times in his years hiking and I asked him what those experiences have been like. He explained by telling me about the time he and several hiking buddies attempted to scale three Adirondack peaks in one day: "Doing three peaks together is a challenge any time of year, but this was during winter. After hiking several hours, we got to an area where the trails broke off in several directions, with fresh snowshoe tracks heading off on each of them. We weren't sure which way to go, but chose a direction and started walking. It was then I realized we were lost.

"The first thing that happens to me when I'm lost is a feeling of frustration: I'm wasting a lot of time, a lot energy, a lot of my thinking and processing, and there's no benefit realized from it. Then, when I come to an area where I can look out over a vista, it hits me: I don't know where I am. This starts the rollercoaster of panic and the feeling of butterflies in my stomach, which leads to confusion: Should I go back? Keep going? I start fearing for my safety: How much time do I have left before dark? Will people know that I'm lost?"

Should hypothermia add to a lost person's dilemma, it can further inhibit their thinking process. Vince continued with his Adirondack scenario to describe what happened to a fellow hiker who experienced hypothermic side effects: "My friend got so disoriented; he kept asking 'Where is the trail?' when the trail was obviously well-established right in front of him. It wasn't until we stopped and got him to drink some hot cider so he had some energy running through him that he was able to snap out of it."

For the Pioneers, chances are they wouldn't be lucky enough to find their missing person drinking a warm beverage or being fully rested. In the case of a lost hunter, this can be a major concern for searchers. "The most dangerous thing we could confront on the search for a lost hunter was finding him with his gun," Steve Ives said. "Once a lost person is in a state of panic, every motion in the woods, every branch moving on a tree is something they see as potentially harmful. If they see a person coming toward them in a bright orange jacket and they are in the wrong state of mind, they may think someone is coming after them; not to save them, but to harm them. Troopers taught us to make ourselves as invisible as we could and try to talk the hunter down before we approached them."

Stress can also impact searchers because team members sometimes work in isolation. More than any other emergency service, search and rescue teams are often required to spread out over a large geographic area, leaving members in the dark about the progress of a search. When dealing with a potentially fatal outcome, the not knowing can take its toll. Burnetta Bennett described the situation of her team being informed that the subject they were looking for, a possible suicide case, had been found:

"It was a surreal feeling as we walked and searched. Finally, we heard on our radios that they had located the person. The radio call was to stand down, which means we had to stay in the woods where we were. I remember sitting down next to a tree and hearing the searchers' voices out in the night, talking back and forth. We sat there in the silence and waited."

There are search scenarios that can be especially challenging because of the time it takes for them to be resolved. With some searches stretching on for months or years, Pioneers can be left carrying the case's unanswered questions within them. Team members return home and try to get some much needed sleep, but the circumstances of a missing person don't just stop playing over and over in a searcher's mind. Hugh Parrow, Jr. often saw this with his parents: "If Mom and Dad went on a search and the person was not found, they'd come home still thinking about it. They wondered if they had properly searched an area or if they missed something."

Eventually getting some sleep was important for more than a Pioneer's physical health, as Steve Ives noted. "Huey and I used to have dreams about the searches that we were on. The next day, we'd talk about those dreams and often they would result in changing our search plans or fine-tuning them."

Huey furthered explained how his mind often worked overtime: "I'd always review the paperwork that we had from the search before I turned in for the night. So I'd go to bed with the details and facts fresh in my mind." As Pioneer Jim Crombach noted: "The mind doesn't shut off when you go to sleep."

Team members learned that they needed to prepare themselves for the inevitability that some searches may never end in a rescue; the missing person they were hoping to bring home might never be found. Jim Crombach spoke of the difficulty accepting this truth: "It's a hard thing for a volunteer to keep coming up against, this unknown and loss. Of all the volunteer organizations, I think search and rescue has the highest percentage of unsolved cases. You go into the woods with high hopes of saving somebody, and it's hard to walk away without any sense of accomplishment. In these situations, you can't offer closure for the family."

Jeannie Parrow explained her struggle with accepting the outcomes of unresolved searches: "I'm a mother, and I don't care how old a child is, if they were to disappear – how would you feel if it was your child? It changes your whole life. If we as a group could find an answer for the mother, the parents, the family, then it was a good thing. But for those that were never recovered, they stay in our minds – they are still in our minds today. We wonder and wonder what happened to them. We wish we had the answers."

There is one more ending to search and rescue work, which, for many in the profession, is the hardest to come to terms with. Though there is a sense of closure in finding a missing person deceased, it is often an unsettling ending for searchers who've been focused on a successful rescue. Preparing for this type of conclusion is an important part of the Pioneers' training, and it begins with handling the often-disturbing physical aspects of a person's death.

"Whenever we found a deceased person, we knew not to touch them," Huey explained. "We immediately called the law officer in charge and made the area secure until they could come in and do their work. We held the grid line until the officials came, and then the team was released. Our role was done."

Death wasn't only covered in the Pioneers' formal training; it was also discussed philosophically, beginning with the team's first leader. "Dad had a different way of viewing death," Richard Bartholomew explained, "and it was something he passed down to his children and to the team. He believed that death is a fact of life. Bodies deteriorate over time, and at times, it was gross – there's no other way of putting it. But Dad's thinking kept me strong through the hard parts of finding those bodies."

Like searchers who make a live find and share their achievement with the whole team, the reverse is true for those who find their subject deceased: Everyone feels the loss. As I researched this disturbing side of search and rescue, with more and more of the cases I reviewed ending with a death, I added another question for the Pioneers I interviewed. How do search and rescuers manage to continue volunteering when their work often ends with sorrow?

Roger Fox's thoughts on this, which at first may seem harsh and unfeeling, honestly address this difficult situation: "You get used to dealing with it because it's a reality. And if you can't do it, then maybe search and rescue isn't for you. When a case ends in death, I always remind myself that I didn't create the situation and I can only deal with what's already happened. If we can make it better in any way, even if it is just finding the deceased to give the family some closure, that's the best we can do. Even in the darkest moments, if you can only make the situation a touch better, then you've done your job. And that's what you need to take away from it."

In a document summarizing the first ten years of the Pioneers' work, the number of live finds and deceased recoveries were noted. Of the 59 searches which resulted in the Pioneers activating teams to look for a missing person, only 24 were found alive. Of the 35 deaths, eight had drowned, five were reported suicides, 13 had perished while they were lost, one was murdered, three were hoaxes and five were never found. In just the first decade of their existence, that was a lot of emotional strain for Pioneers to bear.

I think back to Scott Morehouse's comment about Pioneers often being face-to-face with family members at the search site. They wait for searchers at the end of each day, relying on them for answers. What kind of training can prepare a search volunteer for the look on a family member's face when what they have to offer is news of a death? What happens to Pioneers when they return home carrying these feelings inside?

"The only way you can deal with it is to talk," Sue Fox suggested. "It's wonderful that Roger and I do this rescue work together because we can talk. And you have a team that you are with and they understand what it's like. We've worked together to

124

bring out bodies multiple times, so the team understands. You didn't cause the situation and you're bringing that person home to give the family someone to bury. Through it all, you talk it out."

"After a search we'd all meet at Mimi's, the local diner in Fulton, and have a cup of coffee and relax," remembered Richard Bartholomew. "And then we'd debrief. We'd let the adrenaline wear off. Dad would also critique the search after it was over. He wondered what we could do better or what we could pay more attention to."

Those cups of coffee and meals together were important for the team's morale and for the members to remain strong after difficult scenarios. Fresh off the strenuous hiking through forests and swamps, searchers would look for the nearest opportunity to meet, have a warm meal and relax, maybe even blow off a little steam. Dale Currier talked about one such experience at the Barnes Corner Hotel, which he described as "a restaurant in the Tug Hill Plateau known for their steaks."

"We figured it would be a great meal and we sure were hungry," Dale said. "Ten of us walked into the restaurant and were told they didn't have room, but I think it was because we were muddy and smelly. So I asked the person at the door, 'If the president came, would you have room for him?' 'Of course,' she said. 'Well,' I said, 'he's not coming.' We sat down to eat."

Social events helped the Oswego County team find a balance to the stresses of those difficult searches. Their annual awards dinner, which honored the team members who had gone above and beyond in support of the Pioneers' goals, also provided some fun and fellowship. Christmastime offered the team's holiday party, with members taking turns hosting the event. Former members of the search team were invited to these occasions, and while the conversation included their memories of both satisfying and disappointing searches, it was done in a relaxed atmosphere with good cheer and respect for one another.

After parties were over, though, it was back into the fields and forests when the next callout for a search was received. Team members told me about something they called "compassion fatigue," the accumulated stress a person can experience when they've been in search and rescue for many years. Those same team members pointed out that one way to heal from this fatigue is to focus on the gratitude shared by a missing person's loved ones. Pioneers didn't only get letters of thanks from families of a live rescue. Here's a note of appreciation from the parents of Michael E. Doyle, who in 2009, after being despondent over personal matters, took his life:

"We, along with all members of our family, thank you for the effort you put forth in the search for our son. Your many kindnesses to each of us during this extremely difficult time is greatly appreciated."

Letters can also serve to ease stress by being a reminder to search and rescuers of the important work they do. When eight-year-old Aaron March decided to run away, the Pioneer group, along with the New Haven Fire Department, Onondaga County Air One pilots and a canine unit were called in to search for him. In order to teach the boy a lesson of how poorly-chosen actions can affect so many people, Aaron's parents insisted he write a letter of apology. In an eight-year-old's block letter handwriting, Aaron spelled out what he had learned:

> "Thank you for all the time you were looking for me on Monday. I'm sorry for scaring you and for running away."
> Your friend,
> Aaron March

Those and other letters were beacons of hope as I reviewed the Pioneers' scrapbooks. As a chronological record of the team's important searches, I felt a little bit of that emotional fatigue reading page after page of newspaper clippings, many with disturbing details of missing people never found. The inclusion of letters of thanks is a testimony to the wisdom of those who compiled this record of the Pioneers' work. To me, it proves that the team cared enough to balance the tough stuff with the good. Here's one more letter I found, this one from Steve Ives, who served as co-coordinator of the Pioneers in 1975. To me, it is an example of the healing role leaders can have:

To the members of Oswego County Pioneer Land Search and Rescue Team.

I would like to express my gratitude for the great effort exerted by you on the search for Nona Natke on September 9 and 10.

Remember the swamp you went through on the 9th, the stagnant water, the mud up to your waist, the briar patch you crawled through on your hands and knees? Remember how it felt after two days of hoping she was alive to hear the message that her body had been found?

We, as members, put in 343 man-hours on this search and it personally cost us $1,000.00 in lost time at work and travel expenses. We are the only ones who will ever really appreciate the determination and dedication required in a search.

In closing, I would just like to say that I am proud to be a member of our team. Working with you and for you has been and will continue to be one of the highlights of my life.

Respectfully yours,

Steve Ives

Ending this chapter covering the array of emotions Pioneers deal with was a bit of a challenge until I remembered an aspect of search and rescue work team members shared with me. Searches could take them deep into the beauty of nature. Though several members unapologetically mentioned this fact, I wasn't sure it belonged in a book that was covering the gruesome details of uncovering dead bodies. But I can see how, just like those thoughtful letters of gratitude, appreciation of the environments Pioneers are privy to, is also important.

"Your senses were tuned into nature," remembered Richard Bartholomew. "You'd hear the chipmunks, squirrels and birds. You could smell the fresh-cut hay, the water from the creeks and swamps. And I could appreciate the beauty of it while searching. Along with it being a labor of love, being on a search was also enjoyable."

Steve Ives was also candid about how enjoying nature can be part of a searcher's experience: "There are places in New York State I have seen that I bet no one would ever step into unless they were lost. These are beautiful places, and I'd often think that if it weren't for these searches, I'd never have seen them. While I'm out in these locations, I'll feel the privilege it's been to do search work, and what always 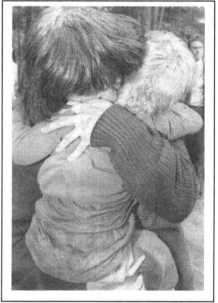 comes back to my mind is the most important reason I'm there: "Helping that family of a missing person."

Chapter Eight

Expanding the World of Search and Rescue

The Pioneers have always been, first and foremost, a search and rescue team that conducts its work on foot, with its volunteers pledging to travel into and through precarious settings. However, from the very beginning, the team was committed to exploring other search techniques as well, starting with an innovative technology that was used when Douglas Legg went missing. While hundreds of people spent weeks searching for the boy on land, a select few were doing so from above.

Infrared photography was just developing as a viable search method when Douglas disappeared. In the town of Rome, New York, a hundred miles southwest of the Santanoni Preserve, an organization calling themselves the Rome Reconnaissance Association (RRA) heard about the challenges searchers were facing. The RRA had been working with Rome's Griffiss Air Force Base to test their new aerial survey technique, a method of photo mapping which could locate 'warm bodies' on the ground. The leaders of the RRA offered their services to the Legg search's coordinators, but as we know, they were unable to help locate Douglas.

When the RRA learned about a search and rescue team organizing in Oswego County, they contacted the county's Civil Defense office to ask about developing a training partnership with the Pioneers. Bart Bartholomew favorably responded to the Rome group's inquiry, and within six months of the Pioneers' founding, the two groups were partners in this new search and rescue technology.

A 1972 *Valley News* reporter covered the inaugural training for the use of this new science, calling it "the most extensive search and rescue exercise ever attempted in Oswego County." The article noted that it may have been "the first time a simulated search of this magnitude has ever been done in the state." Bart voiced his high praise for the RRA and for the other participants in the exciting training event. The Pioneers were the lead organization, sending 25 team members on a practice search for four adults and two children.

The training began on Sunday, March 12 when a pilot took to the sky from Rome's Air Force Base, flying over a designated area where the "missing persons" were thought to be. The photographer on board sent his search findings – black and white photos with points of concentrated light – to the Pioneer's command center in Fulton. The land search began as a helicopter directed the teams from above. When the subjects were quickly found, all who participated in the training deemed it a success.

A helicopter lands at the Oswego County offices in Fulton during a combined aerial and land search and rescue training.

News of the innovative search technique travelled beyond Oswego County when an April 1972 article in Syracuse's *Herald-American* covered the successful collaboration between the Pioneers and the RRA. Entitled "Hot Spots Zero in on 'Lost' Man," the *Herald-American* reporter was at the two groups' second training and offered more on this innovative science:

> "It was early morning when an Air Force C-131 twin-engine plane took off from Griffiss Air Force Base to methodically comb the Fulton area from more than 1,000 feet above the snowy, tree-studded landscape. Below, hidden by the trees, six men wandered, 'lost.' Infrared photo equipment in the aircraft recorded their locations, allowing skilled searchers to rescue them only hours later in an exercise that could spell the difference between life and death for a child lost and near hysteria in terrain like the heavily-wooded Adirondacks.

> "The lost men, members of Oswego County Pioneer Land Search and Rescue Team, showed up as tiny dots of light – hot spots – on the infrared photos which recorded the men's body heat against a darker background of the frozen land which appeared gray on the photos. RRA men readied topographical maps on which they would mark hot spot locations for the five ground search teams. On print, there were several hot spots of various shapes, sizes and brightness. The differences were due to the amount of heat generated by each source. An open fire would appear as a large bright spot, a human's body as a dim pinpoint."

Not only did working with the science of infrared photography add a new search tool to the Pioneers' strategies, but it also ushered in a different perspective team members had of themselves: "It was the first time our little 'ragtag outfit' worked with all these different groups on such a big and complicated operation," Steve Ives said. "It was just great to think I was actually part of it and that maybe this search and rescue thing was going to be much bigger than I ever imagined."

The infrared trainings continued. Huey Parrow recalled the details of one at Pine Lake, near the town of Greig, New York. "Again, we worked with the special team from Rome Airbase. Our group, along with the Lewis County Search and Rescue team, trained under the guidance of Head Ranger Robert Bailey from Lowville/Lewis County area. For this training, two members of the New York State trail-cleaning crew were sent out the day before to set up a campsite with a campfire, a lit Coleman lantern and themselves in bedrolls. Also in this area were beaver, deer, coyotes, and large rocks warmed from the summer day.

Pioneers and Rome Reconnaissance Association members study infrared maps during a search training.

"That night, the military plane flew over the campsite, took the infrared photos and returned to Rome Airbase, where other staff studied them and phoned the DEC with their results. Ranger Bailey and our search teams then went into the area to locate the subjects and objects the photos had shown."

Other search techniques the Pioneers incorporated into their training were done to specifically address the unique terrain the group anticipated encountering. "Because the areas we had to search, such as the Adirondacks, had cliffs or ridges, we took up rappelling," Huey explained. "A few of the team were already familiar with this specialized method of scaling steep landscapes, and since we didn't have an instructor, these guys coached us and we learned on our own. Later, we improved our skills by training with the Syracuse and Fulton Fire Departments and then headed out to places like Old Forge and Salmon River Falls for practice."

Jim Crombach was among those early Pioneer rappellers and he recalled that, "at that time, with the exception of the forest rangers, nobody was doing rope rescues. My wife and I did the Salmon River Falls training, which, in some parts, was difficult. There were spots where the wall jutted in and you were just dangling there. The only safety system was a rope reaching the bottom of the cliff where an individual was helping to control the rope."

Pioneers train in rappelling at Stillwater Reservoir.

Richard Bartholomew was a young teen when he participated in the same rappelling exercise. "Huey and Ralph Larkin taught us how to repel," Richard remembered. "We would go over the face of the cliff several times until it became comfortable, and then several times more to make sure we knew it. I got scuffed up a little bit because I was a little scared and had an adrenaline rush going."

The desire to practice rappelling until the group felt prepared prompted Pioneers to secure training sites wherever possible. Team member Deana Ives' father was a Fulton firefighter and "with his help, we rappelled off Towpath Towers," Jim Crombach said. Pioneers scaling the 11-story high-rise facility in the middle of the city surely offered quite a spectacle for passersby.

The newly-trained rappellers knew that learning to climb was only step one in their training; rescue techniques had to be added to their rope skills. For this, they turned to the Oswego County Civil Defense office. An October 1972 newspaper article mentioned a rappelling training held for the Pioneers. The Civil Defense staff donated the heavy-duty safety belts and rope, and provided instruction in rope tying, lashing and simulated rescues. This allowed the team to incorporate aspects of a search into their exercises, such as using rappelling to raise a stretcher holding a person injured from a fall.

Rappelling skills were an important addition to the Pioneers' search methods year round, and the team knew that for the winter months they'd need to expand on these rope-rescue techniques. Jim Crombach explained that "we also had someone who was a semi-pro mountain and ice climber. He'd been down in the Andes winter climbing and he took us to the Adirondack's Bald Mountain to train. By the end of the day, we were able to climb up twenty or thirty feet that we never would have thought we could do when we started."

The Pioneers didn't have to use their ice-climbing skills when they were called out to help northern New York during the disastrous ice storm of 1998, but they certainly needed to know how to traverse over frozen terrain. "My first memory of that event was driving up Route 81 heading to Watertown," said Steve Ives. "The area looked like a war zone. Trees were down and every single telephone pole had just snapped in two. Even metal towers were bent like pretzels from the weight of the ice. We needed our hard hats for that search – whatever ice had formed overhead, if it fell and you got hit by it, you'd be out of business."

"We met at the Watertown Emergency Management office," Howard Bennett said, "and they assigned us communities to assist, but we were also there to offer whatever help they needed. Burnetta and I were assigned a village near Black River, which had overflowed into some of the main roadways, so we went from house to house with the local fire department trying to get people to evacuate. We also shut off gas lines to avoid explosions and put out a few house fires."

Roger and Sue Fox were in a theatre enjoying the movie *Titanic* when his pager went off with the call to head north to help in the aftermath of the ice storm. "We ended up in Alexandria Bay," Roger said, "in a municipal building which, by operating a few generators, they'd converted into a command and logistics center. One of the issues with this particular rescue effort was that many of the key municipal employees – the fire departments and such – were all trying to solve community problems while handling the effects of the storm on their families. They couldn't do both and it was taking a terrible toll on some of them.

"There was no power to the community and restoration would take weeks, and without power, there was no water. Roads were impassable. Help would be a long time coming as the disaster affected millions of residents across multiple counties in New York, as well as other U.S. states and Canadian provinces. We were able to relieve them of some of their duties, while helping to put together a long-term strategy for getting through this disaster.

"This wasn't something our search team had specifically trained for, but by working with the local communities, we took on and dealt with problems one at a time. A few days later, we returned home with a situation that was much better off than how we found it. By that time, outside assistance had started to filter in and our services were no longer needed."

When the Pioneers weren't expanding their training techniques and helping with unique search and rescue situations, they were offering their knowhow to groups outside the emergency management field. The team often became a "go to" group for special events taking place in wilderness environments, especially in areas where rescues might one day be necessary. Before the team had celebrated its one-year anniversary, it was asked to give a program at an Oswego County Boy Scout Troop spring camporee. The all-day program was set up at Gulliver's Pond in Palermo, New York, a rustic setting Pioneers were familiar with from previous trainings. The team offered the boys instruction on map and compass, search and rescue techniques, first aid, and radio communications. It culminated with the 300 youngsters in attendance applying what they'd learned in a simulated search.

The Pioneers also took part in northern Oswego County's Woodsmen Field Days. Along with search and rescue teams from Lewis County and the town of Boonville, Pioneer team members helped with the annual outdoor event by monitoring its Salmon River whitewater races. An August 1975 *Palladium-Times* article pointed out that "among the many spectators on hand for Saturday's whitewater canoe race will be members of Oswego County Pioneer Land Search and Rescue team. But for the Pioneers, it'll be more than a spectator sport. The team will be ready to rescue canoeists who overturn or spill during the challenging race along the scenic, but swift-flowing river."

The Pioneers were not only there to protect race participants. "The team was also ready to rescue someone who might fall into the Salmon River Falls gorge or similar ravines," Jeannie Parrow explained. She described the team members stationed at various vantage points along the river, ready for any emergency which may arise in the seven-mile-long race.* Little did the team know as they took their places to monitor race proceedings, that a more urgent call for their expertise would take them from this recreational activity and send them due north, straight into the Adirondacks.

---

* In a 2016-version of this type of Pioneer support, Roger Fox mentioned how today's team helps with "a race in the Finger Lakes region. On this 50-mile race, we man the checkpoints and make sure everyone is accounted for. From time to time, people stray off the course, some of whom aren't outdoor types."

As canoeists raced down Salmon River, 17 members of the Pioneers rushed to join 60 other volunteers in the search for Herkimer County resident James Whittlesey. Mr. Whittlesey, who newspaper accounts reported as disoriented while walking the 1,100 acres of his heavily-wooded land, had been missing for over 50 hours. After the searchers followed his tracks more than eight miles from his starting point, the 88-year-old man was found in surprisingly good condition.

The Pioneers even became a sponsor of an outdoor winter event. From Bart Bartholomew's connections with the Fulton YMCA and other civic organizations, in February 1980, the team helped coordinate the city's Winter Festival. (The event was held annually for a number of years.) A brochure for the event indicated sponsorship by the Pioneers along with the American Red Cross and Fulton Amateur Radio Club. The fun included a hockey tournament, open skating, a basketball foul shooting contest, softball games, cross-country skiing, snowball-rolling contest, broomball and a winter run. The Pioneers were also on hand to demonstrate their rope rescue techniques.

Winter 1980 was a busy season for the Pioneers. In January of that year, it was announced that the team would provide support for the Winter Olympics, held at Lake Placid, New York. Noting that 90% of the state police and DEC rangers were committed to securing the immediate Olympic area, a newspaper lauded the Pioneers and other New York-based search teams for agreeing to handle rescue emergencies throughout the state. Taking the lead, the Pioneers held a special statewide meeting to review their responsibilities during the six-week Olympic event.

Steve Ives explained in the article how a rescue call during the sporting games would differ from regular situations: "Normally, the planning, mapping and other coordinating work is done by state police or DEC rangers. However, most of the state police force and all the rangers have been committed to providing security within the eight-mile circle centered on Lake Placid during the Olympics, so our group will be assuming those responsibilities...I look at it as another challenge."

The Pioneers were even called to provide their talents at a rock concert. August 1999 was the thirtieth anniversary of Woodstock, and a commemorative event was held at the former Griffiss Air Force Base. The team was recruited to do a search following the event. According to an article in *PuLSAR,* a newsletter created by Pioneer team members, their job was to ensure that no subjects were still on the base. The concern was for individuals who might be still in tents or remote locations and suffering from illness, heat or alcohol and drug-related health problems. Part of the rational for using a search and rescue team was that, given the events of the night before, non-uniformed (i.e. non-threatening) trained personnel would have less problems.

When a person decides to join a search and rescue team, they are likely motivated by the thought of saving people's lives by braving dangerous terrain day or night. They volunteer to rescue the innocent child, the disoriented grandparent, the wayward soul – but the subject was always *somebody.* Come to find out, searches aren't just for people.* "My very first search was to rescue ducks," Howard Bennett admitted. "When my pager went off, notifying me of a search, I was all excited. I called in to get the details and was told, 'We've got some ducks on a nearly-frozen pond and we can't get them off.' 'Oh, okay,' I said, a bit disappointed."

----

* In my interview with Roger Fox, we discussed the Pioneers' original by-laws which, in fact, did state the group would search for wildlife in trouble. When Fox took a leadership role with the team, he made sure to amend that search aspect: "No more ducks, no more tortoises, no more cats up a tree."

Howard decided to join in, despite the absence of a human subject to search for: "We started out the rescue attempt in a flat-bottomed boat, but the ice was too thick and we couldn't break through to the middle of the pond where the ducks had gathered. We decided to go to the opposite side of the pond, hoping to scare them to a safer place, but they wanted to stay in the middle of the ice. Finally, we took shovels, circled the pond and started throwing dirt out onto the ice. That gave the ducks enough traction and off they went. It wasn't what I was expecting for my first rescue, but it was kind of fun."

There was a second case of a Pioneers' rescue of our feathered friends, this one involving a swan. In recent years, black-billed trumpeter swans have made their summer home in a wetland pond located along County Route 6 in Volney. The swans' young, known as cygnets, spend their first year at that location, then fly south with their parents in the autumn. In 2012, one of the cygnets had been born with a deformed wing and was not able to join its family on their journey south. Those living in the area who had taken an interest in the birds knew this young swan would have starved, frozen or been eaten by coyotes that winter. To prevent this from happening, the local search and rescue team came to mind and a call was made to Steve Ives.

"I was contacted because I was a Pioneer and knew the resources available for different types of emergencies, including boat rescues. I made some calls and found Dick Drosse, an environmentalist who had been involved with a number of local wildlife causes over the years. Dick and I contacted some canoeists and kayakers and they agreed to help."

Bonnie Sommers is one of the neighbors near the pond, and over the years she has kept track of the habits and health of the birds, earning the name "The Swan Lady." She had noticed the deform-winged swan's troubles, and with her husband Glenn, Dick Drosse and Steve Ives, she organized a rescue party to capture it.

"We made our first attempt at the end of November," Dick

Drosse explained, "but a layer of ice had set on the pond and made it impossible to maneuver. The swan moved into the brush and hid. Luckily, we had enough of a thaw in the next two weeks that the ice melted."

Bonnie Sommers shared the group's next rescue attempt: "This time, there were seven kayakers and canoers and we needed all their help since there was about five acres of pond area to break through. The boaters used their paddles and the boats themselves to get through the ice and reach the swan. It was almost comical as the boats tried to close in, but I was also nervous about the safety of the baby bird. Finally, by encircling it and slowly moving in, the swan was safely captured. What was

amazing was how calm and docile it was through it all. After being examined, the bird was turned loose at a Nedrow pond where people can observe wildlife in their habitats."

Swan rescue on County Route 6, Volney.

Not all animals wind up on the receiving end of a search and rescue team's efforts. In fact, there's one particular animal species that instinctively knows how to perform the precise work Pioneers are involved with. It wasn't long after the team was founded that the group welcomed into their training and fieldwork some new members, ones who were naturally suited for the world of search and rescue: dogs.

With their sense of smell 20 to 100 times greater than humans, dogs have long been considered an excellent resource for a variety of search-related needs. Centuries before professional search and rescue teams ever thought of using them, dogs were assisting hunters in the wild to track, locate and retrieve game. Once search groups realized that a trained dog could thoroughly cover as much territory as several human teams, man's best friend began using its powerful sense to the benefit of rescue work.

The science behind why a dog has such an uncanny ability to track the scent of a living creature is still not completely known, but researchers believe it is their ability to detect "skin rafts": scent-carrying dead skin cells, evaporated perspiration and gases released by bacterial action. As long as a "scent generator" exists, which, in the case of search and rescue, is the missing person, canines trained as air-scent dogs can be highly effective in locating them. They can be utilized in a search at any point, including weeks, months or even years later.

In search and rescue situations, air-scent dogs help by picking up traces of a lost person's scent that drifts in the air. When the dog finds the scent, it's referred to as "getting a hit." The dog is trained to follow the scent, which forms a "cone" created by airflow, with the person's most concentrated scent closer to their body. Dogs run back and forth in this cone as the scent narrows its way to the missing person.

Pioneer Jim Crombach was involved with the team's air-scent dog trainings held at Norm Hayden's property and he witnessed the dogs in action: "We had to empty the area of everybody since the dogs would scent on any of us, so our group collected at the top of a valley. Down below, on the other side of the valley, an individual was completely hidden behind a log. The dogs were sent upwind and immediately they ran from side to side. If one of the dogs lost the scent, it would turn around, go back and start again. Within twenty minutes, one of the dogs found the person."

Another specially-trained search and rescue dog is known as a trailing or tracking dog. These canines can be trained to discriminate one scent from another, only beginning to search after being given a sample of a specific person's scent, such as from a piece of their clothing. The trailing dog then picks up and follows only that scent. The scent's heavier-than-air particles will normally be close to the ground or on nearby foliage, so the trailing dog will frequently have its "nose to the ground." Bloodhounds are often trained as trailing or tracking dogs.

There are other specifically-trained canines that are helpful in search and rescue. A disaster dog is trained to find human scent in unusual environments, including collapsed structures and areas affected by tornadoes or earthquakes. A cadaver dog reacts to the scent of a dead human. Water search dogs are trained to detect human scent that is in or coming up from a body of water, focusing on the scent of bodily gases that rise. These dogs and their trainer or handler normally work from a boat or along the shoreline.

An April 1994 *Post-Standard* article about the search for a missing Fort Drum soldier described the use of a water search dog. The soldier disappeared while fishing on Black Lake in northern New York. His fishing boat capsized in high waves, dumping him and his fishing buddy into the 40-degree water. The soldier's friend made it to shore, but he did not. After the friend described to authorities what happened, they pinpointed an area of the lake where the soldier was presumed to have gone under. Jake, trained as a cadaver dog, was taken to the area and soon he "showed interest" by biting and pawing at the water. After divers tried for several hours to locate the soldier, the search ended. Several months later, fishermen discovered his body in the same area Jake was drawn to by his strong sense of smell.

Howard Bennett remembered how dogs were used on a search for a Cayuga County missing person, who, he said, "had some emotional problems. The man had told a few people that if he ever went missing, nobody would find him. We were called in to assist by the Cayuga County Sheriff's Department and found signs near a deep quarry where it appeared someone had slipped off the bank. Dogs were brought into the area with rowboats and they hit on a scent. We radioed this back to shore and a flag was tied in that spot. They brought in divers, but because the area was so murky and full of dead trees and such, they were unable to ever actually locate him."

When Howard and his wife Burnetta joined the team in the early '90s, Burnetta was planning on becoming a typical land search volunteer. But a twist of fate changed all that. "I've always loved dogs," Burnetta explained. "Around the time we joined the Pioneers, my sister's Irish setter had delivered a litter of pups and she pointed out one she'd saved for me. It was a long-eared setter and I thought she was just beautiful. I named her Shone.

"The day I got Shone, we were leaving for a Pioneer search and rescue event where teams from all over New York State came together to share ideas and trainings. I brought Shone with me, and since she was a tiny little thing and it was so cold out, I kept her zipped up in my coat. I watched the dog demonstrations and thought they were neat. That spring, I went to a couple dog trainings, thinking they were good places to socialize Shone. One of the dog handlers said, 'Hey, let's try your dog out.' They put Shone out in a field some distance from where I was standing and she ran right to me. Next, they had me hide in the brush, and when she came running over, I gave her a treat. That's how it all started.

"Shone and I really got into training. We'd go to nearby trails and practice three days a week. She was classic in the way she adapted to searches. I would yell, 'Find!' and a bark would come out of her that she never did except for searches. If Shone was on a search and got distracted by the scent of a squirrel or if she ran up to another searcher, I'd say, 'Leave it!' She'd look at me, thinking, and then she'd go on searching. From all those days of practice, she'd started to read my signs and I started reading hers. I was never as in tune with a dog as I was with Shone."

Burnetta and Shone was part of several Pioneer searches until about six months after they had started training. "She developed hip dysplasia," Burnetta said, "but our vet urged me to continue the trainings; he said it would keep her going longer." Burnetta

143

did find ways to keep Shone active, including taking her to schools for demonstrations. "I'd tell the kids, 'Now watch,' and Shone would find her subject and come back to tag me. The kids got such a kick out of it. We even played this game later in her life, when she was too old to go out on searches. Shone passed away when she was twelve."

Burnetta Bennett and Shone.

Along with Shone, the Pioneers have been fortunate to have other dogs assist them in trainings and on searches. Huey Parrow mentioned an early Pioneer, Donald Phillips, and his German Shepherd. Roger Fox remembered these owners and their canine partners who served as helpful Pioneers: Steve Lathrop and his German Shepherd, Vlux: Dave Claridge's several German Shepherds; Dave Hatfield and his German Shepherd, Danka; Christine Fox and her mixed breed, Brandy; Ray Hines' German Shepherd, Keisha; and Diane DeLeon's Golden Retriever, Lindy.

Roger also explained to me that for many years, "there was no single standard that dogs had to meet to be considered search and rescue canines. Basically, if a team member had a canine with a vest, it could be considered 'operational.' Needless to say, that caused significant problems with the credibility of these dogs and their handlers. Somewhere around 2004, the New York State Federation of Search and Rescue Teams adopted a single standard and mandated compliance for a canine to be considered operational. When that happened, the list of operational canine units went from around 70 to 17, which was all for the good."

Today, the Pioneer team does not have a canine unit, but there is still interest in working with search dogs among members of the team. When Thom Benedetto joined the group in 2013, canine search support was in the back of his mind. Like Burnetta Bennett, Thom didn't start out thinking he'd become a rescue dog trainer; in fact, he wasn't even planning on joining the Pioneers.

"My wife and I were visiting our daughter's school for an open house," Thom recalled. "I noticed that Sue Fox was doing a presentation on Woods Smart, a wilderness training program for children." Benedetto had met Sue before and decided to attend her program, where he learned about the Pioneers and the fact that they were recruiting for an upcoming training. After her presentation, Thom asked Sue if it was too late to register for the upcoming class. "She gave me the application that night, which was a Tuesday, and the first session started that Thursday. I got in under the wire and completed the required training."

Since Thom was one of the current-day Pioneers I interviewed, I wanted to know if his interest in joining a search and rescue team was similar to those of the founders. "For me, it marries my love of the outdoors with some important skills: survival, orienteering, mapping and coming together to help people. When I worked for Oswego County's district attorney, I had been a deputy coroner and worked closely with police agencies, fire departments, and ambulance corps. Being a first responder in search and rescue has many similarities."

The year after Thom became a Pioneer, his wife Patty joined him. For both Benedettos, there was another incentive to their involvement: the canine element of search and rescue. In 2012, the couple adopted a black lab named Leela and from their first interactions with her, they noticed she was special. "Leela had a high hunt drive and a high play drive," Thom explained, "two important aspects in a good search dog." The couple began exploring canine search and rescue.

Soon, the Benedettos were attending training sessions with

Eagle Valley Search Dogs, a volunteer professional canine search and rescue team based in the Hudson Valley. Thom and Patty found out there were additional trainings they would need to complete, which they are currently working on. They've also spent time training as "flankers," who serve as the eyes and ears of a canine handler on a search. This allows the handler to concentrate on their search dog.

As Thom and Patty became more immersed in canine search training, they decided to adopt a second dog. In April 2016, Philip, a yellow lab, joined the busy Benedetto household. Currently, both dogs are in training; Patty working primarily with Leela, and Thom with Philip. "It takes a lot to get a dog ready for search and rescue," Thom said. "We built a workout area at our home where the dogs get regular practice in agility, obedience and training specific to search work."

The Benedettos with Philip and Leela.

The goal for the Benedettos is to become properly trained and certified so that there will be operational search and rescue dogs available in Oswego County. It's a safe bet that Thom and Patty will be instrumental in making this happen. Recently, their youngest daughter, Caralyn, has shown an interest in Philip and Leela's training. "Caralyn attends a lot of the canine workshops with us," said Thom, "and she'll be attending a week-long Junior Canine Handler Academy in the coming months."

It looks like dogs will be important members of the Pioneer team for many years to come.

Chapter Nine

Gaining Respect in Oswego County and Beyond

"When I was coordinator of the Pioneers," Steve Ives said, "the families we helped or the law enforcement agencies leading a search would often ask, 'What can we do for you? You came all the way from Fulton to help us and we want to thank you.' The thing I always asked was for them to mention the name of our group in reports and news releases so people knew we were there to help. I don't know how many times we'd be listed in the paper as 'volunteers.' It would say, 'Subject was found by the state police...and volunteers.' There was nothing to signify that the Oswego County Pioneer Search and Rescue Team helped. It seemed that people never knew about us."

Steve and I were covering the part of the team's history when it moved from a small-town volunteer group to a statewide leader in search and rescue operations. I'd read some of the newspaper articles he'd referred to and also found no mention of the team by name. At times, it was only after talking with Pioneer members that I was able to confirm their involvement with a particular search or a missing person's rescue or recovery. I had a lot of questions about the team's struggle to be recognized; first and foremost, I wanted to know what initiated the Pioneers' eventual fine reputation?

Steve and other Pioneers suggested it was their proficiency with Type III search techniques that first drew attention to the group. When other emergency rescue organizations observed the team efficiently executing their grid searches, they began to appreciate the professionalism of the Pioneers. This acknowledgement of their legitimacy came slowly, especially since, in the early years, the team often found themselves working with other volunteers who were untrained.

"Sometimes these other agencies would show up for a search with 20 or 30 people, which was the same or more than we had on our team," Jim Crombach said. "The person in command of these other volunteers was used to being in charge and he didn't easily hand over the control of his men. We would attempt to blend these volunteers in with our team, which could be troublesome for our leaders who needed to be sure that when they put people on a grid, they could be completely satisfied with how the search was carried out. With these other volunteers, at the end of day, it could be hard to reliably say we'd covered every inch of ground."

Pioneer leaders tried to be appreciative of the extra help they were getting on grid line searches, but, at times, professionalism had to trump kindness. Huey Parrow told me a story about this sort of predicament: "A county deputy sheriff was once assigned to my team. The guy was spit-and-polish: showing up neatly dressed in a vest, coat and nicely-laced boots. We headed off on this search, and as I often did when my team was on the line, I went back and forth to see how they were doing. I found this guy walking *around* a swamp. I went up to him and said, 'Sir, if you are on this team, you will go through that swamp. Otherwise, I will send you back and make a report.' The guy complied with my request and we later became friends. Turns out we were both tough and by the book."

Over time, it was this conviction to the team's systematic search techniques that gave the Pioneers the attention they were seeking. State troopers, police officers and firefighters began recognizing this new group's effectiveness and efficiency. When the team began working closely with DEC forest rangers, whose job includes the well-being of people in the wilderness, an awareness of the Pioneers' value grew. In fact, it is a forest ranger's work which most closely matches that of search and rescue teams. Since 1891, when President Benjamin Harrison announced the Federal Forest Reserve Act and rangers were charged with its implementation, their work has been defined by three things: forest preservation, fire prevention, and search and rescue.

One of my goals while researching this book was to learn firsthand about a forest ranger's job and their association with teams like the Pioneers. As he had done for me time and again, Huey Parrow provided an inroad to my achieving this goal. In my interviews with Huey, he frequently mentioned the names of forest rangers the Pioneers had worked with and agreed to try to track down the whereabouts of these men, some who he'd last worked with over a quarter-century ago.

Sure enough, within a few weeks of his offer, Huey contacted me; he'd found a ranger willing to tell me his story. There was a bonus to Huey's find: this ranger agreed to meet with me at his home on the Stillwater Reservoir, a body of water in the Tug Hill area where the Pioneers held some early trainings. The Reservoir is a three-hour drive from Fulton, heading northeast – I was going back into the Adirondacks.

Joining Huey and I on that adventure were his wife Jeannie and Steve Ives. We got an early start on the morning of July 19, which just happened to be Huey's 80th birthday. I was at the wheel, and without a map or GPS, I was also a little nervous that no one brought written directions. I soon learned, though, that they wouldn't be necessary. In what turned out to be a unique type of internal mapping system, all three of these former Pioneers began pointing out landmarks along the way: locations of other searches, eating and drinking establishments where the team gathered to either celebrate a live find or commiserate over an unsolved search. They let me know miles ahead of a turnoff I needed to make, suggesting I look for a certain church or one-room schoolhouse. I relaxed; I was obviously with people who knew their way around the Adirondacks.

As we were driving, Huey pulled out a piece of paper with his now-familiar handwritten notes. Setting the paper down on my dashboard, he told me it consisted of information about all the rangers he had personally worked with. He recited their names and the regions they covered: Robert Bailey, Cameron, New York; Loren Hamlin, Jefferson County; Cliff Mattis, Copenhagen, New York; Wilber Peters, Homer, New York; and the ranger we were on our way to see, Terry Perkins, from the Stillwater Reservoir. Huey had also taken the time to research each ranger's personal data, including date of birth, and in some cases, date of death. He emphasized that each of these men had been a resource to the team; my interview with Terry would inform me about just one of many who helped shape the Pioneers.

I was able to appreciate the value of this road trip with these Pioneer founders before we even reached Stillwater. There was a spot on our travel route that Huey was anxious to show me. As we drive on tree-lined roadways, he told me about a tombstone we'd be passing that he wanted me to see. "Just east of Lowville," Huey explained, "there's a marker of the burial spot for a search victim from the 1800s, a little boy named Nathanial Tripp."

As I expected, Huey knew the exact road to turn off and even how far I'd have to drive to find the marker. Within sight from the road, we spotted a neatly-mowed area, and in it, a foot-high headstone; a perfect height for the nine-year-old boy it memorializes. We gathered around it, struggling to make out its inscription, but the stone is too worn to read. Somehow, however, it uncovered a memory for Steve:

"I once attended a search and rescue training sponsored by forest rangers and the slideshow portion of the program opened with a photo of this headstone. I remember the ranger saying, 'This is why we do search and rescue, so we never have to bury another child who found themselves lost.' " The four of us stood quietly for a moment or two. Huey knelt down, gently touching the stone.

Stillwater Reservoir offered a picture perfect day, bright sun sprinkling diamonds across the water. Standing in the parking lot waiting for Terry, we watched boaters head in to stock up on supplies for their campsites along the shoreline. (The only way to get to these sites is by water.) There's a line of mailboxes for year-round residents to stay connected to the rest of the world. While we took in the scenery, Terry Perkins approached our group and tentatively asked if one of us was Huey. They two haven't seen each other in decades.

Terry, fit and animated for a man in his 70s, informed us that we'd need to take a boat ride to get to his home. He and his wife Diane are the only occupants of an island a mile or so from the Reservoir parking lot. As Terry explained how life led him to his career, our boat approached an island almost totally tree-covered; an idyllic home for this retired forest ranger.

Terry explained that the surroundings of his childhood home, east of Troy, New York, looked a lot like Tug Hill. As with most kids sixty years ago, he was always out playing in the woods and water. When he was 13 years old, something happened to a family member that profoundly influenced Terry's becoming a forest ranger.

"My uncle and his buddy were fishing in the waters of West Canada Lake," Terry said. "Their boat overturned and they disappeared. I spent that summer with the ranger stationed there, searching for them in the lake. We found my uncle's friend's body a few months later when it came to the water's surface, but we never found my uncle. While working with the ranger, I decided I wanted to have a job like that."

Terry graduated high school, took a summer job teaching hunter safety at a conservation education camp and then went to work in the fish and wildlife management area. Later, he transitioned over to the DEC, slowly accumulating the work experience needed to bypass the associate's degree requirement for becoming a ranger. Terry took the ranger's exam in 1967 and accepted his job at Stillwater Reservoir, where he would serve for

38 years.

"I oversaw about 250 square miles, which is rather small compared to other regions," Terry explained. "But because this area is almost all state land with very little access into the woods, it is a lot to be responsible for." Terry began telling us about his search and rescue work by mentioning the Douglas Legg case. "It was a very high-profile event and, in some ways, it was an embarrassment to the rangers; actually to all of New York State, including the governor. It looked like we didn't know who should have been in the lead, the state police or the forest rangers."

After the failed attempt to find Douglas, Terry was involved with the development of New York's three special search and rescue teams; the Blue Fox being his group. "I was a hunter, so I was pretty good at tracking, and the state wanted certain rangers to get extra training and lead those teams, which turned out to be a bad idea. All rangers should be experts in search and rescue and those special teams didn't last long."

I asked Terry to share his opinion of a volunteer search and rescue team's value: "Some teams, like the Pioneers, were often a good-sized group, which was something we forest rangers needed. There weren't a lot of us to do the searching, so having trained volunteers to help in an intensive search was critical."

As we settled into our conversation in Terry's spacious log cabin home, he asked me if I noticed a ridge of small mountains while we were on our boat ride. I did, and he proceeded to tell the story of a search that, for him, illustrates why having professional volunteer search and rescue teams available to forest rangers is so important:

"One November in the 1980s, a man named Edgar Thabault was hunting with some buddies at Gregg's Lake, about five miles from my workstation at Stillwater. The hunters had rented a cabin about a quarter-mile from the lake in an old logging area. Edgar was up in age, with a heart condition and trouble walking. His buddies had gone out to start their day, but he stayed at camp because of his heart. If he was going to go out at all, he would have just walked a bit. It seems that around 10 o'clock that morning, Edgar did head out, but his friends were convinced that he couldn't have gone more than a couple hundred yards, if that.

"When the hunters came back, they couldn't find Edgar. The men looked around, fired some shots, but got no response. They figured he'd return, but after a while they decided to notify the authorities. I got notice of his disappearance that night and was told that one ranger was going to do an air search while we searched on land. I joined in by walking there since it was just on the other side of the mountain ridge."

Terry started searching by noon the next day, and said he didn't know it at the time, but he walked within 200 feet of where Edgar Thabault had collapsed and died. "We spent the month of November searching for him until the snow got too deep to do so. Sometimes, I'd stay at the hunters' campsite and sometimes I'd come back home and return the next day, but I searched every day."

The Pioneers joined the rangers, spending two weekends searching for the man, also staying in the general area around the hunters' campground. But, as Terry explained, it wasn't the Pioneers or any of the rangers who found the first clue of what happened to Edgar: "Three years later, some hunters found a glacier-deposited rock that was half the size of a living room. It was hollow and you could stand up inside it; it was that large. This was about a mile and a half from Edgar's campsite, which, according to his friends, was way too far for him to have travelled. But, we have learned that people can actually travel much further than might be thought possible when they are in a life-threatening situation. When the hunters found this spot, leaning up against that immense rock was a rifle with one round of ammunition in it.

"The new group of hunters took the rifle to the ranger's office and it was traced to Edgar. The rangers contacted me and we started a new search, beginning from the huge rock. We figured Edgar must have tried to climb to a higher spot to signal the planes that flew overhead searching for him. This would explain

153

why there was only the one round of ammunition left in his gun. He must have tried to signal for help, but it was too far away to be heard. It was determined that Edgar had collapsed from a heart attack. His body was found fully clothed, but he was just a skeleton.

"The search for Edgar Thabault is an example of how organized search and rescue teams can be of great assistance to forest rangers. While the Pioneers would not have been able to save Edgar's life, having more people to search such a large area would have helped. It's a little bit scary on a search to have family or next-door neighbors who are not trained, but want to help. Trained people are so much more reliable; when they'd report back to the command center, we knew their area was done right."

"To have volunteers," Terry concluded, "free of charge, who were trained and willing to work – and the Oswego County group was always willing to respond to our requests – that's the value of a team like the Pioneers."

A visit with retired Forest Ranger Terry Perkins. L to r: Jeannie Parrow, Terry, Steve Ives, Diane Perkins, Huey Parrow.

As appreciation for the service provided by search and rescue teams grew, the Pioneers gained the respect they were looking for. But as the saying goes, be careful what you wish for. No longer mentioned in news reports as an anonymous volunteer group, once communities throughout New York State learned what the Pioneers could offer, the callouts started increasing. "Some of these searches could last for days, weeks or months," Steve Ives said. "It was important to have plenty of people to do them, and early on, when ours was the only team, if a search lasted for an extended period of time, there might be only one Pioneer at the scene, then maybe a few more on weekends. We all had jobs and family, so we couldn't always get away."

Before long, requests for Pioneer search support started coming from throughout the state and beyond. As the team began to function effectively, and with the horror of Douglas Legg's disappearance still on everyone's mind, long-distance requests for the Pioneers increased. Something needed to be done to relieve the Oswego County team before demand for them burned its members out and Bart Bartholomew had an idea.

"Our team has had 30 alerts and 15 actual searches since it started 15 months ago," Bart pointed out in an October 1972 recruitment press release. As part of his plea for new members, he addressed why fresh sets of boots on the ground were needed. "There are nearly 50,000 square miles of land in New York State, over which half is wilderness. That's a lot of area to get lost in." While Bart didn't come right out and say that his search and rescue team couldn't handle the requests to look for missing persons, the article announced an innovative idea of how to prevent that from happening:

"The Pioneers are offering to train representatives from the 62 counties in New York State. By training a few individuals from each county, they can return to their homes and train their own men." Bart also proposed having these teams from different areas rotate being on alert each weekend. "In this way, a few teams can go out on a search one weekend and not be called back the following weekend," the Pioneer leader explained.

Bart's press release didn't hide the fact of what it takes to develop the skill level of search and rescuers, noting that "it takes about a year to develop a good search team." He then swiftly added his opinion of current emergency search standards in New York State: "We are at least 40 years behind the times with search and rescue teams." Bart's comment about his state's deficiency was in reference to California's advanced training and established emergency rescue groups. He ended his request for new recruits with an inspiring challenge: "The time has come for each county to take the responsibility for its citizens and start a search team of its own."

With this passionate call for support, Bart and the Pioneers once again became search and rescue leaders. In January 1973, a statewide workshop was held in Fulton. Its mission? The founding of the New York State Federation of Search and Rescue Teams. Several regions from throughout the state responded favorably to the workshop idea: Geneva, Lyons, Malone, the Adirondack Mountain Club (ADK), Thompkins County, the Thousand Islands, ADK of Onondaga County, a horse rescue team from Franklin County and a team from Camden, New York aptly named "The Snowrunners."

Attending that first meeting were representatives from eight organizations. Most, like the three DEC forest ranger-led teams and one each from Tompkins County and West Leyden, were just forming. Huey Parrow added a few other teams who were early supporters of the Federation: "Massasagua, who were out of Rochester, Thompkins County, and a team out of Albany." He also pointed out a second reason why the Pioneers were strong advocates for a united New York State search and rescue organization:

"We had no control over these other teams who were just forming and some of them were inexperienced. If we went to another area in the state that had a search team, they'd take the lead of organizing the volunteers and we'd work under them.

Once the Federation was organized, it could help those inexperienced teams properly train."

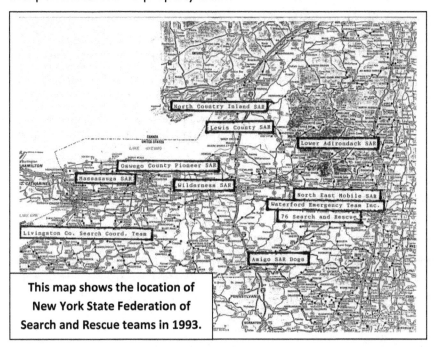

This map shows the location of New York State Federation of Search and Rescue teams in 1993.

Consistent training standards were among the Federation's growing pains. Steve Ives, who was one of the first elected Federation leaders, remembered presiding over the disagreements that erupted at the new organization's planning meetings: "I was trying to keep the group unified, but one of the things they would fight about was who thought they had the best team. There were different ways to train, different things that teams thought were important for searches, and sometimes there was this attitude of 'I know how to do such and such type of training.' Those kinds of things needed to be tempered because, in fact, each of them *did* have something they could offer. One of the things the Federation decided early on was to come up with standards all teams should have, and as its leader, I helped those kinds of decisions to be made."

Other Oswego County Pioneers assumed leadership roles for the statewide group. Jeannie Parrow offered her expertise as a communication officer; her husband Huey's map and compass skills were a popular training. At first, the Federation almost functioned as an extension of the Oswego County team, but over time, it became its own entity. "Today, there are 28 teams in the Federation across New York State," said Sue Fox, "and teams are still forming. There are specialty groups such as dog teams and an equestrian team."

The current Federation even extends itself across borders to work with other states in the northeast. Scott Morehouse is on the Federation Board of Directors and mentioned the far-reaching standards the organization aspires to today: "If a team is willing to come into New York to help, they can belong to the Federation. We have teams from New Jersey, Pennsylvania and Connecticut who come forward when there is an incident." It works reciprocally, too, as Thom Benedetto explained: "As part of the Federation, Pioneers participate in searches throughout the state, but members have also helped out beyond its borders."

The need for statewide search and rescue training standards prompted the Federation to make it one of their top priorities. When the first such event was offered to all New York State teams, the Pioneers were again at the planning table, and the result was an event known as COMFED, the Combined Federation of Search and Rescue Teams of New York State. Included in COMFED's original plans was an idea that continues today: The teams would meet to train twice a year, each spring and fall, with the training taking place in different New York State regions. Teams took turns hosting the event at a site of their choosing, which often reflected the wilderness aspect of search and rescue.

When Western New York's Massasauga Search and Rescue Team hosted COMFED in 1976, it was held at the Carlton Hill Management Area, a 9,000-acre state-owned forest. Newspaper coverage of the event noted the rustic setting for visiting search and rescue teams: pitched tents were clustered in an area with no modern amenities. The base camp shelter was a 20x15-foot plastic-covered framework with a latrine. Everything else had to be brought in to the camp: water, food and bedding. Not the comforts of home, to be sure, but search and rescuers who were there to test their skills didn't mind.

By the time visitors arrived for the first day of training, Massasauga team members had already slipped into the woods to become "subjects" for other teams to search and rescue. Two people portrayed a married couple. The man feigned an injury and hid in a gorge so it appeared he'd gotten trapped there; his "wife" was a short distance away, simulating hysterics. Another subject assumed the role of an escaped mental patient and succeeded in evading his rescuers for quite some time.

When the Pioneers got the opportunity to host a COMFED, they wanted to provide lost-person simulations that outdid what other state teams had offered. While this provided the Oswego County team some practical planning for scenarios they might encounter, it was also fun. "One of my highlights with the Pioneers was when we hosted a COMFED," said Jim Crombach. "We held it at an abandoned Boy Scout camp and I helped set up the training for three separate scenarios. Steve Ives and I teamed up for one where I played the part of a person with mental limitations; Steve was my brother. As part of the situation, I climbed a tree and wouldn't come down. I was just crying for Steve, who ran for help from the visiting teams. One woman spent two hours until she finally talked me down. Another team didn't have any luck with that, so they set up ropes, climbed up and took me down."

The fun and friendship continued after the day's training was completed. Visiting teams relaxed with fellow search and rescuers and their families. "These events really fit into our team philosophy," Steve Ives mentioned. "In some ways, the Pioneers were like a search and rescue family, so if our kids could be with us, that was good. We attended these events as families and it was almost like we were going away for a weekend camping trip."

Jim Crombach recalled one COMFED that challenged how much of a family atmosphere team members could handle. The training took place in early autumn, so no one expected winter weather to disrupt the event, but as Jim explained, it did: "Steve and Deana Ives and their two children, and my wife, our two kids and I spent the night together in the tent – with two nursing babies. We woke up with two inches of snow on the tent in October."

In the mid-1990s, with the Oswego County team gaining respect both locally and statewide, founding Pioneers were met with yet another challenge. These men and women who were in their 50s and 60s, and who had learned to search with map and compass and not much else, were expected to accept a revolutionary shift in how they operated: along with the rest of the world, search and rescue strategies were being rewritten by modern technology.

Chapter Ten

Modern Day Searching

"The things the Pioneers tried to do in their early days were the right things to do," Roger Fox said, reflecting on his impressions of the team when he joined in 1994, its twenty-third year. "But, the world had changed and the Pioneers had been so used to doing the same thing and operating the same way, it was almost like they were isolated from the rest of the world."

Roger and his wife Sue were sharing their memories with me in April of 2016, while the two were in the middle of packing their house for a move south. The Foxes are pulling back from their active role with the Pioneers this year, and as I sat at their dining room table cluttered with paperwork and objects to keep, donate or discard, they spoke about the team's move toward more modern search and rescue methods.

Roger's involvement with modernizing the Pioneers was influenced by his career path, beginning with his service to our country in the United States Navy. After graduating from the U.S. Naval Academy and then attending Naval Flight School, Roger served six years as a helicopter pilot. His duties introduced him to maritime search and rescue and anti-submarine warfare. During our interview, Roger explained how this training was important to his contributions to the Pioneers. He started by clarifying how maritime warfare relates to land search and rescue efforts.

"Early in World War II, the Allies were losing the battle for the Atlantic," Roger said. "They had no tactical strategy to successfully counter the U-boat menace until a research group in England started to take a much more scientific approach to the problem. It was basically a 'know your enemy' strategy, which included these questions: Where should you look for the enemy? How often do they surface? How detectable are they when they do? How deep can they go? Do they surface at night when they can be more easily detected? Much of this search theory was classified information during the war, but in 1950s the theory and its applications were revealed. A lot of that search theory was found to be applicable to what rescue teams were trying to do, and over the course of the last 30 or 40 years it has been adapted to land search and rescue."

After serving ten years in the military, Roger went to work as a computer programmer. When he joined the Pioneers at age 42, he brought those skills to the team, as well. "Over the years, I got intimately familiar with a lot of up-and-coming technology like Geographic Information Systems, a computer program that displays data collected by Global Positioning System (GPS) satellites. When I joined the Pioneers, I asked, 'Why are we limiting ourselves to paper maps? Why can't we use computer mapping and try to improve our capabilities?' "

Roger's wife Sue, age 44 when she joined the Pioneers, also brought her previous work and volunteer experiences to the team. Sue obtained a degree in physical education, a masters in Sports and Health Management, and then shifted her career focus to elementary school, where she taught for 30 years. The Foxes raised two daughters and during their formative years, Sue became a Girl Scout leader, serving as an outdoor trainer for the Central New York Girl Scout Council. When she and Roger saw an article about the Pioneers that Ralph Larkin had put in newspapers, it caught their eye.

"Ralph's press release asked if anyone liked being in the woods," Sue recalled, "and Roger and I did a lot of hiking in the Adirondacks. Since our children were older, we had time to consider other activities." The Foxes showed up at Gulliver's Pond, where the Pioneers were doing some training. There, they met the group and other recruits and got their first lessons in search and rescue work, including map and compass and how to manage a grid. A new chapter of the Oswego County Pioneer Search and Rescue Team had begun.

Roger and Sue spent the next twenty years helping to improve and build the search management capabilities of the team through training, the use of computer technology, more capable communication systems and a commitment to continued learning. Now that those changes are firmly established, it's difficult for anyone learning about the Pioneers today to imagine how revolutionary those changes were. There is one person, though, who is in the position to comment on the striking differences between original Pioneer protocol and the team's current search and rescue standards. Dale Currier has the distinction of being a Pioneer on two separate occasions.

I had tracked Dale down after seeing his name in the Pioneer archives, finding out that he is currently the director of Oswego County Emergency Management, an organization with strong ties to search and rescue work. Dale and I had planned a phone interview, and when I called his office, he apologized ahead of time if his memories of first joining the team were muddled. After explaining that he'd spent a long night on an emergency management issue, I offered to reschedule our talk, but he said that wasn't necessary. Within the first few minutes of our conversation, Dale was describing those early years with clarity:

"In the 1970s, I was a student at SUNY Oswego and part of the college's SAVAC ambulance corp. I met members of the Pioneer team during an EMT class I was teaching. During one session, the Pioneers were telling me about their team, and since I'd grown up in the Adirondacks and had been on searches up there, they invited me to join."

Dale served with the Pioneers until employment opportunities took him out of the Oswego County area. He married, raised a family, and somewhere around 2005, he found himself with free time, looking to do volunteer work. Dale met Sue and Roger Fox, who were manning the Pioneer's recruitment table at an event, and mentioned he'd once belonged to their group. The Foxes told him about an upcoming training at Happy Valley Wildlife Management Area. "Why don't you come join us?" they asked.

"I liked the idea of seeing what the search team had morphed into," Dale said, regarding his motivation to attend the training. "I also wondered if I had any skills they could use." He spent the next five years with the Pioneers.* While with the Pioneers his second time, Dale served as a training officer, and it was in that role that he got to see the many changes his team had undergone since the '70s, beginning with something as basic as how they dressed for a rescue:

"Back when I first joined, you'd go in the woods wearing big heavy hunting boots or leather boots meant for construction sites, not long-distance hikes. Our shirts, pants and coats were wool and heavy; if they got wet, they got heavier. Today, you look at people on the team and their footwear is lightweight; since they're walking on Gore-Tex, their feet stay dry. You have nylon and other synthetics for pants and shirts versus cotton, which when it gets wet, it isn't good for your body. This not only makes it more comfortable for the searcher, but also safer, which allows them to be functional and more effective for longer periods of time."

Dale also observed the improvements in food preparation and packaging since the '70s: "In the early days, if I knew I was going out on a search, I'd pack three or four peanut butter and jelly sandwiches and that would be it. They worked because they were easy to carry, didn't require refrigeration, and I got some sugar and protein. I'd be okay for a while. Today, already loaded in my backpack are energy bars. It's a food that's been scientifically crafted to give needed nutrients, and it's properly stored so it can last for years."

---

* Another job change required Dale to spend a lot of time in the Albany area. As a dedicated search and rescue volunteer, he was also involved with a rescue team there.

Dale's memories helped me form a bridge that connects the Pioneers' founding members with today's current team. In the nearly half century that separates them, hundreds of volunteers spent time on the team; some for a few months, others for decades. As I interviewed Pioneers from the different eras, I began to notice similarities in their stories and I came to see that, despite so much of our world having changed since 1971, how a volunteer answers the call to search and rescue has not. Here's a few examples of how today's Pioneers found their way to the team.

Joe Homola, raised among the farm fields and woods outside Cicero, New York, had a childhood that sounds like many of the early Pioneers. "We didn't have the internet back when I was a kid, so we'd go outside, make forts and sleep in the woods," Joe wrote in an email exchange we conducted about his association with the Pioneers. He mentioned that he was also very involved with the Boy Scouts, and at age 13, he attended a DEC Conservation Camp, successfully completing his hunter safety course.

Joe's love of the outdoors continues today. He's been a volunteer for the Nordic Ski Patrol, which is part of the National Ski Patrol system, for 30 years. In the 1980s, Joe took a Wildland Search Course through the DEC, allowing him to be a certified volunteer for their searches. As an Onondaga County resident, he approached their Wilderness Search and Rescue Team about 15 years ago, but its leaders didn't think he could give enough time to their organization due to his involvement with Ski Patrol. Then Joe met Roger Fox.

"I first heard about Oswego County Search and Rescue in 2006 when I was looking to renew my Wildland Search certification. The Pioneers were offering the class and I got in touch with Roger. While taking the course, I talked with him about joining the Pioneers, and the more I talked with him, the more I learned about his experience and background. He seemed like a good person to learn from. I also wanted to make sure he and the team knew I was with Nordic, which he said wouldn't be a problem. They were willing to have me and I was willing to give them my time." Still an active member of the Pioneers today, Joe leads some of the team's trainings.

Scott Morehouse, the Pioneers' current coordinator, also had life experiences that warranted his joining the team in 2012. Scott grew up on a farm outside Ithaca and remembered spending much of his childhood tracking horses and cows. After high school, he began to develop skills which would move him closer to search and rescue work.

"I had an interest in being a conservation officer, so I originally went to college for forestry," Scott explained. "I ended up with dual majors, earning degrees in forestry and civil engineering. At that time, however, the state was in the process of laying off conservation officers, so I spent many years in engineering and land surveying around the country."

Scott also mentioned a lifelong conviction to give back to his community, "using the skill set that God has given me to help others in need. Search and rescue has fulfilled that for me. Working for the families experiencing their worst day, helping to find their loved one is returning God's gift to them."

In his relatively short time with the Pioneers, Scott has spent a good deal of it in leadership roles, serving as the team's assistant coordinator for two years under Roger Fox. By this time, the Foxes had started pulling back from their leadership role with the group, but as Scott pointed out, "Roger still monitors our events, and even though he's not with us for all the searches, he's always just a phone call away."

Aaron Albrecht, who we met in this book's chapter entitled "At the Heart of Every Search," was 25 years old when he joined the Pioneers in 2011, just one year older than Steve Ives when he helped found the team. Aaron remembered the reaction from some of the team when he showed up for his first meeting: "When I walked into the room, they said, 'Oh yes, young blood!' But Aaron's young age didn't inhibit his ability to become an effective search and rescuer, given how he'd spent his first 20 years.

"My grandparents owned the Jellystone Park campground, so I had spent a lot of time outdoors. I was also a Boy Scout and always liked the first aid and map and compass skills I learned there." Aaron also always had a desire to help people in his community, but the obvious volunteer choice, his local fire department, didn't appeal to him: "I wasn't too keen about running into a burning building."

"I knew Oswego County had a rescue team because I'd seen Roger driving the Pioneers' truck through town a few times," Aaron explained. "When the 2010 search for Jenni-Lyn Watson, a college student from Liverpool, New York, turned into a high-profile criminal case, I saw the Pioneers on the news. That's what finally got me to check out search and rescue." By that time, Aaron was out of college and working full time. When he joined the Pioneers, the eligibility requirements were lax, and Aaron admitted he probably shouldn't have been on his first search.

"A woman from East Syracuse had been in the Inlet area," Aaron said. "She'd gone up on a Friday to the Limekiln State Campgrounds to take pictures and never made it back to her car. The forest rangers started searching for her over the weekend and turned up nothing. The following Tuesday night, they called in for all the state federation teams and I was able to get time off work. I went there to see what it was all about."

Aaron was the only person from Oswego County who made it to the search and described his first experience as "quite the sight to see. All these people showed up, including about 30 Federation searchers and 30 forest rangers from all over the state. There were a couple guys I met from the Lower Adirondack Search Team and one worked for the DEC. When I told him I was new to search and rescue, he took me under his wing. The first thing he said was 'Eat! Eat! You're going to need fuel because you'll be out all day hiking through the snow.' "

Keeping his belly full wasn't all Aaron had to worry about when he headed out into the snowy search. "Luckily, I ended up being paired with the DEC guy, and our group was sent to the first grid. They put me in the middle of the line in order to watch me, and they made me feel like I was part of the search. We went from nine a.m. until three in the afternoon, stopping about twenty minutes to eat lunch. The other guys had radios and I could hear that another team had found her body. I later found out that she had died one grid block over from where we were searching. For my first search, it was good that my team didn't find her. I was already taking in a whole lot that day."

Over the next five years, Aaron learned quickly and began assuming Pioneer leadership roles. In 2012, he became certified as a team leader, joined the advisory board in 2013 and assumed the role of treasurer the following year. In 2016, he began his term as the team's co-coordinator, which means he is eligible to become the Pioneers' leader within the next few years. Aaron and his wife may want to start a family soon, and he knows a child will affect the amount of time he'll have available to devote to the team. Like the Pioneers he follows, Aaron gives all that he can while he can.

Remember the phone tree that the original Pioneers put in place to alert team members of a search? Or how about the primitive walkie-talkies that sometimes worked and sometimes didn't? And the beat-up van they bought for fifty dollars and some change? These sufficed for the Pioneers, in the sense that "something was better than nothing," but search and rescue sure has come a long way in the team's 45 years.

In the 1990s, Pioneer phone trees were supplemented with pagers donated by the New York State Police, which Howard

Bennett remembered as a big step for the team: "If we got paged, we called the coordinator or a field officer to find out the specifics of where to meet." Roger Fox agreed the pagers had value, but noted that they left a lot to be desired:

"The pagers given to our team were activated out of the Oneida County State Police Barracks. When the pager tripped, since it didn't have any verbal announcement, the only thing you knew to do was call Oneida. Most of the time when we'd call down there, the dispatcher would say, 'Search and rescue? What the hell are you calling us for?' They didn't even know they were responsible for paging us."

Howard credits Roger with the next big advancement in the team's communications system: "Roger knew someone from Onondaga County's Wilderness Search and Rescue Team who was an employee of Leo-Mac Radio. The two men were able to vastly improve upon our communications by working with our county to install repeaters on a couple of existing radio towers. This en-

Howard Bennett in the Pioneers' mobile command center.

hanced our ability to communicate not only amongst ourselves, but also with the state forest rangers who utilized similar frequencies. When Oswego County upgraded its old radio systems to a common high frequency 800 system, they made a provision for adding search and rescue to it. Unfortunately, the county didn't allocate any equipment to the Pioneers, so we had to procure some on our own."

Dale Currier, with his 30-year gap between volunteer turns as a Pioneer, has also witnessed the tremendous changes in the communications field. But before he explained what *has* changed, Dale pointed out something that hasn't: map and compass. "It's been around since the days of Christopher Columbus," Dale pointed out, "but technology, especially Global Positioning Systems, certainly changed *how* we use map and compass. We still had to know the mapping basics, but GPS really made it more effective."

I'm not very computer savvy, so I asked Dale to tell me in laymen's terms how GPS aids search and rescue efforts. "On a search, you can carry a GPS unit with you," he explained. "When you come in from the field, you can take the unit, download it into a computer and it will tell you within a few yards of where you walked on that search. Then the team can look at this information superimposed on a map and say, 'If a person was here, we should have seen them.' Or, 'Look, here's a hole that we missed; we need to search that area again.' In the old days, you tried to write on a map where you'd searched and accuracy was probably around 25 percent, whereas with GPS, it's more like 90 percent."

Joe Homola helped me understand this new technology by comparing it to an old board game we used to play as kids: "It's like the game Battleship. You use the GPS's coordinates to narrow your search area, getting closer and closer until you hit your mark. In our case, the mark is a missing person."

How GPS has revolutionized search and rescue methods is further illustrated in Roger Fox's recollections of this November 2003 case: "A 40'ish-year-old woman from the Camillus area was reported missing by her husband. Early the next morning, her abandoned car was discovered on an access road to the Camillus Forest Unique Area. An aerial search by Onondaga County's Air One was conducted using thermal imaging and visual searching, but the subject was not located. The Pioneers and Wilderness Search and Rescue from Onondaga County were activated and a Type I search was initiated with no success.

"The next day, " Roger continued, "better resources became available and a Type III search was implemented. Still, by the end of the day, no sign of the subject had been found. New teams were brought in and one of the team leaders had a GPS unit, which he used to record the track as they performed their assignment. He shared his GPS information with us during the search's debriefing.

"At the time, not everyone had a GPS and their use was not an integral part of our operations, but I was doing the debriefs and had the computer software to download the individual's GPS. As we were discussing his team's area coverage for the day, the leader indicated that they had searched the entire segment and were confident the subject was not there. Preparing to record that segment task as completed, I took a look at the leader's GPS track and noticed that it did not match up with the team's assigned block. I asked him to describe how they had determined their initial starting point, and as it turned out, the team had searched the wrong segment! The next morning, the area was searched again, and within 15 minutes of that search team starting its operations, the subject was located alive."

Roger explained that without the GPS track, searchers would not have returned to that segment for days, if at all. The subject may never have been found. "From then on," Roger concluded, "I became a big believer in the importance of GPS in documenting every search task. The Pioneers purchased several GPS units that we could utilize ourselves or loan out on a search to other teams who didn't have them. It was that important."

Those who've used GPS in search and rescue admit it doesn't always work, especially in the dense woodlands of northern Oswego County and the Adirondacks, where so many searches take place. These areas' thick trees can prevent equipment from connecting with satellite signals, and then, as Dale Currier conceded, "it's back to the basics."

I got to experience this interruption of service during my trip to the Santanoni Preserve on the anniversary of Douglas Legg's disappearance. Carrying a smartphone in order to keep track of our hiking and trail exploration through my phone's GPS, I found myself with no signal throughout most of the day.

Because of GPS's tenuous abilities, Steve Ives informed me that although he understands the importance of the technology in rescue work, he prefers to search by combining old-fashioned methods with modern tools: "I'm more comfortable if I can look at a map and see the whole trip laid out. I can determine where I've got to make my turns and what kind of landmarks I can expect to come across. After I do that, I'll still use GPS, but in my mind I know where I'm going, so if it gets me off course, it can't take me too far off because I've looked at the route I should be taking."

Though becoming increasingly popular as a navigation tool, not everyone is familiar with how GPS works. But nearly every person today has a cellphone, and companies like Apple and Microsoft keep coming up with innovative ways they can enhance how we live. "Smartphones, while they aren't a failsafe in regards to people being lost, have really changed how we know where we are," Scott Morehouse remarked.

I had assumed that cellphones were part of present-day search and rescue operations and several current Pioneers filled me in on how. Dale Currier: "With cellphones, searchers know that if they call someone's phone and get no response, they can contact 911, who can 'ping' the nonresponsive person's phone. (A "ping" identifies a phone's location by tracking where its last signal came from.) The dispatcher can then radio back to searchers: 'Here's where the phone is.' "

Pretty amazing, I told Dale, and he concurred with me by describing his reaction to the first time Pioneers tested the use of a cellphone in search training: "I was chosen to be the missing subject and we decided I should find a place on Battle Island Golf Course outside Fulton. The area has some pretty dense clusters of trees and I found a remote spot, called 911 on my flip phone and the Pioneers went into action. From 911, the team was able to get a reading of my location and they found me in 45 minutes. I remember looking at what now would be considered an 'ancient' flip phone, thinking they were going to change how search and rescues would be carried out from then on."

Another way cellphones have altered rescue efforts involves the decision of when to send out a search team. Once phones started being carried into the world, a searcher could actually communicate with their missing person. "Sometimes, a person has called 911 on a cellphone to say they are lost," Dale explained. "We call the phone back and ask the person: 'Are you hurt?' 'No.' 'Are you warm?' 'Yes.' Using that information, we figure it's a nice summer night, there's no bad weather coming in, nobody's hurt and it's one o'clock in the morning. Let's wait until after sunrise, when it's safer to rescue someone."

Cellphones have also become a determining factor in whether a search and rescue team is even called out to find a missing person. Thom Benedetto explained why by relating this incident involving snowmobilers: "The group was riding in northern Oswego County and thought they had gotten lost, so they used a cellphone to contact 911. Today, when someone calls the 911 Center and identifies themselves as lost, search and rescue teams are automatically dispatched. But it turned out the snowmobilers also contacted family members and determined that they weren't really lost, they were just slightly off the trail system. In a case like that, there was no full search team callout. The police were quickly able to resolve the call once they learned that the snowmobilers were able to carry out a self-rescue with assistance by family members over the phone."

A February 1998 *Post-Standard* article covered one of the first successful rescue efforts due to the cellphone. The circumstances of the search started like many other missing person situations: Four hikers were lost in Highland Forest, a nearly 3,000-acre Onondaga County park. The group, three teens from the Elmcrest Children's Center and their counselor, had hit the trails in mid-afternoon. They left without a map, compass, water or even warm jackets – but they did have a cellphone. When the group didn't show up for dinner, the Center called for help, and from the police officer's first phone contact with the hikers, the rescue was nearly certain. The phone enabled the counselor to describe where they first picked up the trail and the general direction they headed. By early evening, the four were back in the facility's parking lot, shaken, but uninjured.

Success stories like these prove that cellphones are indeed a powerful tool for search and rescue. But like we've seen with other technological advances, there is a downside to these modern communication devices. With phone companies claiming better service and wider coverage, mobile phones have given people a false sense of safety, as Dale Currier noted: "Nowadays, people hike into a wilderness area like the Adirondacks without being well-prepared. They'll think, 'I'm good. I've got my phone, so if I get into the trouble, I'll call 911 and someone will save me.' But we know cell coverage doesn't work everywhere."

Roger Fox clarified what Dale was referring to: "Cellphones have the ability to provide precise location information to 911, but there are a lot of 'if's' in there. First, is it a newer cellphone with a built-in GPS, or an older style? Does the cellphone itself have a good GPS signal or is it sending the *last* good location it recorded? Are its location services turned on so it can provide any positional information to the Center? If it can't, then the cellphone service provider may only be able to estimate the phone's location relative to the nearest tower. Where, exactly, is that cellphone tower located? Does the Center have to talk the caller through changing their phone's setup to get that information?"

There are other ways that a cellphone's ability to aid in a rescue can be compromised. "In May 2016, we were dispatched to a canoeist on the Redfield Reservoir who had to put ashore due to rough water and became lost," Roger explained. "He called his brother using a cellphone and actually provided a screen shot of his location. The brother called the 911 Center to make a report. The Center was unable to get a call back on the cellphone, but was able to ping it and get an intermittent location. Search and

Rescue, along with the New York State Police, were dispatched to the site.

"Using a GPS with the location entered, after a half-mile through the woods, rescuers arrived at the phone's location, but there was no sign of the subject or the canoe. A search of the shoreline and surrounding area turned up nothing. The 911 Center still had intermittent location information from the phone in that area. Further investigation revealed that the subject's car was not at the boat launch where he had put in. A call to his home phone found him there, cooking dinner.

"After initially calling his brother for his assistance, the water on the Reservoir had calmed down enough for the subject to paddle his way back to the boat launch. In the process of getting into his canoe to return, he lost his cellphone in the Reservoir. So," Roger concluded, "we can add another condition with regards to cellular location information: the phone has to be *with* the subject."

Of course, modern technology will never be able to address a major concern for search and rescuers: the behavior of a missing person. At a recent Pioneer business meeting, I observed members discussing their concern over a particularly frustrating callout for a search. A hunter was lost somewhere in the Oswego County woodlands and sent a text to 911 for help. The dispatcher followed protocol for a distressed caller's text and asked the hunter to call into the 911 Center. This would allow dispatch to establish communications with the missing person and provide vital information to the search team. The hunter, using some pretty strong language, texted back his refusal to call in, which meant the Pioneers would need to resort to more traditional search methods; in other words, they would need to start from scratch.

All in all, though, advances in technology have not only helped the Pioneers search more efficiently, but it has also enhanced the team's relationship with other agencies. "Today, search and rescue teams use the same management structures that all emergency support systems – police, fire, EMT – use," Dale Currier said. "When the Pioneers show up at a search site, everything is going to be set up and managed in the same way."

Dale is referring to what is known as the Incident Management System, a standardized approach to the command, control, and coordination during emergency situations when responders from one or multiple agencies are involved. Though the system has been in place for decades, the need for its effectiveness really became important after major disasters like Hurricane Katrina, the 9/11 terrorist attacks and Hurricane Sandy.

"The Incident Management System assures that the most competent individual(s) will be in charge," said Roger Fox. "They will identify the strategy and tactics to resolve the incident and activate the most efficient utilization of the resources available to do that. The System develops one plan and everyone is on the same page."

There's one more way in which modern technology and improved search and rescue protocol assists a team like the Pioneers. It involves compliance with various laws and regulations. Increasingly, the case of a missing person has potential legal implications. "Every search today is organized under the direction of a specific law enforcement agency and they must initially determine whether or not criminal activity is involved," Thom Benedetto pointed out. "Everything we do must be properly documented. There is also potential for lawsuits, so proper training is important. Generally, as long as a searcher reasonably undertakes his or her responsibilities within the scope of their skill level and training, they aren't likely to be held liable."

Talking about modern communication devices and advancements in technology got me thinking about the future of search and rescue. What's the next new search tool coming down the pike, I wondered. A conversation with current Pioneer member Patti Ruffos, who is researching one particular new resource, gave me a clue.

"Drones now come with GPS and cameras," Patti said. "With them, our search and rescue team will be able to hone in on a missing person, radio that information back to the command center and then head out on foot. Developing this tool will need FAA approval because search and rescue practices are considered a commercial use of the new technology, but it holds a lot of potential."

As I visualized what Patti described, I felt like I'd just been given a bird's-eye view of a futuristic search and rescue world.

Chapter Eleven

Training for Today's Search and Rescue

"You had to be breathing," Roger Fox joked when I asked what the Pioneers' requirements were when he joined the team in 1994. "Literally, there was no formal training at the time, except the DEC's eight-hour Basic Wildland Search Skills course."

I did a little research on this DEC course and found that it, indeed, covers just basic skills. Having learned about everything searchers need to be aware of before they enter the woods, eight hours seems like it wouldn't even scratch the surface of adequate training. I asked a few more early Pioneers about the kind of preparation they received when they joined the team, and Howard Bennett's introduction to search and rescue work sounded similar to Roger's:

"Showing an interest was the only requirement. I contacted Ralph Larkin and he invited me to a meeting. After you attended a certain number of meetings and trainings, you became an official member."

Thinking back on what I'd learned about the founding Pioneers' extensive training regimen – first aid, the three types of grid searches, simulated rescues in the backwoods – I wondered if something had changed between 1971 and the mid-'90s. No, things hadn't changed, I found out; I'd just neglected to ask those early Pioneers what the training requirements were back when they founded the team. There were none, they explained, but what *did* matter, as Howard confirmed with memories of his first training, was that all members were expected to learn and grow:

"We had mock searches and drills. We learned how to search by grid pattern. Of course, at that time, it was all old-school: map, compass, string and flagging tape."

Dale Currier made a particularly colorful comment about the difference between the Pioneers' 1970s "old school" training to 2000's more modern version by comparing them to how airplanes have been flown over the years: "In the early days of aviation, pilots, such as the old barnstormers, learned to fly their planes in a few hours. They'd fly around, landing where they wanted to, leapfrogging from place to place. Today, pilots are highly-trained. They use GPS and other technology to more effectively fly and land. They plan their flights and must adhere to rules about what elevation they can be at depending on the direction they are travelling."

Eventually, the Pioneers' training criteria became more comprehensive, as well as mandatory. By the time Joe Homola joined in 2006, the team's trainings were offered monthly. "There were by-laws written stating that to be on the team you had to express an interest, take the DEC course and attend three events, either trainings or meetings."

Aaron Albrecht found the same three-events rule when he joined the Pioneers in 2011, but added the requirement of an application and references to vouch for the new candidate's abilities. "After your third event, you were accepted on the team," Aaron explained. "Then you'd get your training as you went along. There were several different classes you needed to complete, but not within a deadline. And there was no formal graduation at that time, not like is done with today's Academy."

Aaron was talking about the Pioneers' comprehensive training program for new recruits, the latest example of how the Oswego County team continues to be innovators in search and rescue. Like many other important advancements throughout the Pioneers' nearly half-century of operation, this one was inspired by a search and rescue effort that ended tragically.

"The first Academy took place the year following the disappearance and search for Jenni-Lyn Watson," Joe Homola explained. Jenni-Lyn was a nineteen-year-old Liverpool, New York resident who disappeared from her parents' home in 2010, while on Thanksgiving break. Joe explained that the search went on for over a week until her body was discovered and investigations led officials to charge her boyfriend with the college student's murder.

Jenni-Lyn's search was a high-profile case, and along with extensive newspaper and TV coverage, the new social media phenomenon known as Facebook added 5,000 people to those who were following it. "It was a search that sticks out in my mind as major," Joe pointed out. "The first Search and Rescue Academy happened to be that next spring and there was a large turnout, at least partially because of her disappearance."

Planned and run primarily by Onondaga County's Wilderness Search and Rescue Team, the Pioneers provided classroom and field instructors for that first Academy. It was the first organized and comprehensive training school of its kind in New York State. The Academy's success was so evident that the two teams, Wilderness and the Pioneers, decided to conduct it annually, alternating the lead agency.

In the spring and early summer of 2016, the sixteen-week program ran for its fifth time, and Scott Morehouse, who is one of the Academy's instructors, shared the course design with me: "Classroom sessions covering CPR, First Aid and Wilderness First Aid run one night a week at the Emergency Rescue Training Center in Oswego. One or two weekends a month, there are field trainings on what students have learned in class."

Scott shared a flowchart of the full Academy course roster and I looked over the names of other classes: Clothing, Survival, Equipment; Map Coordinates Systems and GPS; Crime Scene Awareness; Communications and 911; Project Lifesaver; Lost Person Behavior. About a dozen different instructors are involved in the training. My first thought: this is lightyears away from those simulated searches to find a makeshift dummy in the woods. Even as I think this, Scott honored the original Pioneers by describing what sounds a lot like the founders' first trainings:

"We put a lot of emphasis on land navigation because the use of map and compass is still very important. We do that particular training throughout the Academy, and on the last day, the students are totally on their own. We set up markers, which are just pieces of florescent tape hanging in trees half-mile or so apart. Each student is given a different course to find these markers and each segment is different with regards to the equipment they can use to navigate.

"At each location, students are queried regarding where they are on the map, including their calculated bearings to the next location. Additionally, they must demonstrate their survival skills, including fire-making and shelter building.   It's like their final exam in the field."

On a Saturday in May 2016, I attended a daylong Academy training at Happy Valley Wildlife Management Area in northern Oswego County. Consisting of just under 10,000 acres of woodland, the Management Area is a perfect spot for potential Pioneer team members to learn how to search and rescue.

"Happy Valley is a popular place for both hunters and novice hikers to go," said Roger Fox, another Academy instructor. "The area has a rich history and even has its own resident ghost, or at least that's what some believe, and that brings in people who follow that kind of thing. Some years, about 50 percent of the calls we get for search and rescue in Oswego County happen in Happy Valley."

As I pulled into the Management Area's gravel parking lot, I could see why half of all callouts in Oswego County are to this wilderness area. Besides a couple of storage buildings, I was looking at trees – miles and miles of them. Later, I found out the dirt trails Academy students will search on are not marked, just like one would find in parts of the Adirondacks. As class members arrived, I imagined what was going on in their minds as they prepared for a full day of training. While we waited for the program to begin, I introduced myself to several of the 15 recruits, wanting to learn what drives someone to volunteer for such a lengthy search and rescue training.

The student's ages are all over the map, ranging from teens to retirees. The same with their occupations: critical care nurse, bus driver, teacher, public information clerk. One of the class is looking to become a firefighter in his town, and the youngest candidate, age eighteen, had become an Eagle Scout, so search and rescue seemed like his logical next step. Not surprisingly, all the candidates have one thing in common: like their Pioneer "ancestors," they love the outdoors and the day's training would be a nice break from the hours they'd spent in the classroom and required homework readings.

Scott Morehouse opened the class by explaining the agenda for the day. The eight hours would begin with four 1-hour sessions of small group work: technical ropes rescue, basic map and compass, fire-making and shelter building, and familiarizing themselves with GPS. The remainder of the day would further build on those skills as the students would be challenged to navigate through the woods on a simulated search.

I joined one of the four small groups and headed over to technical ropes training, where I met Pioneer Tom Fazzio, the assistant for that class. "Being on the Pioneer team definitely has an element of book smart," Tom told me, "but it's really all about being street smart." As I rotated through the four morning sessions, watching recruits earn their street-smart credentials, my head was spinning. The amount of material being covered was overwhelming: practicing proper knots for a rope rescue, calculating the compass bearing from one location to another and then following it, punching in the right codes to program a GPS.

I know the students have been studying these important facets of search and rescue for months, but I also know the difference between reading about a skill and mastering it. I spent my lunchtime trying to comprehend it all and found out that a similar weekend training included stations where students worked on other essential skills: radio communications, setting up the command trailer, travelling to a particular location using coordinates provided.

As the afternoon session began, clouds were forming overhead. People were checking their weather apps and there was discussion about not continuing the program. The decision to carry on was wise; Academy leaders knew that recruits needed to understand how inclement weather is part of search and rescue. Facilitators reminded the group that, fair weather or not, once the simulated search was described to them, other than making sure they were safe, the 15 were on their own.

The missing person scenario sounded believable based on the search and rescue events I'd been studying for months: two women in their 60s had gone out for a hike in Happy Valley. They'd stayed on the trails, but when one woman was injured by a falling tree limb, her friend panicked and wandered off the trail trying to get back for help. Her one call to 911 sent a signal of her location, but then her phone died. "Find both women, assess their situation and get them the help they need," Roger Fox challenged the class.

The students broke into three groups: command center, search team, and a backup team, who would serve in any capacity required during the search. I began by looking in on the command center team, who climbed into the Pioneers' state-of-the-art trailer. Scott Morehouse explained that the vehicle contains everything needed for a search: basics like string for grid lines, rope, flagging, first aid and food supplies. A generator provides power and there are backup batteries, if needed. The center has an internet connection, two computer screens, multiple printers, maps and several radios. Roger Fox explained the reason for so many radios:

"We travel to many locations that are outside our county and there is no one common radio system across New York. In Oswego County, we are lucky enough to utilize a radio system that is common to every agency in the county. With one radio, we can talk to all the people that we need to. Even in our surrounding counties, the same system is utilized. As we travel further from Central New York, we have to be prepared, minimal-

The Pioneers' mobile command center.

ly, to talk with our own team personnel. It's not only for search management, but also for safety purposes. Having a variety of radio systems located in our command trailer gives us a great deal of flexibility when we are working with agencies in areas outside of our county."

After observing the Academy students as they power up the command center, I joined the group heading into the woods, watching as its newly-appointed leader organized his team of four searchers. A grid line was formed as it started to rain, and now wearing waterproof parkas, they fanned out on either side of the trail. I noted some tentativeness in this team; their calls of the missing people's names were weak at first. The grid line kept breaking up, with some members getting ahead of others. A candy bar wrapper was overlooked until one of the facilitators suggested they keep their eyes on the ground. I empathize with the group; actually searching in the field is a lot different than sitting in a classroom thinking about it.

When the searchers located the first woman – the uninjured person who'd called for help – they found her in a state of hysteria. "Where's my friend! Is she alright?" the woman pleaded. There was chaos for a while, until somebody remembered the backup team and a call was made for them to escort the woman back to safety *and* remove her over-the-top anxiety from their mission at hand. Eventually, the search team found the second woman (a first-aid mannequin filled this role), unconscious but alive. A nurse on the team assessed her and provided treatment. A call to the command center for assistance obtained additional manpower with equipment. The group then put the injured person on the "stokes," a stretcher-like piece of equipment, radioed for an ambulance to be brought in, and carried her to the trailhead.

By this time, the rain was pretty heavy, but the full group still gathered in the parking lot to debrief. The students talked about the awkwardness of being in their new roles. They asked good questions about what they could have done differently. They also all looked tired. I know I was. But as Roger Fox said in the wrap-up, "It's all about the practice. No situation is the same as the last, but with each one you learn something new about what you can do, what to 'pack in your bag' and how to rely on your teammates."

If the students I observed in this training finish the Academy program successfully, they'll have logged over 100 hours of classroom and in-the-field experience. "If there had been an Academy when I started, I don't know if I'd be on this team today," Aaron Albrecht admitted. "It's a lot of hours to devote in a small amount of time, and one of the reasons I joined the team when I did was that there wasn't a lot of upfront training involved. Now, it's a four-month commitment."

Over the five years the Academy has been running, Scott Morehouse said about 90 percent of the students make it all the way through. But he added the fact that about 50 percent of them will drop out once they spend some time on the team: "A lot of people are intimidated by the reality of search and rescue. Searches can be very hard, and for others, it just isn't what they thought it was." What Scott was explaining sounds a lot like what I heard from Pioneer founders about some of *their* first recruits.

There's also a financial commitment required of today's potential search and rescuers. "The cost of the Academy is $100, paid by the individual," Scott explained. "The Academy provides study books and other items, but by the time you finish the course and start buying gear – boots, backpacks and all that – it's going to cost a person around $500. And this is an all-volunteer group," he reminded me.

Still, with all the financial and time commitments, there are people who welcome the Academy's challenges. All 15 people I watched maneuver through their training day at Happy Valley successfully completed the course. In 2016, the Pioneers and its partner in the program, Wilderness Search and Rescue, have properly prepared the next generation of professional search and rescuers. And the success of the Academy is spreading beyond Central New York. "This is something that a lot of the other New York State search and rescue teams are adopting," Aaron pointed out.

At least partially due to the success of the Academy, the Pioneers have seen an influx of new members. In 2016, twenty-seven volunteers were on the team's roster, but the majority of them were new to the group. "Our team was a fairly old team until a couple of years ago," Scott Morehouse said, "but we've seen a transition lately. There's a lot of enthusiasm and it's a cohesive unit. This team will take us into the future, but it was people like Bart Bartholomew, Huey Parrow and Steve Ives who started us on this road..."

As thorough as the Academy sounds to a bystander like me, today's Pioneers are quick to point out that graduating from its program should never be seen as the end of a dedicated team member's training. Pioneers are encouraged to continue learning when new classes are offered, as well as attending refresher courses to keep skill levels high. "The team did about 1,000 hours of training last year," Scott Morehouse said. "We also have two specialty groups: the canine group and the Mantracking group, and combined they added another 650 hours." Joe Homola pointed out that there are "more advanced courses, such as Managing the Lost Person Incident, which gives team members the skills to actually run a search."

There's also the DEC's Searcher 1 certification, which Thom Benedetto has earned. Those with this special training qualify to be a search team's "crew boss," today's title for what Pioneers used to call a team leader. Thom pointed out that "when a person meets the Searcher 1 criteria established by the DEC, they must take a test to prove competency. The Pioneers were the first team in the state to develop a specific Searcher 1 training curriculum. Through the Academy, members receive all of the necessary training to successfully pass the Searcher 1 test."

All these additional trainings are important since the New York State Federation of Search and Rescue Teams is now overseeing the development of search standards and their implementation. Now that these standards have been set, Federation officials overseeing any search within the state can check to see which volunteers have proper certificates. "At a search site, when a person signs in on the state form, it asks for their certifications," Scott explained. "There are rescue team members in the state who haven't received this certification and are not a part of the Federation. That's okay, but the law enforcement agency in charge of the search needs to know that."

Law enforcement will be paying close attention to a volunteer's certification, especially because liability has become such an important factor in search and rescue today. Scott explained why: "Let's say someone is missing and there's 170 acres to search. Local authorities call in an uncertified group to help and they search the entire area without find the missing person. A month later, the subject's body is discovered in that area, only a quarter mile from where he was last seen. In this situation, a big liability comes into play, so authorities need to be careful who they call to be involved in a search."

Developing the Academy and creating a strong Federation of

Search and Rescue Teams are not the only feathers in the Pioneers' training cap. Team members old and new that I spoke with kept revealing names of unique-sounding search programs they've been associated with. Whenever a Pioneer mentioned a program I hadn't heard of, I'd jot it down and make sure to research it. Sort of like I was following a trail, which according to Steve Ives, is what "Mantracking" is all about. After Steve mentioned his involvement in that program, I did a quick Google search and discovered that Mantracking is a relatively new search and rescue technique based on a very old practice.

Indeed, people have been relying on clues left on the ground or snow for as long as they have been hunting for food. Prehistoric trackers taught themselves to recognize and follow an animal through its tracks, scat, traces of feathers or fur, sounds and scents. A skilled tracker was able to study these clues, figure out the animal's route and eventually capture their prey. Eventually, these tracking skills were transferred to the hunt for humans, with military and intelligence agencies utilizing them first. Gradually, the skills were adapted for non-combat purposes, including an evolving division of emergency services known as search and rescue.

"Mantracking was first used by search and rescue teams in the Midwestern United States," Steve explained. He's been leading this innovate work for the Pioneers for several years and considers the technique a science. "On a search, a good Mantracker can walk into any area and figure out what happened there in the last 12 hours. Before I got into Mantracking, I thought I was a pretty good searcher, but it turns out I was just seeing the same things everybody else does."

Steve spent a lot of time developing his fine-tuned Mantracking techniques by going to places like the State Fair, just watching how people walk and what kind of trails they leave behind. In time, he became more adept at his search skills: "Now I can figure out what's on the ground, like depressions from footprints. And not only on grass or snow; there are things to notice on an asphalt parking lot: stones that have been disrupted or the dampness where they've been overturned."

That's not to say Steve doesn't doubt his tracking abilities now and then. He told me about a Mantracking training scheduled to take place in his expansive backyard. On the morning of the practice search, Steve mowed the lawn, forgetting that the foot tracks the group would be trying to follow had been laid down the night before. He was worried that he'd ruined the training, but Steve recalled the teacher for the course saying, "If we're really good, we should be able to still see where those tracks were made." And, Steve said, they did.

Pioneers use their Mantracking skills on a search.

I wanted to hear about how Mantracking has influenced a Pioneer search and Steve referred to one that took place in Hannibal: "A teenager had run away from his family's trailer. He was barefoot when last seen and I was assigned, along with another tracker, to check the grounds. We found his footprints in two places: by a creek and behind the mailbox post, where one print was heading in the direction of the trailer. We surmised the boy was in one or the other location and reported that information to the state police.

"We found out later that the boy had been evading the

190

authorities, and somehow in the confusion, he was able to return to the trailer. The police said it would be awhile before they could search inside; something about it being a criminal case if the search took place in a residence. We figured we were going to have to start dredging the creek, but just before we did, the authorities were allowed to reenter the trailer. And there was the missing teenager, hiding under a bed which was thought to have already been checked."

Joe Homola pointed out the combination of knowledge and art that makes up Mantracking: "There are definitely skills you need to have for it, and it's quite impressive to see what Mantrackers can do on a search. Roger Fox always said that if you arrive at a search taking place alongside a road and a Mantracker has already searched one side of that road, you just cut your search in half."

Steve and a few other local search and rescuers have taken their gift for Mantracking to the next level, becoming certified to teach the skill. They offer classes periodically for the Pioneers, other search teams, the DEC police and forest rangers. They've even travelled to the west coast to further their understanding of the skill. For Steve, his interest in Mantracking has kept him motivated to continue with search and rescue. Forty-five years later, one of the founding Pioneers is still blazing new trails.

The Pioneers have always been first and foremost a search and rescue operation, putting their skills into play *after* a person is lost. But from its inception, the team has also been a leader in the prevention of someone becoming the next missing person case. Advocating for safety first can be found in an early Pioneer press release, which quoted Bart Bartholomew: "Every day, there are more hunters, campers and people with environmental concerns spending more time in the wilderness. Most people become lost because they do not know how to dress, read a compass accurately or what to do when they are lost." Bart's article then offered some basic prevention measures, dispelled myths of woodland dangers, and made a call for cool heads while in the wild.

Twenty-five years after Bartholomew encouraged hiking safety, the Pioneers were continuing to share his advice, especially when providing community presentations. In 1996, the team, led by Roger and Sue Fox, created a program to get their message out to a group who were often most vulnerable in the woods: young children. The Pioneers called their presentation Woods Smart.

"We modeled it after a successful program in California called Hug-a-Tree," Roger said. "Our first talk was given to fourth graders at Leighton Elementary School in Oswego. We used hand-drawn posters, a few simple props and a dog from our canine unit. From there, we started doing programs at wellness or school career days."

Woods Smart teaches children how to keep from getting lost, but if they do, the program also covers how to remain safe until rescuers arrive. Several Pioneers were trained in how to lead it, including Burnetta Bennett, who explained why she thought Woods Smart was so important: "For me, it went all the way back to Douglas Legg. Here was this little boy who was never found and he was always on my mind as I went out on searches."

After providing the program for many youth groups, the Pioneers felt confident they were doing an effective job. There was talk that Woods Smart was really making a difference in Oswego County and the number of callouts for lost children had seemed to drop. But no one knew for sure how meaningful the program was until the night of February 4, 1999.

That evening, Roger and Sue Fox's pagers went off, alerting them, along with the Parish Volunteer Fire Department and McFee Ambulance, of an incident. "We were aware this incident might be a search," Roger said, "so we called McFee, who informed us they were just as in the dark as we were. A few minutes later, we heard a call over the sheriff's frequency dispatching a unit to the Parish area for a missing children incident. When names of the children were given – Rebecca Mintonye and Samantha Barber – Sue recognized one of them as a girl in her class. Given the time of day and weather conditions, we called dispatch immediately to let them know the Pioneers would be sending someone right away. Sue and I responded immediately and the team followed.

"Within five minutes, we arrived at the home of one of the girls. The scene was already a bustle of activity with fire and law enforcement arriving and quite a few family members and friends at the house. When we entered the kitchen, where the command center had been set up, we got a quick briefing from both the deputy and a fire chief. The eight-year-old girls had last been seen playing around the house at about 1530." *

An hour and a half later, when the girls were called for dinner, they did not respond. After searching and calling for them without luck, as darkness closed in, 911 was called. Last seen dressed in light coats and sneakers, and with the afternoon's mild weather turning colder, fears for their safety were rising. Sue and Roger stepped outside with a deputy to discuss the circumstances under which the children might have become missing. Sue knew report cards had recently been issued; perhaps one of the girls was upset from that and had run away or was hiding. Also, with a popular snowmobile trail passing behind the house, the potential of criminal activity had to be considered.

Roger explained what happened next: "It was decided that Sue and I would travel down the road to interview the other mother and find out if she might have any insight into the girls' whereabouts." Nothing of substance resulted from that interview

---

* Emergency service personnel, including search and rescue teams, use military time when communicating and recording data.

and the Foxes headed back to the command center. The fire department and other volunteers arrived to search roads and snowmobile trails. A nearby creek was identified as a possible hazard, so a team was quickly formed to investigate it. After the Foxes reviewed topo maps, they decided to get additional help, including a canine unit, into the field as quickly as possible.

"The wind was coming out of the southwest, so the dog would have had a good chance of picking up any scent," Roger said. "Onondaga County's Air One was now overhead lighting up the area and searching from the air. The logging trail we had been travelling on was covered in knee-deep snow. With the thawing and refreezing that had been going on, sometimes we were able to easily walk on top, other times we sunk through to our knees. All this time, we had been calling out to the girls with no response.

"Finally, we thought we heard a weak answer to one of our calls. I immediately got on the radio to see if Sue's team had been shouting. They had not, so we called out again and got another faint response. Sue called back immediately to let us know that they had also heard someone and both teams headed for the voices. Getting off the trail, the conditions were a bit worse and it required a great deal of bushwhacking in the direction of the calls. Stopping every few minutes, we could hear the voices well enough to discern that there was more than one person and that they sounded like young girls."

Roger's team reached the children first. "As we started over a small rise, the girls became visible through the trees in the beams of our flashlights. We immediately called the command center to let them know we had made contact and the girls appeared to be in good condition."

The youngsters were found huddled under a large pine tree. Roger did a quick assessment of them – their socks, shoes and pants were quite wet and both children were shivering. "I got my pack off and started taking out the spare clothes I carry. I got Rebecca's shoes and socks off and checked her feet. They were cold and wet, but she still had good feeling in them. I placed a pair of wool socks on her and tried to pull them up as far as I could underneath her wet pant legs. With Samantha, we placed gloves on her feet as she wasn't going to be doing any walking and I was out of socks."

Roger also had an energy bar in his pack and gave the girls some along with water. When Sue's team arrived, both children recognized their teacher and were excited to see her. Then they mentioned the Woods Smart program. "They told us that they knew to stay in one place and someone would be coming for them," Roger explained. "They also said they had found a tree and stayed with it."

Air One figured out the shortest route for the group to get back and the team headed out. Both girls were small enough for piggyback rides, and with extra weight on their backs, the two men carrying them continually broke through the crusted snow. The group finally made it to the roadway, where ambulance and rescue vehicles were waiting.

"Out of the woods, girls safely in the ambulance, it now became time to think about what we had just accomplished," Roger concluded. "There were a lot of handshakes and 'atta-boys' or 'atta-girls,' and needless to say, there were a lot of happy people back at the house. The ambulance went there first so the parents could see their children before they headed off to the hospital to be checked out."

Once news of the rescue made it around the region, accolades for The Oswego County team came pouring in. Along with the Parish Fire Department, McFee Ambulance, 911, and Oswego County Sheriff's Department, the Pioneers were recognized by Oswego County Legislature for their search and rescue efforts. Sue Fox, on behalf of the team, received recognition from the American Red Cross, and the New York State United Teachers, which puts out a publication, *New York Teacher.* Sue was featured in their March 1999 issue, with her school district's President of the Faculty Association Barry Glickstein affirming that "elementary teachers should instruct students about safety through programs like Woods Smart. We're mostly a wooded county and it's very easy for young kids to get lost."

The most heartfelt acknowledgement of the Pioneers' Woods Smart program came from the two girls themselves. Found in the team's scrapbook is a letter written in neat grade-school printing: "Dear Search and Rescue Team. Thank you for rescuing us. Thank you for warming us up. Thank you for finding us. We were in the newspaper and on the radio. I learned not to go in the woods, only if it is an emergency or if we are with a grownup. We thought that we weren't going to make it through the night. Thank you from Rebecca Mintonye and Samantha Barber."

"When we came up with the Woods Smart program," Roger Fox said, "we had a very modest goal: Prevent one child from getting lost or assist one child in being found more quickly. With this rescue, we achieved that goal times two." *

Sue Fox, with elementary school friends Rebecca Mintonye and Samantha Barber.

---

* When the Fox's niece graduated in 2008, they attended her ceremony. "As we waited for the graduates to make their procession into the stadium," Roger said, "a girl broke from the line. 'Mrs. Fox! Mrs. Fox!,' she yelled, running up to Sue and hugging her tightly. We spoke for a few minutes, congratulated her on her success, now and in the future, and she returned to the line. The graduate? Samantha Barber. This is why we do what we do."

Today, Woods Smart continues to help young children make wise choices. A brochure promoting the program spells out its key points, including these preventative measures that parents should review with their children:

> Always tell your parents or another adult where you will be.
> Buddy up – never go off alone.
> Be prepared: take your backpack with a jacket, hat, something to eat/drink and a small first-aid kit.
> Stay on a familiar path.
> Be wise. Look around. Notice landmarks. Be aware of time/weather/darkness.
> If lost, find a tree and stay there.
> Stay together as a group.
> Button up your jacket.
> Make a survival bed.
> Make yourself bigger. Hang something bright, keep colorful clothing on the outside. If in an open space, build a big "X" or "SOS."
> To parents: Mark off a perimeter for your children to know where it is and isn't okay to walk. Footprint your child.

Not content with just keeping their eye on youngsters, the Pioneers have also sought ways to help others who are especially vulnerable to the dangers of the outdoors, including the elderly. Statistics show the population of the United States continuing to age. Baby boomers are entering their later years, and along with that, comes an increase in people diagnosed with dementia and Alzheimer's. The Alzheimer's Association states that more than 60 percent of people with dementia will wander from home at some point and about half of them remain unfound after 24 hours, putting them at serious risk for injury or death.

An August 2010 *Post-Standard* article, with its headline "Program Helps People with Dementia," explained how the Pioneers have become partners with an agency offering support for those with compromised mental abilities. The article included an interview with Patricia Major, who told reporters that she worried every time her husband, who suffered from dementia, took off on his lawn tractor. "He has gone down the road, and when he gets there, he can't remember how he got there," she said. "I'm trying to be under his feet every minute, but sometimes I have to sit down."

Patricia was interested in signing up for Project Lifesaver, a program Oswego County's 911 Emergency Communications Department had adopted to help find people who wander from their homes. The article explained how Project Lifesaver works:

A person with dementia, Alzheimer's, autism or another cognitive deficit, wears a special bracelet that carries a tiny radio transmitter. If the person goes missing, their loved one calls 911, which has a list of everyone in the Lifesaver program. The 911 Center then dispatches both law enforcement and the Pioneers, all of whom are trained and equipped to operate the Project Lifesaver Tracking units.

Roger Fox informed me that Oswego County implements the program differently than most counties by ensuring the tracking equipment is available at several locations and that all law enforcement agencies have trained personnel available when dispatch makes a callout. Additionally, the county's Pioneers are one of only two search and rescue teams in New York State who are certified Project Lifesaver agencies.

"While Project Lifesaver is centered in Oswego County, we don't worry about municipal boundaries," Roger Fox explained. "We have weather in this region that may only give us a 30-minute window to find a lost subject alive, so we can't afford to delay the response in any way. We'd rather have more equipment and operators respond immediately, than none."

Joe Homola helped me visualize how the Project Lifesaver

tracking equipment works by referring to an old TV show: "Remember Marlon Perkins and the show *Wild Kingdom?* They put radio trackers on animals and used a radio directional finder to locate them. That's where the technology of Lifesaver is from." Joe is an instructor for the project, and as part of his explanation of its benefits, he noted how Pioneers access the radio's tracking information during search and rescue calls: "Using the wristwatch device, we are able to track a missing person from about a mile away. Since we began using the program, a lost person wearing this device has always been found."

I told Joe that I found this new search aid pretty remarkable, but I'm even more impressed when he added: "The average find time has been 30 minutes."

Programs like Woods Smart and Project Lifesaver are examples of how today's Pioneers continue to advance in the search and rescue world. Scott Morehouse noted that as rescue teams become established, they often specialize and he mentioned other ways the Pioneers are contributing to the emergency services field:

"Here in Oswego County, besides highly-capable searchers, we specialize in search management. There are not too many teams who have the command capabilities we have. Being able to communicate sounds like a simple thing, but it's not simple when you're in the middle of the Adirondacks or in northern Oswego County. Our command center can be miles from where our searchers are, but our equipment can still coordinate, map and plot it all for those in the field."

Just like Pioneer founder Huey Parrow's map and compass skills and his cofounder Steve Ives' ability to find compromise in a group, today's Pioneers have their own special talents, and Scott noted a few of these: "Joe Homola has some great winter survival skills from his work on a ski patrol team. Patrick McCurdy is a medical physician's assistant who's been on a California rescue team and has extensive wilderness first aid and rope rescue training. Roger Fox has turned this team into a group that is very competent in both search management and searcher resources because of his skill set and ability to teach so well. Sue Fox has brought medical insight and searching techniques to the team."

Trainings like the Academy, outreach presentations such as Woods Smart, and team members' specialized trainings not only demand a lot of the Pioneers' time, but also put a strain on their financial resources. As I considered the group's innovative programs and continued need for equipment updates, I remembered the early Pioneers' almost-negligible budget. For 45 years, the team has functioned as an all-volunteer, nonprofit outfit. How has it managed to stay afloat?

One important factor in the Pioneers' financial stability has never changed: Each team member still takes care of their own search and rescue essentials: training fees, uniforms and personal equipment. At times, grants have helped the group cover major expenses such as replacing the command center vehicle and upgrading radio communication systems. Beyond that, the team raises money the way most not-for-profits do, one fundraiser at a time.

In 2006, the Pioneers celebrated their 35th anniversary, and the Syracuse *Post-Standard* captured an event held at the Parish Firehouse to honor the group and also to raise some money. The paper's reporter interviewed Roger Fox, who was flipping pancakes to feed the event's supporters. When asked about funding sources, Roger explained "our bare-bone budget is about $2,000 a year just for operating expenses. Money comes from fundraisers like this pancake breakfast and chicken barbeques sponsored by the Oswego Elks Club. We do some raffles and we basically beg. We also participate in public events like the Central Square Apple Festival."

I was familiar with this annual Oswego County event, and during my interview with Thom Benedetto, he clarified the Pioneers' involvement in the festival: "The Lioness Club of Central Square is the event sponsor and they like to have organizations such as ours come to help. It's a way of letting the public see who we are. They always make a donation to the Pioneers as a thank you and it has become one of our annual events. As the relationship between the Pioneers and the Lioness Club grew, our Wooly Worms Race was created."

Now in its third year, this imaginative race was the brainchild of Roger and Sue Fox, who had seen this type of event in their travels down south. "Through the years, wooly worms have been used to predict the severity of winters throughout the United States," Roger explained. "Wooly worm races in North Carolina, Kentucky and other states have determined the fastest, strongest, most representative worm to predict the winter weather severity. Central New York has its own brutal winters and we've got our own wooly worms, born and bred to the unique climate we live in. No south-of-the-Mason-Dixon-line wooly worm can even come close to giving us an idea of what the winter ahead holds for us. We need our own champion: The Central New York wooly worm of wooly worms!"

The contest can get heated – that is if you can find enough of the worms when the annual race takes place in late September. "You see a lot of them around in August," Thom Benedetto said, "but wooly worms aren't always plentiful as autumn sets in. We've been known to start gathering a supply in the summer and put them in training as the big event gets closer."

It's a lot of fun, prizes for the lucky winners, and some much-needed financial support for the Pioneers, allowing them to carry out effective trainings and develop new search techniques, ever focusing on the goal of finding their missing person.

One final note regarding the Pioneers' extensive and diversified training: As important as it has been for the team to specialize, it wouldn't function without those members who take their place on a grid line, carrying out the nuts and bolts of a search. Though they don't have an official title (some refer to themselves as "groundpounders"), everyone who joins the Oswego County team starts off in this positon. In fact, some spend years as a Pioneer and never perform any other duty but putting one foot in front of the other, eyes to the ground, searching every inch that lies before them. They look a lot like their counterparts from 1971, and over the years, these team members have helped the Pioneers tackle some of New York State's most perplexing searches.

Chapter Twelve

Landmark Pioneer Searches

Since Douglas Legg's disappearance, the Pioneers have responded to hundreds of callouts for their support in finding a missing person. Some searches, like Douglas's, made headlines for weeks; others hardly got a mention. But when the Pioneers look back on their history, as I witnessed with interview after interview, each search holds special meaning. Often, after listening to their memories of a specific case, I would turn to the team's scrapbooks. Studying the contents of these bursting-at-the-seams books, I'd find newspaper accounts of the searches Pioneers were excited to tell me about. Additionally, in the team's extensive files, I reviewed thick folders containing hastily-written or neatly typed notes of those searches, including the names of Pioneers in attendance, significant details about the missing person garnered from family members, topo maps with sketched-in search routes, and summary reports, where it was revealed if the search ended with a live find, the person succumbed, or if the case was to remain open.

By combining these thorough records with team members' recollections, I offer the following overviews of some key Pioneer searches, which, to me, make up the compelling chapters of The Oswego County Pioneer Search and Rescue Team's history.

May 1972   Jack Blake

"The first large search we went on as a team was for Jack Blake," Huey Parrow said, swiftly adding, "It did not go well."

Sitting with Huey during an interview, I could tell he had a lot to say about the team's first important search, but before I could really understand his and other Pioneers' memories of the Jack Blake case, I needed to learn the circumstances of his disappearance. I was 16 when Jack went missing and wasn't much interested in reading the paper or watching the news. But when I turned to the Pioneer scrapbooks and found over a dozen shocking newspaper headlines alongside Jack's photo, I discovered why his search captured Upstate New York's attention much as had happened with Douglas Legg.

Ten-year-old Jack Blake, one of nine children from an impoverished Watertown family, went missing on May 4, 1972. Early theories suggested the boy ran away from home. (Jack disappeared in the '70s, I had to remind myself, before a missing child automatically meant abduction.) Police searched the area where young Blake was last seen without success. When officials appeared ready to give up on the case, the boy's mother voiced sharp criticism of their work. The decision was made to expand the search and a call was put out for help. Over 50 volunteers showed up; 23 of them were Oswego County Pioneers.

When the team arrived in Watertown, their first objective was to do something Bart Bartholomew and other early Pioneer leaders insisted was vital to executing a thorough search: talk with the subject's family. "Interviewing Jack Blake's mother was not something law enforcement would have suggested," explained Steve Ives, "but we wanted to help as much as we could and she really wanted to talk."

Mrs. Blake's theories of what happened to her son, largely ignored by police, proved to be foreboding. Jeannie Parrow was on the search and she recalled talking with Jack's mother: "She told me she knew the man who murdered her son. She also said there were children playing in the area where Jack went missing and claimed they saw this same man take the boy into the woods."

"We took this information to the police officer in charge and he kind of blew us off," Huey said. "We wanted to start searching in the area where Jack had last been seen, but the officer said that area had already been covered and sent us to do grid searching elsewhere. We disagreed, but did as we were told. In our opinion, we were not used to our capacity."

Notes from the Pioneers' Jack Blake file support the frustration voiced by the Parrows and Steve Ives. A summary of family and Watertown resident interviews conducted by Pioneer members suggested that one neighbor of the Blakes, a man who they said portrayed himself as a caretaker for the family, gave false or exaggerated statements to authorities. Other people familiar with the Blakes suggested that police had downplayed the importance of the case because the family was poor and the children often in trouble. After one day of searching, the team returned to Oswego County, frustrated by the confusion and lack of tangible evidence. A week later, four members of the Pioneers returned to try to retrace Jack's steps and rethink what might have happened to the boy. Nothing new was uncovered, and the Pioneers returned home, again in frustration.

"It was the first time we got into a search where we questioned the methods being used by the lead agency," remarked Steve Ives. "On our way home after searching, Bart, Huey, Jeannie and I were discussing the case. I said, 'I think we should have stood up and done what we thought we should do.' After making that statement, I found that we all felt that way, but we were brand new and didn't push it."

Information from the scrapbooks fleshed out what the Pioneers told me really happened to Jack Blake. Organized searches were called off on May 12, but volunteers continued to hunt for Jack on their own. On the 15th, when clothing was found that matched those of the boy, the search was reopened. The next day, his parents announced to media that they had asked a man with "ESP powers" from New Jersey to come help them. By June 5, posters with the boy's photo were released. All summer, theories of what was behind the discovery of Jack's clothing spread throughout Watertown and beyond.

In September, bloodstained trousers too large to fit a child were found near the original search area. Soon after, police discovered a decomposed body and word quickly spread that it was the Blake boy's. The investigation intensified, and for the first time, authorities linked Jack's death to a man named Arthur J. Shawcross. A week earlier, Shawcross had been identified as the alleged killer of another child, Karen Ann Hill, when her body was discovered under a Watertown bridge. Soon after, Jack's father confirmed that Shawcross had taken his son fishing several times in the past. Shawcross was jailed, the bloody clothing found was confirmed as his, and tests on the bloodstains were positively linked to Jack Blake.

Steve Ives wrapped up the tragic but important lesson the Pioneers learned from their first major involvement with rescue work: "It was the search where we learned to believe in our training and in ourselves. We did a lot of growing up because of it. It turns out our intuition was right, and if we had spoken up perhaps the life of the little girl killed by Shawcross could have been prevented."

February 1973   Thomas McNamara

The disappearance of Thomas McNamara took the Pioneers out of their typical woodland terrain, but it wasn't just unfamiliar territory that made this search unique. The team was used to being given sketchy details about a missing person, but when the Pioneers were called to the city of Oswego to search for McNamara, an Air Force veteran, the description they were given of the man turned out to be strangely inaccurate.

The initial report of a missing person, called in on February 14 to Oswego police, was made by McNamara's mother, who offered only a few specifics. She described her son as a "clean-cut young man," and that, on the evening of his disappearance, he was "agitated." Later that night, the family heard a crash from Thomas's bedroom; he'd jumped through the first-story window. "He was wearing dungarees," was the only other detail his mother could offer authorities.

Outside the McNamara home, Oswego police quickly found a trail of blood that indicated their subject had started off running at a fast pace. When the Pioneers were called in to assist the police on the second day, they also began their search at the McNamara's and Steve Ives remembered how amazed he was of the young man's stride: "We followed his footsteps for several blocks and his prints were seven and a half feet apart."

Two blocks from the house, McNamara's slipper socks were found, and in a nearby park, more blood had collected, suggesting he'd stopped, perhaps to catch his breath. The blood trail then picked up and again was lost south of McNamara's home, behind the Oswego Catholic High School and the county's Mental Health Facility. The area was a mix of closely-clustered trees and abandoned fields, a setting the Pioneers were accustomed to working in. But just as they were forming their first grid line, the team was handed an additional challenge. During their search, lake-effect snow had started falling, and in the matter of a few hours, the city known for its intense winter storms found itself with an eight-inch blanket of fresh snow.

The Pioneers persevered, eventually uncovering an Air Force-type olive-green parka with blood and vomit stains. About 40 feet from the jacket, a pair of brown corduroy pants, similarly soiled, were found. They were not the dungarees the subject had been described as wearing, but when the corduroys were positively identified by McNamara's brother, the search team believed they were in the right area.

As I reviewed the information I'd collected about McNamara, one detail didn't make sense: Why had the man stripped off his clothing? Weather statistics for Oswego during that mid-February time period showed that, along with heavy snow, temperatures had plummeted below zero. Could McNamara actually have gotten overheated?

Dale Currier, who has spent much of his career in emergency management, provided me with a credible explanation: "In cold weather, when hypothermia sets in, people actually feel a sensation of being warm. If this persists, they'll start to remove their clothing." *

New theories about McNamara's disappearance that were spreading through Oswego added to the already-puzzling search situation for the Pioneers. "There was now talk that the young man may have been hiding at his girlfriend's home, but she told authorities she hadn't seen him," Huey Parrow explained. "There was also a rumor that he had taken drugs, experimenting with something known as 'the San Francisco Speedball,' a deadly combination of heroin and LSD." In their efforts to properly execute the search, Pioneers had contacted the Air Force to find out the reason for the young man's discharge. "We were told they would not disclose any information," Huey added.

Much like how Pioneers would contemplate such a confusing case as this one, I reviewed my notes and started putting together the facts that had been uncovered: the mother's report of her son's agitation, the suspected drug use, the realities of hypothermia. I was getting a good lesson in what it takes to crack a search mystery like McNamara's.

Further explaining the unfolding case, Huey noted that "it snowed heavily until there was several feet on the ground. We were assisted by Rochester's Massasauga Search and Rescue Team and some fire department groups. (Newspaper coverage indicated that nearly 50 people participated in the McNamara search.) It was extremely cold, but we continued all day using

---

* Medical professionals and emergency specialists have a name for this bizarre behavior: paradoxical undressing.

our Type III shoulder-to-shoulder search pattern. With the heavy snow accumulation, the team used things like ski poles, walking sticks or anything we could find at home, such as ½-inch PVC pipe, to probe. While we had no luck in finding our subject, no one wanted to give up."

On February 21, after a week of sporadic searching when Pioneers could get time off from work, a clear bare footprint and blood was found where snow had settled. The search intensified and more footprints were identified, but they turned out to be made by a pair of shoes, no doubt from one of the many volunteer searchers. On February 25, after multiple walk-throughs in the area with no fresh evidence uncovered, the search was officially ended and volunteers were released. The plan was to resume searching in the spring, but one Pioneer was not about to accept that decision.

"Ralph Larkin wanted to go back up to that area to re-search it," Jeannie Parrow explained. "Ralph was a stickler for trying to solve these sorts of mysteries, so a few days later, after the heavy snowfall had stopped and the accumulation had settled a bit, he went back on his own."

Larkin's initiative proved significant. Beginning in the area where the single footprint had been found, he expanded his one-man search to a nearby hilly area and discovered that one of its slopes contained several natural depressions. In one of those good-sized hollows, Larkin discovered McNamara's body. With the heavy snowfall, even something as large as an adult was smoothly blanketed over on the hill's decline. Only after enough snow had compacted was Larkin able to spot a portion of the man's body; naked as suspected, but instead of the short-cropped hair searchers were told he would have, McNamara's long locks were tied back with a ribbon. The Pioneers never learned why his original description was so incorrect.

"To this day, I still think about that search," said Steve Ives. "Shortly after Ralph found the man, some of us went back to the site. We wanted to see how we could have missed him in our original searching. We saw our prod marks made by the poles and some were very close to where his body was found. Then I noticed something that made sense to me: Near where McNamara died, there was a little sapling. I looked at it and looked at the slope of the hill, and it seemed like the most natural thing: Someone was searching along, prodding the snow and came to this spot. In order to keep from tumbling down the hill, they must have grabbed onto the sapling and pulled themselves around that area, stopping their prodding for just a few feet. I could see how we missed finding McNamara's body."

November 1973   James Howard

It was James Howard's photograph in the Pioneers' scrapbook that caught my eye while reviewing the details of his disappearance. As reports of the ongoing search were released, media used the same photo of the missing 19-year-old: his blonde longish hair falling easily around his face, his innocent eyes looking straight into the camera. I thought of Howard's family in Antwerp, New York, and wondered what it must have been like as information about their loved one became known.

On Friday evening, November 23, after a day of hunting near the Fort Drum military complex outside Watertown, New York, James Howard went missing. His four hunting buddies later told police that after their group had travelled some distance, they stopped to take a rest. When they resumed in a single file format, Howard took up the rear. After about a mile, the four men in front noticed he hadn't stayed with the group, so they retraced their tracks, searching through the night. Howard's choice of clothing didn't help; his hip-boots and a green Army fatigue jacket blended into the landscape. No sign of their friend was found.

Saturday morning, the teen's father was called. He notified police and the official search began. Newspaper descriptions of the area where the men were hunting was of swamps, sections of rolling hills and clusters of hardwoods. Not terrain that would have been considered unusual to the Pioneers, but the area that bordered it – a military base – certainly was.

When Fort Drum personnel properly interviewed the members of Howard's hunting group, the men's story changed. While hunting, they crossed over into the Fort Drum facility, realized they were in a restricted area and scattered to avoid being found. That was how Howard got separated from the group, they admitted.

Now, officials were really worried. Fort Drum brass cautioned the searchers that the area had been posted as restricted because it was used as their main artillery impact range. Newspapers described "untold amounts of highly-explosive ammunition and unexploded mortars and rockets" scattered in the area. The ammunition was difficult to detect and the slightest movement could unexpectedly set them off. The decision was made that only specially-trained military personnel could access the area, with one exception: the Oswego County Pioneers would be allowed to assist in the dangerous search.

Huey Parrow described how the Pioneers were instructed to conduct their search and rescue plan: "We were taken into the command center and told, 'Here's what you'll find in this field. Don't touch them, don't step on them. Some are duds, but some are alive.' We had to sign releases that we would not hold the military responsible on this search."

After the Pioneers put their agreement in writing, they were placed in a vehicle called a Gama Goat. My Google search of this odd name turned up photographs of Jeep-like oversized vehicles powered by six-wheel-drive. They were described as semi-amphibious army vehicles known for their ability to traverse over exceptionally rough and muddy terrain. I pictured the Pioneers looking down from their open air perches, where, as Huey explained, "we started seeing these things sticking out of the ground."

While newspaper accounts didn't mention the Gama Goat, it did cover a few details that tied James Howard to the location, including the discovery of two cartridges from a British Enfield rifle, which matched the bullets Howard's gun used. The search continued both in the vehicle and out, but after old wells were pumped dry and ravines and wooded areas were examined, no sign of the missing hunter turned up.

In total, 17 members of the Pioneers responded in the first days of the search. They worked alongside Fort Drum's 327th Ordinance Battalion, the Carthage Ordinance Battalion, and later, after no new clues were uncovered, a team with bloodhounds. But with much of the search spent in steadily-falling rain, any chance of the dogs picking up a scent had been washed away.

For 16 days, members of the Pioneer team helped thoroughly inspect the area. As November turned into December, rescuers began worrying about the arrival of snow. That would certainly hinder the search, especially in those explosive ammunition areas. When the feared snowfall did blanket the area, conditions were deemed too dangerous and the official search was terminated. "I went back several times with DEC rangers to keep looking for his body," Huey said. "We never had any luck."

It would be spring before Howard was finally discovered in a deep creek. Though officials concluded that it was ice-covered when he attempted to cross it, he'd most likely misjudged the ice's thickness, broke through and drowned.

Reading the final report of the Howard case, I closed the scrapbook that preserved those pictures of James, understanding how, for the Pioneers, images like the young man's innocent face keep memories of his search forever burning in their minds.

December 1978 Plane Crash Victims

Newspaper headlines greeting Upstate New York residents

the day after Christmas 1978 were anything but joyful. "Plane Crashes at 3,100 Feet on Nye Mountain. Three Killed," reported Syracuse's *Post-Standard.* Perhaps it was because the accident occurred on the most holy of holidays, or maybe it was that crash details were buried for months in a wintry Adirondack setting, but the sorrowful story continued to spread across the country, eventually turning up as a feature in the March 1979 issue of *People* magazine, which summarized the flight's demise:

> "At 4:30 p.m. Christmas Day, a twin-engine Piper Navajo Chieftain took off from Metro Airport in Detroit and headed east toward Saranac Lake, N.Y., in the heart of the snow-covered Adirondack Mountains. On board were Cris Ray, 26, head of a Key West, Florida construction company; his friend Kip Teifer, 26; their pilot Dick Pierce, 32; and two dogs, Crip and Aqui. By the time the group neared Adirondack Airport two and a half hours later, on their way to a skiing vacation at nearby Lake Placid, winds were gusting up to 90 miles an hour. The airfield was deserted, the runway had not been plowed and the landing lights were covered by drifts. The little plane passed over the airport, then disappeared into the night."

According to *People*, on the day after the plane's disappearance, Kip Teifer's sister, Lisa Teifer, who was also Cris Ray's fiancé, got news of the suspected crash from New York State police. When she was told the plane had not yet been located, Lisa flew from Florida to participate in the search, and 12 days later, with no clues and near-continuous snow making the search impossible, rescue operations ended. However, unknown to Lisa and others, during their search, a dog had been spotted foraging for food in garbage cans at Lake Placid. A local newspaper covered the details:

> "Although temperatures ranged down to minus 40, the searchers were heartened by the appearance of a dog who wandered up to a farmhouse on January 4. The owners of the farm notified the local dog warden, who contacted state police, and soon a positive identification was made: The brown mongrel, with one blue eye and one brown, was Aqui, one of the dogs that had disappeared with the plane. Hopes rose for the possible survival of the plane's occupants and Lisa Teifer urged officials to not give up the search."

Though the state police and DEC officials stressed the slim possibility of human survivors, private pilots planned to continue search flights. The DEC, whose forest rangers knew the Adirondack terrain better than anyone, was asked to take the lead in searching for the downed plane. Once the decision to resume the search was given in mid-February 1979, the DEC knew just who to call for the risky land search to locate the plane's wreckage. The Pioneers had been waiting for the call.

"Before we even headed up to Lake Placid, there was a lot of investigation our group did," Steve Ives recalled. "We got the reports from state police and looked them over until we had a plan in place." At my interview with Steve, he shared a thick folder of information the Pioneers had collected both before and during their search, including police reports and transcripts of interviews team members had conducted with people living near the presumed crash site. One neighbor's statement jumped out at me: "The roar of the plane was so loud I thought it was going to crash in my backyard."

The Pioneers' paperwork even included an interview with a psychic, who had been contacted by the Teifer family. From her

California home, the clairvoyant provided searchers with a sketched map indicating the point where she "saw" the plane wreckage. I asked Pioneers if they remembered this woman's sketch and here's how Steve Ives replied: "I saw the sketch and thought it looked like hundreds of areas in the Adirondacks. It really had nothing to make it easier to find the plane's location." The final pages of Ives' paperwork were topo maps used by the Pioneers to sketch out a trail they would attempt to blaze to their targeted search endpoint.

The team left Fulton on Saturday, February 16, arriving late at a Lake Placid church that offered the searchers overnight lodging. Before they headed out the next morning, Huey Parrow uncovered one more valuable piece of information: "We were able to get hold of some details about the airport the plane was supposed to fly into, including a set of flight plans for their landing. Even a novice could determine from reading them that the plans were incorrect. If the pilot missed their initial landing at the airport, which happened in this case, the instructions were to raise the plane's elevation a certain number of feet. But Nye Mountain was higher in elevation than the plan's indicated."

"When we realized the approach given by the airport was at an elevation insufficient to clear the mountaintop, we placed the plane to have crashed at a specific point on the mountain," Steve Ives added. The Pioneers adjusted their search plan, and that afternoon the team headed up Nye Mountain, with Steve leading the way. "I have never been on a search with so much snow in my life," he remembered.

Indeed, the area's winter of 1978-'79 was stormy and frigid, but beyond towering snowfall totals, there was also an added factor to the Pioneers' search attempt in that particular section of the Adirondacks. "Because the area had been deemed Forever Wild," Jeannie Parrow said, "there were no ATVs or other vehicles to take searchers in. We had to snowshoe quite a distance before we could even get to the mountain."

"We had brought our altimeter with us," Steve continued,

"which we used to keep track of how far up the mountain we'd gone. We reached the base of a rock cliff and were pretty certain we were just beneath the point where the plane crashed." As they set off for the final push on their search, the Pioneers met another major setback. One of the searchers, a volunteer from the National Guard who was not trained in search and rescue, sprained her ankle. Considering the size of the group and the limited daylight left, the Pioneers were forced to turn around.

By the next day, worsening weather prevented the team from finishing their search before returning home to family and jobs. Within a week, an aerial search party picked up where the Pioneers had left off and found the plane wreckage, "right where we thought it would be," Steve said. In the spring of that year, the Pioneers returned to Nye Mountain, and by this time, as Huey explained, "it had been rumored there were drugs on the plane and we just wanted to see for ourselves what had transpired."

A May 1979 *Post-Standard* article clarified what the Pioneers had heard, with its headline stating: "$12,000, Drugs Removed From Plane." The article explained how state investigators had to be lowered by helicopter to remove the victims. (Autopsies of the three men determined they'd died in the crash, probably at impact.) Also found amongst the plane wreckage was the suspected cash and drugs. Pointing out the dangerous location of the plane's crash, the article also noted that, due to the impossibility of getting recovery equipment to the site, the wreckage would not be removed.

The question of why the pilot missed his planned airport landing was not addressed in the article and there was no mention of the Pioneers' theory of the incorrect flight elevation information. The article ended with one more reference to the treacherous conditions involved in Adirondack searches by clarifying why the rescue crew had to use a helicopter to reach the site. 'That's the only way to get to the scene, unless you're a mountain goat,' a trooper explained."

Apparently, that trooper hadn't met the Pioneers of Oswego

County, who were not going to let a challenging climb stand in the way of searching for their missing person.

Once I had agreed to write about the Pioneers' long history of rescue work, I couldn't wait to sit with team members, listening as they described their personal sacrifice in often grueling environments; each search ending with a sense of accomplishment. How fulfilling it would be to offer readers the stories of those who'd been lost and then reunited with loved ones. These are wonderful images and such stories do exist, but as I soon discovered, things haven't always turned out as satisfying for the Pioneers. In fact, there are searches that have ended with something harder to accept than death.

At 7:30 a.m. on Friday, February 2, Christine Lane called state police from her Lansing, New York apartment, frantically explaining to officials what had happened earlier that morning after she'd taken her 23-month-old daughter, Aliza May Bush, for a walk. Returning home, Ms. Lane said she went to the bathroom and when she came out, Aliza was gone. Within an hour of her call, state police and nearly 100 firefighters began searching for the little girl. The first clue they discovered turned up in a driveway near Lane's apartment. It was a pink mitten, confirmed by the mother to be her daughter's. Police suspected an abduction.

By Saturday, dozens of search teams were sent out, instructed to thoroughly patrol the area while calling out the child's name, but softly, so as to not frighten her. Two helicopters hovered over the area and search dogs hunted for the child's scent. By midday, the number of volunteers grew to over 300, the concern for Aliza heightened by another criminal case that had the Lansing community up in arms. Just a few months before Aliza's disappearance, a murderous episode took place in Dryden, New

York, just 60 miles from Lansing. Brutal killings of the Harris family – a mother, father and two children – were disturbingly fresh in people's minds. On February 7, five days after Aliza's disappearance, a suspect in the Harris case was identified. Rumors began that investigators had found a link between Aliza's disappearance and the murders just an hour north.

On February 4, the Oswego County Pioneers headed out into fog, sleet and falling snow to join the search for Aliza. The team's paperwork from the search included a handwritten list of questions Pioneers had brainstormed before even setting foot in Lansing: "Why was the mother out walking the child before seven a.m.? Why hadn't more people reported this little girl alone on the street? Had the mother found the apartment door opened or closed?" The questions were followed by a statement: "I don't think this mother is telling the whole story."

The paperwork also identified Steve Ives as a group leader, with his team assigned to cover an area referred to as "Block 26," using Type III's precise search method. The first report, made three days after Aliza's disappearance, offered a measure of optimism: "Yesterday, tremendous progress was made in the primary search area. By the end of the operational period, over 40 crews had been dispatched. Any clues they turned up will be worked more extensively today and Type III grids will expand via the road systems."

Posters that were distributed throughout New York State were included with the report. They show a precious photo of Aliza in winter clothing, and listed the identifiable details of the child: "Two years old, approximately 40 pounds (later documents listed her weight at 20 pounds), three feet tall, blonde hair and blue eyes." Also listed was her mother's description of what Aliza would be wearing: "gray sweatpants, pink winter jacket, pink and white hat with a blue tassel, pink boots"...and, I hopefully imagined, one pink mitten.

The search continued through the weekend, with dogs picking up a light scent in an area where a set of tracks appeared to match Aliza's boot size. The tracks led to an open field near the subject's apartment, then ended. Searching continued until Monday, February 5, when authorities deemed a thorough search had been conducted and volunteers were sent home.

On Wednesday, February 7, a strange new clue in Aliza's disappearance reopened the case. A pink mitten – the twin of what had been found on the search's first day – arrived in a postal package at Christine Lane's apartment. The package was postmarked February 6 at the Elmira Post Office, which served the Lansing area. Authorities considered it proof Aliza was still alive. Christine spoke to the media, pleading for Aliza's return, concluding her statement with a description of the gifts she had readied for her daughter's third birthday, February 19. But four days shy of that hoped-for birthday party, Aliza Bush's body was found, the true story of her disappearance and death suddenly taking a gruesome twist.

Ordered to take a second lie detector test, Christine Lane's role in her daughter's death was finally revealed. (Lane's first test, which she passed, was conducted shortly after Aliza's disappearance.) Emotionally broken, Christine shared with investigators a strikingly different story of her daughter's demise. In the early morning of February 2, Christine got up to use the bathroom and checked on Aliza in her crib, finding her tangled in her bedclothes, dead. Autopsy reports later revealed that the child had suffocated.

Shortly after her tearful confession, Christine led officials to the site where she had hidden her daughter's body. Newspapers reported the scene, with Ms. Lane flanked by an FBI agent and a county investigator, walking through a field into a wooded area. She led them through dense trees, pointed to a thick pile of brush near a pine tree and quietly backed away, not wanting to witness as the men located Aliza's body double-wrapped in plastic bags.

But there was more that authorities learned about Christine Lane which would fully indict her in Aliza's death. She confessed to mailing herself the mitten to distract searchers once they got dangerously close to the site of her daughter's body. Further autopsy examinations determined that the child's suffocation was the result of smothering. In March of 1990, a grand jury charged Lane with two counts of second-degree murder. For the citizens of Lancing and those following the story far beyond the community, Christine Lane's sentence of 25 years to life for her daughter's murder closed the disturbing case. But not for the Pioneers.

Looking back on the search for Aliza Bush, Steve Ives remembered his team crawling on their hands and knees through the wintry marsh and thick brush: "It was one of the harder searches to handle physically because of the weather – I remember my hands going into that ice cold water in the swampy areas. But nobody wanted to give up because of this little girl; we wanted to return her to her family. Her grandfather greeted us every day with hot chocolate and sandwiches. He was so grateful for what we were doing."

Considering the unsettling details of Aliza's death, Steve added: "Christine Lane had to be one of the best liars; she was so convincing and it was really difficult to fathom that a mother could have done that. But after it was all over, the grandfather said something like, 'Of all the people on the earth who would do something like this, I believe my daughter could.' "

Sitting with Steve as he recalled the search details, I found it hard to compose myself. How do even the most dedicated members of a search and rescue team go on in the face of these situations? Perhaps Steve read my horror at what he'd shared and made a final comment in the case of Aliza Bush: "There are things you might see in life and it all depends on what you are able to handle. Some people can deal with it and some people can't."

August 1993   Sara Anne Wood

Three years later, Steve Ives' statement about a person's

ability to handle the horrendous outcome of difficult searches came back to haunt him. It wasn't only Steve who was deeply disturbed by the disappearance and still-unsolved mystery of what happened to 12-year-old Sara Anne Wood. When she disappeared on August 18 while riding her bicycle on a quiet road near her Frankfort, New York home, the whole world felt the despair of yet another missing child.

After Douglas Legg's disappearance, and the Jack Blake and Aliza Bush cases, people hoped for the best, but prepared for the worst. Volunteers came out by the hundreds to participate in searches, which often began with divinely-inspired words from Sara's father, Bob Wood. The searchers combed the western New York region, with media reporting each day's progress. Intently following the news was a future Oswego County Pioneer.

"I was in college when the Sara Anne Wood search was going on," Scott Morehouse said. "Though I was interested in becoming involved in it, I was busy in college – but it stuck with me over the years." Little did Morehouse know, but his first job after college graduation would put him eerily close to the Sara Anne case and the world of search and rescue.

"I was working in civil engineering," Scott recalled, "and while we were surveying in the area near where Sara Anne went missing, we found a brand new bicycle in a pond. We reported it to police, thinking that someone must have stolen it. Later, they came to us and said, 'We need to talk to you guys.' It turned out to be Sara's bike and they traced its location to her disappearance and the man they would eventually name as her abductor."

Scott was talking about Louis Lent, a janitor from Massachusetts who was convicted in the girl's murder. The case dragged on for years, until finally, in 1996, Lent confessed to kidnapping, sexually assaulting and killing Sara – but he refused to reveal where he buried her body. Lent had also been convicted in a number of other abduction/murders and was sentenced to life without parole. Today, he remains in a Massachusetts prison, still tightlipped about the location of Sara Anne's body, only stating she was not buried alone.

In 2013, at the request of New York State police, the Herkimer County DA's office and New York State forest rangers, the Pioneers led a team of cadaver canines to a remote location in the Adirondacks to search for signs of Sara. The state police were acting on an incident that had been reported several years before. A vehicle had been seen on a remote trail about the time Sara went missing and it fit the description of Lewis Lent's car. Roger Fox was one of the Pioneers on the search and shared his memories of this latest attempt to find Sara's remains:

"We spent two days covering a three-square-mile area at a location that requires 'Hummers' to access it. The canines showed interest at one location the first day and a forensic team processed it.* Realistically, given the time frame, the highly acidic nature of the Adirondack soil, and animal activity, the chance of finding discernible, visual evidence related to Sara was highly unlikely, but we tried."

Despite the unsettling outcome of the search, efforts to keep hope alive for other children who become lost are now more organized because of Sara. In a movement led by her father, the Sara Anne Wood Foundation was created to offer a clearinghouse for information on missing children, greatly reducing the time it takes to communicate details of the subject and their disappear-

---

* Roger added a note about cadaver dog searches: "It's hard to explain why, when cadaver dogs express an interest in an area, they don't always find what you're looking for. On this search, the dog followed its nose and then sat down, which was his trained indication he'd found something. The handler brushed away some leaf cover and located an old Band-Aid. 'See,' the handler said, 'this is the problem. I can't tell you whose blood is on the Band-Aid or when it was dropped. Neither can the dog. They can only tell us there's scent on the item that they are trained to find. The dogs are doing what they are supposed to be doing.' "

ance. Annually, the Foundation sponsors its Ride for Missing Children, a bicycle marathon inspired by the little girl who went for a ride on a pleasant afternoon and never returned.

Organizations and events like those created in Sara Anne's memory offer her mourners and the mourners of other abducted children a way to heal by helping. They also provide inspiration for the search teams who continue to work towards a happier ending for missing children and their families. But for Steve Ives, after 22 years with the Pioneers, the circumstances of Sara Anne's disappearance challenged his commitment to search and rescue.

"The Sara Anne Wood search hit me hard," Steve confided. "It was like she was my daughter. After the final search for her, I cried like a baby because I thought about her dad, who came out and prayed with every one of the search teams. We wanted so much to find her for her family and it was so awful.

"When we first started the Pioneers, it was supposed to be to find lost hunters and lost kids; searches that would get positive results. We never thought it was going to be criminal searches. The Sara Anne Wood search got to some very experienced troopers, police officers and search and rescue people. And it really got to me. I backed off from the group for a while to get my head together."

April 1994 Heidi Allen

Shaken by the tragic outcome of the search for Sara Anne Wood, the Pioneers didn't have much time to regain their composure. Less than a year later, rescue volunteers were called into action to help solve what *The Post-Standard* recently referred to as "the biggest mystery in Oswego County." On Easter Sunday, April 3, 18-year-old Heidi Allen was working the morning shift at a convenience store in the town of New Haven. Heidi handled the shift on her own, opening the business in a predawn darkness. By eight a.m., she was reported missing.

Oswego County sheriffs arrived at the scene, quickly suspected an abduction and began their investigation. As with the Sara Anne Wood case, public awareness swiftly spread. Volunteers poured in, including future Pioneer Howard Bennett. "My children had gone to school with Heidi and we lived right around the corner from the store where she was abducted," Howard explained. From the first call for community support, whenever Bennett wasn't at work, he searched. "Because I was quite familiar with the area, law enforcement saw that I knew my way around and they made me a team leader. We searched along roads and in people's homes."

In the weeks following Heidi's disappearance, Howard estimates volunteers ended up searching "a good-sized section of Oswego County. We were bussed to areas quite a distance from the site of her abduction, and one of the roads we searched was where the Thibodeaus lived." The Thibodeau brothers, Richard and Gary, became suspects in Heidi's disappearance; they were eventually arrested and charged with her kidnapping and murder.

Separate jury trials were held for each brother, and in June 1995, Gary was convicted of the charges and sentenced to 25 years to life. As this book goes to press, he is appealing his conviction to the New York State Supreme Court. Richard Thibodeau fared better; three months after his conviction, he was found not guilty.

Howard Bennett searched for Heidi a total of six days, during which he interacted with other volunteers, including some Pioneers. "I worked at Nestlé with Ralph Larkin and he was always trying to recruit new members for the team," Howard explained. "For me, the Heidi Allen abduction was the catalyst that pushed me to join the Pioneers." Howard remained with the team until 2003, only stepping down when he took a job at the Oswego County Sherriff's Department.

Two other future Pioneers also offered their help: Roger and Sue Fox. "With our work schedules, we initially volunteered on a

Saturday and Sunday," Roger said, "but we ended up spending a lot of time on the search, somewhat because of the personal connection we felt: Our daughter, who was 16 at the time, had spent the weekend with a friend who lived in Oswego and was coming home that Easter Sunday morning. She passed right by the convenience store around that time, and Sue and I kept thinking about the randomness of Heidi's abduction."

When I asked Roger what his impressions of the search for Heidi were, the man who would one day be routinely implementing rescue plans for the Pioneers suggested there are two ways to look at it: "Originally, not knowing a lot about search and rescue, it seemed like that's the way things should be. But after many years with the Pioneers, I now say it could have been done better."

Roger's opinion is partly in reference to how search leaders handled the masses of people who felt compelled to volunteer. Another Pioneer involved in the case, Dale Currier, noted: "In my memory, it was the biggest outpouring of people offering to help; people who had never participated in anything like this, but wanted to do something." Dale was faced with a tough decision when he first heard about the call for searchers. "The weekend I was going to volunteer was my daughter's birthday and I was really torn where I should be. My daughter, who was turning eight years old that year, helped me make the decision. 'This girl needs you more than I need you at my birthday party,' she said."

Dale shared more about the compassion which can come when tragedy strikes a community. "When I found out that the New Haven fire barn, which had been designated as the search command center, was basically an empty building, I called over to the nuke plants, where I worked. We had just cleaned up some of the offices and I asked what had been done with all the desks and such. After finding out they had been put in storage, I explained what the command center needed and it wasn't long before a truck pulled up with furniture and other things to help organize the search."

Among the paperwork found in the Pioneers' thick folder on the Heidi Allen search is the inaugural issue of *SearchLines,* billed as "the official newsletter of the New York State Federation of Search and Rescue Teams." The newsletter was part of the Federation's efforts to provide its teams support and networking opportunities. Their publication's first front-page article was titled "The Search for Heidi Allen." Noting that Pioneers were on the scene Easter Sunday, the article goes on to say that, by April 14, preparation of all search areas was the Oswego County team's responsibility. Huey Parrow was in charge of map work and Steve Ives was the search's field officer. Here's how Steve recalled his duties:

"I was in charge of people searching for clues in certain areas. We spent about a week doing this, and much like the Sara Anne Wood search, this one was difficult. We so wanted to help the Allen family, who were involved from the start."

I contacted Lisa Buske, Heidi's sister, to ask her perspective on the Pioneer's work during the search. Lisa, who was 22 at the time of the abduction, began with acknowledging she doesn't remember a lot about the Pioneers' work. "During their involvement with my sister's kidnapping, I was numb and merely going through the motions," Lisa said. "I wasn't at a place to make decisions or to lead, so other family members and our community interacted with the Pioneer team. But I do know that, in addition to utilizing their skills to help in the search and potential rescue of my sister, they trained and led thousands of men, women, and young adults arriving to aide in this process to find Heidi. Their countless hours increased our hopes to find my sister. Although she remains missing more than twenty years later, it is not due to a lack of effort by all involved, especially the Oswego County Search and Rescue Team. I am grateful for all they did."

Even today, the search for Heidi Allen and a definitive answer to her disappearance continues. Recent court proceedings have reopened the case, as Sue Fox explained to me. Over the years,

Sue's role with the Pioneers included the responsibility of compiling reports and related documents, including Heidi's. "All the paperwork we collected from that search is currently being used by the investigative team still trying to crack the case," Sue explained. "The Oswego County Sheriff's Office also called us out last year when they wanted to conduct a search in an area which had been identified as a possible location where harm came to Heidi. The search was not directly for Heidi, but for the remains of a building or its foundation referenced in testimony from recent court proceedings."

Sue told me that in this most recent search, the team provided management and manpower for two days. Any item of interest that was discovered was immediately referred to law enforcement personnel who were standing by to process it and determine whether it was related to Heidi's disappearance. Sue ended her comments with a statement that I'm beginning to see is often the troubling final word for Pioneers: "We came up empty-handed."

November 1995   James Matott

The search for James Matott included several key elements in what I've come to understand are the realities of search and rescue work: the rigorous training a professional search team must undertake, the sketchy information they are often given about their subject's disappearance, the unfortunate tendency of having to search in inclement weather, and the undying spirit of volunteers who risk their lives for another's. Strangely enough, I may never have known about this dramatic search – it hadn't warranted TV or newspaper coverage when it occurred – if Howard Bennett hadn't been compelled to tell his version of what happened to Matott in an article that appeared months later in the several Oswego County newspapers.

Howard's story, with its headline: "Search and Rescue Team Training Pays Off, Saving a Hunter's Life," began with details of the day Matott went missing: "On Saturday, November 11, eight members of Oswego County Pioneer Land Search and Rescue Team attended a Basic Wildland Search class sponsored by the New York State DEC. The class is a mandatory team requirement, and those who satisfactorily complete it are registered with the state of New York as trained search and rescue volunteers. All eight members of the Oswego County team satisfied course requirements."

Team members Roger and Sue Fox had joined the Pioneers a year earlier and for both, the class was their first exposure to any formal search training. Roger, who considers the Matott search one of his most memorable, explained what that day stated off like: "It was November, but the weather was unseasonably beautiful; it was an almost-70-degree day. But as we were driving home after class, a storm front moved through, and in a matter of hours, it went from beautiful weather to torrential rain, falling temperatures, tremendous winds, downed trees and multiple power outages.

"About eight p.m., my pager went off. After calling in to the state police, we were told that there was a missing man in the Redfield area, 38-year-old James Matott, who had gone hunting with his friends. Later, we learned that Matott was new to hunting and unfamiliar with the area, so his friends set up what is known as a deer drive. Matott waited in a particular spot and his hunting buddies drove the deer toward him. When the other hunters lost track of their friend, they figured he'd left to go home and so they drove back to Oswego. They didn't discover Matott was missing until later that day when his wife called regarding his whereabouts. When the search began, forest rangers had requested that our team assist them.

"By this time, the storm was really raging and as we were driving down Route 69 toward Redfield, there were power lines arcing and sparking and down. I didn't think we'd make it, especially since we weren't even sure where we were going. For directions we had something really vague: 'It's off County Route 17,' we were told, 'and you'll have to take the snowmobile trail off the road.' We met up with some of our search and rescue people and drove our cars down the snowmobile trail. At one point, I got out and jumped up and down on a wooden bridge to make sure it was going to hold us if we drove across."

Howard Bennett was among the Pioneers waiting when the Foxes arrived, and when I interviewed him about this search, he added his memories of the scene, noting the worsening weather: "By the time we got there, it was beginning to snow. When the other hunters returned to the scene to help us figure out a starting point for the search, the snowfall had altered the look of the terrain. We were just guessing if we were in the right area."

The Pioneers' file on the Matott search included the team's report, which indicated a start time of 11:30 p.m. and listed who else joined the team on the search: seven state police, two NOCA ambulance staff, one firefighter from Redfield, the Oswego County Sheriffs' canine team and four New York State forest rangers. But taking the lead as the group headed out into the now dark and snowy woods, with their newly-trained search methods less than a half-day under their belts, were seven members of the Oswego County Pioneers.

Howard's newspaper article described the forest rangers' surprise when they realized who had arrived on the scene as professional searchers: "Ironically, two of the rangers in charge of the search effort were the instructors for our training, which had ended just four hours prior." The article pointed out that as the rangers briefed the team on the situation and the missing hunter's description, they had a difficult decision to make: Do they allow newly-trained searchers out on what was looking like a difficult mission? In my interview with Howard, he was able to elaborate on the rangers' concern:

"They recognized us from our attendance earlier in the day and one of the rangers said, 'I can't put you people out there;

229

you're newly trained.' But I said, 'What choice do you have? If we don't do this now, we're talking about a body bag search in the morning.' The ranger finally agreed, but told us, 'I'm only going to have you search the roadsides, because I'm reluctant to have this team search in the woods.'

"We went with that and I led the team out. Every once in a while, we'd stop and call out the subject's name. After about the third call, we heard a very faint 'Help me.' Roger was on the west end of the line and closest to where the voice had come from. I radioed back that we had heard a response and were going to go deeper into the woods. We went a little further, called out again, and the response was louder. We took a bearing on it, headed that direction and eventually came across Matott. We found him with his clothing shredded from the thick brush, soaking wet and in early- to mid-stages of hypothermia, using his shotgun as a crutch. We quickly took the gun from him and made sure it was clear.

"We did the best we could putting dry clothes on Matott and called back as to our approximate location and said we were bringing him out. The heavy, wet snow was getting worse and visibility was almost non-existent. As a group, we followed a compass bearing to get us back to the snowmobile trail, supporting Matott along the way. When we hit the trail, the state police car that had been driving up and down the trail found us and Matott was quickly placed inside and taken to a waiting ambulance."

The Pioneers' report recorded the search ending at 3 a.m., but as any Pioneer will tell you, with a search such as that one, it's hard to neatly file it away. Twenty years after taking the lead to find James Matott, Howard still gets emotional when he reflects on it: "It was a great example of a successful search, and it felt so good to know that this person had been reunited with his family. This would not have been the case if the search group hadn't put themselves in danger. By the time we brought him out of the woods, there was a good foot and a half of snow on the ground and he would not have survived the night if we hadn't found him."

Howard ended his newspaper article with this final thought: "The reward? A thank you, a hot cup of coffee and the knowledge that his wife will hold James Matott a little tighter tonight. 'That's all we need,' one Oswego County Pioneer team member noted. 'That's why we do what we do.' "

January 1996   Matthew Tanner

A few months later, the Pioneers would participate in another memorable search, this one important not only due to the team's successful efforts in rescuing their missing person, but also because circumstances that complicated the rescue led to major changes in how Oswego County oversaw search and rescue procedures. When the team was called to the Little John Wildlife Management Area, which straddles the northeastern Oswego County and southern Jefferson County borders, it wasn't just dense forests and brutal weather conditions they faced. Heading out on a bitterly cold Saturday to search for Matthew Tanner, the Pioneers were met with a series of mishaps that were among some of the most frustrating in the team's 25-year history.

It was early afternoon when 14-year-old Matthew headed into the Wildlife Management woods with his mother and brother, looking for three of the family's five Rottweilers that had wandered off. The Management Area, a 7,900-acre state-owned facility, is mostly flat, tree-covered terrain, but its long, narrow swamps and small depressions make foot travel particularly difficult in winter. I checked with my experienced Adirondack climber Vince Markowsky to see if he'd ever hiked Little John. He had, calling it "one of the most desolate areas in the state." I was curious why Vince chose such a strong word as desolate. His answer justified the word choice.

"There's a road that dead ends where the Management Area

begins," Vince explained. "If you hike east from it, there are no other roads or signs of human life until you reach the foothills of the Adirondacks." The name of that dead end road, Vince informed me, is Little John Drive.

"I grew up on Little John Drive," said Matthew Tanner, now 34 years old, who'd agreed to tell me about his experiences being lost in those woods. "We assumed we knew our way around the Management Area, so when I found our dogs' tracks and started following them, I was confident going deeper into the woods."

By late afternoon, with the January daylight quickly fading, Matthew had wandered away from his family. "It had started snowing and it was coming down pretty hard," he continued, "and the temperature dropped. (Records for the day show the thermometer struggled to hit 10 degrees in the Little John area.) When it starts snowing like that where I grew up and you're in the woods, all you can see is white. Any landmarks I knew had vanished, and without any stars in the cloud-covered night sky, there was nothing to help me navigate."

The Tanners' dogs eventually returned home, as did Matthew's mother and brother, but he did not. His parents called the authorities, who relayed the information to the nearby Redfield Fire Department. Howard Bennett was on the search and recalled that "as it got later in the evening, the Pioneers were called in to assist. Our plan was to box in the young boy by surrounding the whole area where he might have gone and then gradually move in."

In 1995, with Oswego County emergency service agencies lacking a cohesive plan for rescuing a missing person, the search for Matthew got confusing. Roger Fox, although he was not on the scene, described the problem which had been hindering search efforts for many years: "The search was conducted as if there was more than one agency in charge, so without a single plan, not everyone was on the same page. This resulted in multiple uncoordinated efforts."

While agencies were struggling with how best to conduct the

search, a *Post-Standard* article captured Matthew's struggles in those woods: "(The teen) had to maneuver in four-foot drifts of snow, and became surrounded by thickets of brush and pond water." Matthew added his memories to that stormy forest scene: "I came to what I thought was a clearing, but it turned out to be an iced-over pond. I fell through up to my chest several times and got soaked. I was getting pretty cold; my pants and socks were frozen and it felt like my feet were frostbitten."

By this point, Matthew had resigned himself to the fact that he was lost, but he didn't panic, relying on what he'd learned growing up near the woods. "Our dad taught us at a young age that if we didn't know where we were, to stay put. I crawled under a pine tree and dozed off a couple of times, which wasn't the best thing to do." The newspaper article noted that Matthew said he sporadically ate snow to keep from dehydrating. "Maybe I did," he told me when I read him that part of the article, "but to be honest, a lot of what happened is a blur."

Pioneer paperwork on the search indicated that authorities called in a helicopter to use their thermal imaging, "but the small, fine snowflakes falling prevented them from getting any images," Matthew's father explained to me. Mr. Tanner was my first contact when I tried to reach Matthew, and he was happy to direct me to his son, but first he had an important memory to share: "We found out later that by the time those helicopters arrived, Matthew's body temperature had dropped so low a thermometer wouldn't have gotten a reading. It's questionable if the infrared technology would have even registered what little heat his body still had."

As evening closed in on midnight, the search looked pretty bleak. Finally, a Redfield fireman who often hunted in the area showed up, put on a pair of snowshoes and headed out. When he noticed some areas of ice where the boy had fallen through, he followed the breaks and found Matthew. But the teen, the Pioneers and other volunteers searching weren't out of the woods yet, literally and figuratively.

"While we were searching," Howard Bennett explained, "we were notified that someone had located Matthew. As we stood there waiting for another team to catch up with us so we could all head out together, my flashlight was shining down and I noticed water seeping through the snow. When I realized we were standing on an ice-covered pond, I radioed the other team to advise them to skirt the area, and then proceeded to get my team off the ice. However, instead of avoiding the spot, the other team, which included firefighters in their heavy full turnout gear, came directly across. We started to hear people breaking through the ice."

The Post-Standard reported nearly 100 volunteers on the search, and for the Pioneers, as Howard described, it became "a rescue to rescue the rescuers. We were out in the middle of the woods and we had people unfamiliar with how to search in those conditions. A rescuer's snowmobile got caught in an icy area and had to be abandoned. I called the DEC, who was one of the agencies leading the command center, to help pinpoint our location and instruct us on which direction to head for the nearest trail. We needed to get help as soon as possible for those who were cold and wet. Also, unfortunately, some of the resources we still needed, like the sheriff's snowmobile patrol, had already packed up and left once Matthew was out of the woods. The search was turning into a real mess."

Foremost, of course, was getting young Tanner medical attention. When he was carried out of the woods, Northern Oswego County Ambulance was on the scene to transport him to Syracuse's Upstate Medical Center. "I was admitted to the burn unit, which is where frostbite is treated," Matthew explained. "I stayed for a couple of days, recuperated just fine and was sent back home."

The Pioneers could now turn their attention to the procedural concerns related to the search. The decision was made to hold a meeting of all participating Oswego County emergency organizations, which Roger Fox called "a watershed event in the

Pioneers' history. At the time, local fire departments were still the primary response agency in a lost person case. Even though the Tanner search outcome was positive, Oswego County Fire Coordinator Bill Denery became aware that there were a lot of issues which happened on the search that needed to be addressed. Bill organized the meeting and this started a conversation between agencies *at a county level*, rather than just between the agencies themselves."

Roger noted that a number of issues were resolved at the meeting, and among the most significant was a change in how search and rescue teams were informed of missing person incidents. "Up until the Matthew Tanner search, the inclusion of teams like the Pioneers was dependent on the lead organization having knowledge of and contacting us. Communications at all levels was poor, to say the least, and search and rescue teams were usually an 'afterthought.' "

Included in this discussion was determining *which* emergency agency was the best suited for a search incident. The talk touched on each agency's training, equipment, clothing, and even fitness. "The response to a lost or missing person can be quite complex," Roger noted. "It requires specialized skills, knowledge, and experience. The county meeting determined that management of these types of incidents should be conducted by individuals who are most capable, not just default to whichever agency responded first. Search and rescue teams would be immediately called in when it was determined an active search was needed. To facilitate this, the teams were to be added to the county dispatch system and to the county communications system."

Those were major changes for the Pioneers, but the county meeting went further. "The fact that several volunteers looking for Matthew required medical attention for frostbite and exposure prompted the realization that searcher safety was a key consideration," Roger continued. "The group's discussion brought to light that safety starts with accountability. Because the Tanner search had no one lead agency, knowing who was on scene, how many people were volunteering, and where they were at all times failed to happen. When Matthew was located and people left the scene, not only did it reduce the number of volunteers available to help the searchers who'd gotten into trouble, but being able to formally end the search became impossible."

Before the county meeting adjourned, the participating agencies acknowledged that they needed to establish an ongoing conversation regarding lost and missing person incidents and that search and rescue teams should be included. With this in mind, Roger said, "Oswego County created a Search and Rescue Committee, consisting of the Pioneer team, fire, forest rangers and county and state law enforcement. They decided to meet quarterly to discuss search incidents. After a year or so, this group 'morphed' into an existing committee, the Law Enforcement Committee. With the advent of the current radio system implemented in 2013, this committee then became the Protocol Review and Advisory Committee."

For all the good that came from this meeting, it hadn't been carried out with just polite conversation. Pioneers in attendance remembered some people yelling and walking out; Roger referred to parts of the evening involving "a good share of bloodletting." Among the attendees raising their voices and leaving were some Pioneers. But, as Roger pointed out, the changes within the Pioneer organization were important, too:

"Team members recognized that we had to change the way we recruited, trained, and responded to incidents. We had to make sure we were providing significant value to the lead organizations that requested our service. Through our interaction with other New York State search teams, we were able to recognize there were different and better ways of training and responding to incidents. Specialized search and rescue management training was acquired, and new technologies, such as GPS and on-line mapping, were investigated and adopted."

That's a lot of positive change resulting from the search for one missing person, and for Matthew Tanner, the search also heralded a new direction in his life. "It was definitely an event that I didn't soon forget. I started looking at life with a little more caution," he stated, then quickly added: "but minor mishaps should never stop anyone from doing anything."

It certainly didn't stop Matthew. After graduating high school, he enlisted in the Air Force and travelled the world. Today, he lives in California and assured me, "I hunt, so I still go into the woods. But when I go, I always take a definite route and don't waiver at all."

Since the dawn of a new century and a new millennium, the Oswego County Pioneers have continued to be involved with some high-profile emergency situations. When terrorists attacked the World Trade Center on September 11, 2001, an outpouring of volunteers looked for ways to help. One of the most unsettling matters at hand was sifting through the areas of New York City buried in debris, and search and rescue canines provided needed support. "We sent 13 dogs from various Federation search and rescue teams," Roger Fox said. "They weren't at the forefront of what was going on, but were involved with trying to find human remains."

Roger, who at the time was heading up the New York State Federation, received phone calls from those wanting to help far from New York City; in one case, over 4,000 miles away: "The Hungarian Spider Rescue Team called me and wondered why they hadn't been activated. So many people wanted to help and didn't know how. When they found our New York State Federation website, they thought we might be involved with providing aid to New York City. We, of course, had no lead in the emergency rescue and support for the city, but we found ways to send those who wanted to help in the right direction."

Though not every search the Pioneers have been involved with over the years turned out as dramatic as those described in this chapter, I was curious to compare them with what the team encounters when heading out for a missing person in today's world. With advances in communication technology and safety standards, I wondered if modern Pioneers were still being called out as frequently as those who came before them, and if so, for what reasons? I didn't have to look far to get my answer.

In keeping with their high standards of maintaining accurate records of their service, the Pioneers annually compile an End-of-Year Report. This document includes the team's significant accomplishments during the year, an account of the group's finances, cooperative searches and trainings with other teams, and something referred to as a "Call Summary," which categorizes and gives a number count for the team's searches that year. In 2015, the Pioneers' Call Summary included:

Forty "notifications," or situations where the team was called. Twenty-nine of those calls turned into actual "activations," where the team participated in the search. (Pioneers informed me that sometimes the missing person is found before a search officially begins.) The youngest subject they searched for was three years old; the oldest was 82. The following is a breakdown of who the Pioneers were searching for in the 29 cases.

Dementia: 5
Elderly (Medical): 2
Autistic: 3
Despondent: 3
Mentally Challenged: 1
Children Lost/Missing: 7
Alcohol/Drugs: 2
Hiker: 3
Fisherman: 1
Hunter: 2

Among these callouts were seven requests for mutual aid from the following counties: three from Onondaga, and one each from Chenango, Livingston, Saratoga and Warren. The Summary also noted that 2015 was a successful year due to the fact that no Oswego County incidents went unresolved and no deaths or significant injuries occurred within the county as the result of a missing person incident.

The 2015 Summary was what I expected to see. After reading and hearing about the Pioneers' long track record of proficiency, I suspected their commitment to search and rescue work would have remained strong. As I was developing the final chapters of this book, I thought that closing with this summary would provide an uplifting conclusion of the team's accomplishments. I thought I might even suggest that, with the advancements of search and rescue technology and the Pioneers' commitment to them, many concerns about the dangers of being lost have been addressed. But something stopped me from ending with those words – or should I say, someone.

In November 2015, the homepage of the New York State DEC website offered this callout for help: "DEC Announces Search for Missing Hunter Could Extend into the Weekend." The posting requested "assistance from experienced volunteers to locate Thomas E. Messick, an 82-year-old hunter lost in the Adirondacks." Details about Messick's disappearance sounded a lot like the missing person cases that fill the Pioneers' scrapbooks and files: At 4:30 p.m. on Sunday, November 15, DEC dispatch received a report that Mr. Messick, of Troy, New York, had failed to meet his hunting party at their designated location and time. Forest rangers and DEC police led over 145 volunteers in the search.

The website mentioned that steep terrain, wet lowlands, thick vegetation, cold temperatures and wind, snow and rain had hindered search efforts, but eventually volunteers grid-searched nearly 2,500 acres (four square miles) and "many more thousands of acres" were covered by the State Police Aviation Unit. The posting concluded with a request for assistance from *trained* volunteers to continue the search.

The Oswego County Pioneers were among the 17

organizations listed as partners in the search for Messick, and Patti Ruffos, a new Pioneer team member, joined in. She remembered her first search this way: "After a three-hour drive to the Horicon, New York command center, I was assigned to a team and searched the entire day. By the time I returned home, it was well after dark, but I felt compelled to contact other members of the Pioneers to explain how the day went. I remember feeling like we were close to finding Mr. Messick."

Surely, I thought, Ruffos' intuition would prove correct. Perhaps Mr. Messick would have succumbed to the elements, but I was certain search and rescue teams would eventually find him. A North Country Public Radio's November 26 update on Messick proved otherwise. After eleven days of searching, there was still no closure on the case, and at the request of the missing man's family, operations were suspended for the Thanksgiving holiday weekend.

Included in the report was an interview with two of Messick's hunting buddies who commented on the day he disappeared. "It was a good day and something went wrong," Roland Gendron stated. "He was just supposed to go up in the woods, sit and wait for deer to come, but instead, he started walking." The second friend, Allen Rasmussen, added: "We have no idea where he disappeared to. It's devastating." Messick's wife Beverly stood by the volunteer sign-in table to say thank you to each searcher. "We are so lucky in this state to have these people," she said. "Certainly we haven't given up hope and I'm sure they'll keep looking."

Search teams did continue through winter, the darkest period of an Upstate New York year. In February 2016, I interviewed Pioneer team member Thom Benedetto who confirmed what seemed unbelievable to me in today's world: Messick was still missing. "Despite the hard work of law enforcement and many volunteers to put the right resources in the area where he was last known to be, Mr. Messick has not been found," Thom said.

While I continued to conduct interviews and research on the book, I kept an eye on the Messick case. On May 27, 2016, with no sign of Messick, the DEC turned again to the media, hoping that with the start of the summer season, visitors to the Adirondacks might come across something to help solve the mystery of their subject's whereabouts. In September, I contacted the DEC to see if there had been any advancement in the search for Messick over the previous four months. A representative from the DEC's Public Involvement and News Department confirmed that Messick was still missing and that no new leads in the case had been uncovered.

As this book goes to press, in November 2016, the hunter out for an enjoyable day in his beloved backwoods crosses the one-year anniversary as a missing person. For the Pioneers, Thomas Messick now joins Douglas Legg and others caught in a disheartening limbo: without a fresh clue to offer hope, his will remain an open search.

Chapter Thirteen

"...the Best Search and Rescue Team"

An early group photo of The Pioneers.

"There's a lot that people don't know about the Pioneers," Dale Currier told me as we were wrapping up our interview. He was responding to the same final question I asked every Pioneer during my conversations with them: What is the legacy of the Oswego County Pioneer Search and Rescue Team? Dale took a moment to collect his thoughts and continued: "Search and rescue isn't like the good work police and fire departments do, which we can hear from their sirens going through streets. We don't read about a lot of searches like we do when a house burns down and firefighters save a family. Search and rescue teams are quiet warriors, if you will, that labor on. Most people don't even know they exist."

Dale is right. I'm not the only person who was unaware of the Pioneers and their accomplishments. In the past year, whenever someone who lives in Central New York asked me about the topic of my next book, I got the same reaction when I explained that I was writing about the Pioneer Search and Rescue Team: puzzlement. The look on their face suggested they felt they should know this group – maybe they'd even heard its name or understand the concept of a search and rescue team – but they really didn't know the Pioneers.

It's not that people haven't tried to acknowledge the team's good work over the years. As early as 1973, a newspaper article quoted New York State Police Sergeant A.D. Slocum's praise for the Pioneers' "invaluable assistance to police agencies throughout the state." Slocum had watched the group grow rapidly in its first 18 months and noted that "we recognize the Pioneers as a good group to call when someone is lost." He referred to several alerts, searches and training exercises the team had participated in with state police, noting how efficiently the two groups worked together.

A few months later, in August 1973, a *Valley News* article covering the second anniversary party for the Pioneers mentioned the team's accomplishments. Two guest speakers, David Russell, executive director of Oswego County Civil Defense, and Alvin Krakau, chairman of the Oswego County Legislature, shared their perceptions of the Pioneers' value. Summing up the team's achievements, Russell remarked, "Yours is a dynamic group whose service has certainly put Oswego County on the map!"

The same year, the Pioneers were formally recognized by the Oswego County Legislature, its resolution stating that the organization "has provided exemplary search and rescue services to this county and state...and has demonstrated, through its performance and professionalism, that it provides an important and lifesaving service to residents of Oswego County and New York State."

Praise for the Pioneers came from beyond county borders, even warranting a statement from New York State's highest elected official. "Soon after we started having successful searches," explained Steve Ives, "Governor Nelson Rockefeller put out a message that anyone in New York State who wanted to form a search and rescue team should do it like we'd done in Oswego County." Groups from around the state listened to Rockefeller, and the Pioneers were happy to share their ideas of how to successfully start a search and rescue team. Included in their suggestions was the importance of developing goals, which was how the team's founders began.

The Pioneers continued to heed their own advice about goalsetting even after they had established themselves as a professional organization. They knew the importance of revisiting and refocusing on their goals and here's how the team looked forward in the January 1998 issue of *PuLSAR*, the official newsletter of the Pioneer team. They stated five goals for the new year:

1) Develop a working relationship with a minimum of 50 percent of the organizations either responsible for or responding to search and rescue work in Oswego County.
2) Provide 100 percent documented training programs to all existing team members and new members when they join.
3) Response by at least 50 percent of the active team membership to at least 80 percent of the searches called in Oswego County.
4) Upgrade current radio communications equipment.
5) Upgrade paging to include page out by Oswego County Fire Control and provide 100 percent paging availability to all of the membership.

In 2006, in an interview with *The Post-Standard* during the Pioneer's thirty-fifth anniversary celebration, Roger Fox had trimmed the team's goals down to two very important topics:

"Our number one goal is to provide the same high level of service we currently do, which means no deaths in Oswego County as a result of search and rescue. In the last three years, we have not had a death as a result of a search and rescue operation. This includes our 16 rescues last year. Across all of New York State, last year there were 33 searches by all search teams and there were 13 deaths. We represent half of the searches, and you'd think at least one of those (fatalities) would have popped up in Oswego County, but it didn't. I attribute that to two things: We get involved very early, and all the agencies work together: law enforcement, fire, forest rangers, and search and rescue."

Roger stated that the team's next goal was to increase membership. "We have about 30 members, all volunteers. That sounds like a lot, but on a daytime activation, if you can get 12 people to show up, that's a lot, because of family and job requirements."

Ten years later, the current Pioneer coordinators are still striving for the team's best. Here's how Scott Morehouse and Aaron Albrecht map out their team's 2016 goals:

1) Continue the education of our team with the Academy, trainings and seminars.
2) Incorporate more people into our training instructor positions and field officer positions.
3) Improve our search management by putting more people through "Managing the Lost Person Incident" classes.
4) Strengthen our Mantracking and low-angle rescue skills.*

* Aaron explained that low-angle rescues are any rope rescues which are less than a vertical rescue, include lowering or raising a stokes basket on a steep incline or pulling someone to safety across an icy surface where traction is limited.

5) Improve existing equipment and put together new communication and navigation equipment.
6) Find a building and/or piece of land to call home, allowing us to do training in our own facility and keep our equipment in one place.
7) Work toward our Woolly Worm Races really taking off to raise money for our yearly expenses.
8) Replace our 1990 GMC truck.

The 2016 Pioneers' final goal, Scott and Aaron agreed, will be a tough one to achieve: addressing the fact that Roger and Sue Fox will be stepping down from the Pioneers. Scott added that "it's going to take several folks stepping up to make the Pioneers run as well as it has in the years under Roger's direction."

Scott's concern reminded me about a conversation I'd had with Steve Ives regarding the team's history. He was explaining to me the transitions he'd seen the Pioneers go through and focused on the mid-'90s, that pivotal period when the team initiated some radical changes.

"The biggest thing that helped the Pioneers succeed and gain respect was Roger Fox," Steve said. "In many ways, Roger was a lot like Bart Bartholomew at the beginning of the Pioneers. Bart was a motivational speaker who got people excited about things. Roger was able to talk with department heads and politicians and he took the team to a whole different level. Today, the Pioneers have ten times the respect

Roger Fox participating in a ropes rescue training.

we had at the beginning."

Roger is quick to downplay his contributions to the team, explaining that a healthy, productive working relationship is a "two-way street." He offered praise for the lead agencies in Oswego County, noting that "they've figured out how to integrate search and rescue into other emergency services. In fact, we are the only county in the state that handles search and rescue in what I feel is the correct way."

It's not just what people have said about Roger's contributions to the Pioneers that have proved his commitment to the team. Time and again, I've seen his influence while reviewing the team's archives. Here's an example from their newsletter, *PuLSAR*, which was published primarily through Roger's effort. Along with news about upcoming trainings and recaps of important searches, Roger tried to include something in each issue that encouraged Pioneers to think about the service they were providing. In the June 1997 edition, he suggested team members take a fresh look at the three words that defined the Pioneers: search and rescue, with emphasis on the word "and."

"Our profession is Search and Rescue," Roger wrote, "but, at times, we may only be tasked with searching...Because of the nature of our profession, we do more actual searching than we do rescuing. Locating the subject is usually the larger effort where we are involved...(but) our obligation to the subject does not end when they are located. Our obligation doesn't even end when other resources show up on the scene. Our role may change, but our mission doesn't end until the subject has been placed under the control of a higher level of emergency services and is absolutely out of danger...We must always be prepared to perform all aspects of our mission: Search and Rescue."

Losing the kind of vision Roger held for the Pioneers will be a significant challenge for the team, but current members are confident in their future. As important as his tenure with the Pioneers has been, Roger is one part of a long and successful history. "Along with Roger's contributions," Scott noted, "the fact that we are still considered a highly-respected search and rescue team goes back to the old-timers who set the standard."

Thom Benedetto echoed Scott's comments about Oswego County Search and Rescue by referring to his team's roots: "The foresight of the early Pioneers to organize is remarkable. Since then, there have certainly been good, qualified search and rescue teams throughout the state, and when we're at a search, we're all in it together. It's not about who's better, it's about what we need to do to get things done. But there's a lot of pride knowing we are part of a team that can trace its roots to the beginning of the search and rescue movement in New York State."

This idea of the Pioneers being first in local search and rescue efforts feeds into a question that has been on my mind since I started this writing project: How do founding members view today's Pioneers? I wasn't sure how to address this touchy subject with those who had worked so hard to establish the team. What if they didn't look so favorably on their modern counterparts? Dale Currier helped to address my question and concerns by describing a recent Academy graduation ceremony. In the audience were members of the founding Pioneers.

"I recognized some of the original team, though I hadn't seen them in thirty years," Dale said. "I saw these old-timers' eyes light up as they observed the next generation continuing on with something they had started, something they put their heart and soul into, as well as their personal resources. Seeing the newest Pioneers was particularly impressive to the original team members, as well as to me, because in this day and age it is getting harder to find people who want to volunteer. The original Pioneers have never lost their interest; you can tell it is near and dear to their hearts."

Steve Ives was one of those "old-timers" watching that Academy graduation and he recalled what was going through his mind as he watched the event: "I was picturing the faces of all the Pioneers from the past; people who are no longer with us. Here was a whole new generation ready to do the work of saving people's lives. I saw a team the original Pioneers could really be proud of."

Dale Currier, after two stints as a Pioneer, still keeps involved with search and rescue work through his current position as director of Oswego County Emergency Management, the modern-day version of the Civil Defense Department that Bart Bartholomew once had ties to. One of Dale's staff recently went through the Academy training, and at his request, the graduate put together a presentation about search and rescue for the Emergency Management staff.

"This was a guy who knew his way around the wilderness," Dale said, "but his opening statement about the Pioneers was that being on the team was a whole lot more involved than he had originally imagined. The commitment to the training and the many other agencies it connected with during searches really made an impression on him. To me, his reaction was a testimony to the fact that Pioneers continue to give their all to achieve their goal."

Dale's opinion of the current Pioneers' commitment to Bart Bartholomew's challenge of becoming "the best search and rescue team" is inspiring. But, to me, the question of whether the team ended up achieving their goal can be more definitively answered by the original members themselves. Here's how a few of those who witnessed the team's early striving toward that goal answered my question about the Pioneers' legacy:

Jim Crombach offered this observation of the team in action, attributing their success to *how* they conducted business: "During my time with the Pioneers, there was very little tension or people not seeing eye-to-eye, which can so often befoul an organization and create a split. But, somehow, we were able to avoid that. Being with search and rescue was an important, but also a fun part of my life. I enjoyed the community it created and I was very sorry when my job took me out of it, because I missed it."

Richard Bartholomew used the popular music of the 1970s to reflect on the diverse group of individuals he got to know in the Pioneers. "John Denver tried to describe nature as best he could in songs like *Rocky Mountain High* and *The Eagle & The Hawk*," Richard noted. It was the same thing with the guys on the rescue team; we came from all walks of life, but we were all together in nature."

I'm a big John Denver fan, but I hadn't ever listened to his music with the Pioneers' search and rescue ideals in mind. After talking with Richard, I played some of Denver's songs and in this verse from *The Eagle & The Hawk*, I got a sense of what the founder's son was saying about the Pioneers:

"Come dance with the west wind and touch on the mountaintops.
Sail o'er the canyons and up to the stars.
And reach for the heavens and hope for the future,
and all that we can be, and not what we are."

Another child of an original Pioneer, Derek Ives, offered this reflection of learning, at such a young age, what being a volunteer means: "The adults on the team had one thing in common: a love of people. I think the word that comes up for me about all the Pioneers is sacrifice. That's the way my mom and dad were, and that's how the Pioneers were. I grew up with that."

Derek put the Pioneers' spirit of volunteerism into action when he attended college to study wilderness recreation. During that time, he worked with at-risk kids and thinks one of his most important duties was being a role model for children who'd never had one. "That's the sort of thing I learned from the Pioneers," Derek said.

Burnetta Bennett answered my question about the Pioneers' legacy with these personal anecdotes: "When I joined the team, I had just received Shone, a crazy female Irish setter pup. The one absolute, unselfish friend a person can have in this selfish world is the one that never deserts them, that never proves ungrateful or treacherous: a dog! I was also inspired to join because of the Heidi Allen search. Lastly, I'm passionate about the woods, and the Pioneers provided a great opportunity to smell the pine and walk the land of upper New York State that I love."

For Howard Bennett, the legacy he sees comes from his memories being on searches: "From the onset of a callout to its conclusion, each search became personal to me, as I believe it did with most team members. It was as though we were looking for a missing member of our own family and I believe it's this caring and compassion that causes trained volunteers to give up their time and resources.

"Each time I arrived on the scene and received details, I would mentally put myself in the place of the missing subject, which helped prepare me to plan and execute my assignment. The elation we as searchers felt each time a subject was found I cannot put into words. Even unsuccessful searches had some reward in knowing we had done all we could do to ease a family's pain. When I changed careers and had to leave the team due to my work schedule, it was a difficult transition to make. I cherish my memories of those days."

Barbara Bartholomew reflected on the Pioneers' legacy by speaking on behalf of her husband: "How very proud Bart would be (and is) to see and hear all the wonderful testimonials regarding the magnificent people who have been and are a part of the team. He always knew they would be, were, and are the most highly-skilled search and rescue team in this United States of America."

Jeannie Parrow's thoughts on the Pioneers' legacy focused on the people she worked alongside: "Everyone who joined the Pioneers had their own special knowledge. Not everybody was an expert, but each had something to give. It takes a special person to do the kind of volunteerism required in search and rescue, and all the people who stuck with the Pioneers had good hearts."

Huey Parrow focused on the family aspect of the Pioneers' legacy: "One thing about our team: we always knew where we were in the woods. We always remembered first to protect ourselves and each other. We searched together, camped out together, laughed together, felt sad together. Everyone was treated the same and given respect, be they male or female. We all worked as one, so it wasn't 'your team' or 'my team,' but 'our team.' I was proud to be a part of it."

"We put ourselves in the hands of our teammates," said Steve Ives.

Steve Ives' thoughts on the Pioneers' legacy starts with the reality of search and rescue, which he became aware of only after a long history with the team: "It turns out there's the good, the bad and the ugly in search and rescue. We all went into this thinking we were going to be looking for lost hunters or little kids. Innocent stuff. But it didn't always turn out that way. Still, I had the opportunity to be shoulder-to-shoulder with some of the best people there ever were, who were out there trying to serve, purely motivated by wanting to help. "Ironically, if it wasn't for the Douglas Legg tragedy, none of this would have happened. What a loss it would have been to my life if we hadn't come together. I think about what we said in Bart's backyard and what the Pioneers are today. It's amazing that it all came true: What we dreamed about actually happened."

Afterword

What the Mountains Taught Me

September 20, 2016. Midday. I'm hiking the San Juan Mountains of Southwest Colorado, having travelled to this "highest state in the union" to isolate myself from the busyness of the world so I can concentrate on writing this book. Through the kindness of friends, I have been given the use of a cottage in the town of Ouray, known as "The Switzerland of America" because of its setting in a narrow valley, bordered on three and a half sides by steep mountains. Here, I am 8,000 feet above sea level, twice that of the Adirondack's Santanoni Preserve, and every day, after several hours of writing, I climb into these mountains to stretch my legs and think about the Pioneers, their history and what I can offer their story.

Today, it struck me how appropriate it is to finish this search and rescue book in a Colorado town. Working from here has put me back in the mountains, back in the familiar setting of where this story began, heading off to Santanoni in search for the link between Douglas Legg and the Pioneers. Of course, the San Juan Mountains are not the Adirondacks. Instead of northern New York's dense forests and endless greenery, Colorado is rock, rock and more rock. But both offer breathtaking vistas from high perches, where my mind is free to imagine what I want this book to say. Today, I got my answer, but I had to come face-to-face with some real danger before I did.

Hiking the San Juan Mountains isn't dangerous in the same way that the Adirondack's swamps, bogs and thick tree cover are. Here in Colorado, the way to stay safe is to avoid slipping off the bare rock of these steep cliffs that drop 1,000 feet or more. Add in the element of changeable weather, and keeping yourself from harm becomes a real challenge. I've noticed a disturbing pattern in Ouray's weather after a few weeks here: right around midday, the wind picks up and whistles through these mountain peaks like a locomotive out of the Wild West.

Today's one of those exceptionally windy days, and to be honest, hiking in it is scary. After 60 years, there's not a lot in the natural world that frightens me anymore. I know how to handle myself in a winter blizzard or thunder and lightning, and I've even learned how to avoid getting lost in the Adirondacks. But being on these San Juan Mountain ledges is new and this rush of fear runs through me. Real head-to-toe fear.

That's when it hits me, or should I say, that's how writing this search and rescue book became more than something to put my mind to. Suddenly, I'm *feeling* it, comprehending each chapter on a deeper level: Douglas Legg's mysterious disappearance, Vince Markowsky's explanation of what it's like to be lost, Matthew Tanner's snowy January night curled up beneath a pine tree, his parents' anxious wait at home, the Pioneers' 45 years of stepping into the unknown.

Fear.

To steady myself as I make my way from cliff to cliff, I search for a stick along the trail. Any old tree limb will do as long as it fits my hand and my height. As I reach for one that will serve my purpose, I suddenly think of Gary Carter, the man who spent 40 days searching for Douglas Legg. When I arrived at Carter's home to interview him, he greeted me with a hand-carved walking stick, personalized with my first name. I was struck by Gary's kindness toward a person he hadn't even met, but I guess someone writing a book about the good that came out of the Douglas Legg tragedy could be a friend of Gary's.

Douglas has been on my mind a lot on this writing retreat. As one of the main subjects of this book, I wanted to paint a picture of him for readers. Fellow writers who'd read my drafts of the sections about Douglas told me they wanted to know more about him. But, with old newspaper accounts offering only sketchy details and his family not comfortable sharing their memories, I was at a loss. I did meet a few people who knew of Douglas: a woman in my writing class whose children went to preschool with him, another who lived two doors down from the Legg family. But it wasn't until just before I left for this trip to Colorado that I met Paul Foster, who had the details about Douglas I was looking for.

Paul is chief of the Fulton Fire Department, so I'd seen his name in the paper a lot and heard about the good service his department provides for our community. But I'd never met him until he stopped me on the street one day. He'd heard I was writing a book about the Pioneers' search and rescue work and wondered if I was going to include information about Douglas. When I told him I was, a smile lit up his face. "I grew up with Dougie," Paul said. "He was my childhood friend." I smiled in return. My picture of Douglas Legg could finally be completed.

"I met Dougie in kindergarten," Paul told me during an interview that took place via a 2,000-mile phone connection from Fulton to Ouray. "He and I were part of a group of five boys who became friends. Dougie was a strong kid, kind of rugged and into the kind of things young boys did: playing football at recess, going to our friends' birthday parties and such.

"When Dougie went missing, it was summer and I hadn't seen him for a while. The day news came out of his disappearance, I had come home from playing and my mom met me on the porch. 'Don't you have a friend named Dougie Legg?' she asked. I said, 'Yeah, why?' 'Well, he got lost in the Adirondacks.' "

Paul paused at this part of his story, which gave me time to consider what I'd just heard. What must have it been like for a child to try to understand his friend just disappearing? Paul answered my question by remembering the many questions that went through his young mind: "How long had Dougie been lost? Are people looking for him? Did he have any food? I was worried, but back then, which was a much more innocent time, we often heard about kids getting lost at the State Fair and such, and they

257

were always found. I figured they would find Dougie."

As hope for Douglas's well-being waned, young children like Paul had to come to terms with a friend no longer in their life. "We went back to school in the fall and there was nothing," Paul stated. "No mention of Dougie's disappearance, no memorial service. Nowadays, there are programs like counseling to help people process the loss, but not back then."

To this day, whenever some mention of Douglas Legg appears in the paper or on TV, Paul pays close attention. As I concluded our interview, he thanked me for the opportunity to share memories of his childhood friend. I was surprised Paul was offering thanks when he was the one doing me the favor, and I asked him why he felt the need to do so. His response helped me realize another reason why I feel it is so important to properly honor the Pioneers.

"Of all I've been through in my life," Paul said, "what happened to Dougie is one of those things that never went away and I've never had a chance to talk with anyone about it. There's never been any closure. You have a friend that disappears and you feel a loss. And that loss never goes away."

Paul's words have played over and over on my daily hikes in Ouray. Today, though, they really sink in and add a final dimension to my belief in what search and rescue teams do. I'm thinking about Paul's loss of Douglas as I glance down at the huge drop just a few feet from where I stand. I think of my family back home and how they would grieve if I were to lose my footing.

Stopping to catch my breath and regain my composure, I think of the Pioneers and how loss has been such an integral part of their work: Losing the trail of a missing person, telling a family that hope is lost, each team member trying to come to terms with it, time and again.

Loss.

Fear and loss are close cousins in the world of search and rescue. They are what keeps calling a team out for each new missing person, which, to me, make the Pioneers soldiers of hope.

They venture out to ease the fear of those lost in the woods and those who will be waiting at the search's end, bracing themselves for an unthinkable loss.

That same fear and loss are with me on today's hike. As I stand on a San Juan Mountain cliff, a stiff wind seriously toying with my life, I grip my walking stick a little tighter, steady my fear and carry on, the Oswego County Pioneer Search and Rescue Team's legacy echoing in these mountains.

APPENDIX

Every Pioneer team member I interviewed mentioned the importance of prevention when people head into the wild. In a book that deals with the realities of getting lost in the woods, I thought it appropriate to include information from search and rescue professionals on

How to Prepare For and Stay Safe in the Woods

- ➢ Check the weather reports before you leave. Weather can quickly change.
- ➢ Dress in non-cotton, light-colored clothes. (Light colors help you to be seen and help you spot ticks if they land on you.) Bring extra clothing, including a rain poncho.
- ➢ Tell someone where you are going and the approximate time you intend on returning.
- ➢ Always include in your backpack: water, pocketknife, watch, whistle, waterproof matches, flashlight, energy food, emergency blanket and first-aid kit. (If you are allergic to bees, take an EpiPen.)
- ➢ Bring your cellphone. Bring an extra cellphone battery, charge stick, or means of recharging your phone. Note: Cellphone service is spotty in the Adirondacks, so don't rely on one. Plan for alternate means of communication, like a whistle, mobile radio, or satellite phone.
- ➢ Carry a map and compass and know how to use them.
- ➢ Choose a hike that's appropriate for you - don't overexert yourself.
- ➢ Have a pre-arranged "turn-around" time to prevent hiking in the dark.
- ➢ Sign in and out at the trailhead registers.
- ➢ Don't travel alone if it can be avoided. It's best to stay with your group.

- Make sure to take water and food breaks to allow your body to rest. Do not drink water from ponds, streams or lakes unless you boil, filter or purify it first.
- Avoid swimming or wading in unfamiliar waters.
- Be on the lookout for invasive and harmful plants, taking care to avoid them and the discomfort they may cause.
- If you become lost, keep calm and warm, stay dry, and stay put to make it easier for a search party to find you. Finding your way out of an unfamiliar area can be difficult. Most people who are lost actually walk in circles, so it's better to stay in one place, reserve your energy and make yourself visible.
- If you feel you can try to find your way out of the woods, remember that following streams downhill will nearly always lead you back to signs of habitation.
- If it appears that you will need to spend the night in the woods, build a campfire to provide heat, light and comfort. A campfire will be invaluable in locating you if you have been reported missing. Aircraft may be used in searching when weather permits and smoky campfires may be spotted from the air.
- If the weather is particularly cold or bad and you must spend the night in the woods, set up camp before darkness falls. Build a small shelter using dead branches, hemlock boughs and leaves. The shelter will serve as a "cocoon" and should be just big enough for you to lie in comfortably.
- In case of an accident, at least one person should remain with the injured person. Know and use basic first-aid techniques. Others in the group should carefully note their location and contact 911.

ACKNOWLEDGEMENTS

Along with those who offered me their Pioneer search and rescue memories, I'd like to also thank:

Amanda Boespflug, New York State United Teachers
CNY Arts, Inc.*
The Downtown Writers Center
The Fulton Public Library
Peter Mathews and Glenn Yamaguchi
Betty Mauté
The New York State Department of Environmental Conservation
The New York State Federation of Search and Rescue Teams
The Onondaga County Historical Association
The Oswego County Libraries
The Oswego County Pioneer Search and Rescue Team
Georgia Popoff
the rivers end bookstore
Erica Schreiner
The Writers Bloc:
       Joe Abbate
       Lisa Davis
       Diane Sokolowski

* This book is the result of a 2016 Individual Artist Commission from CNY Arts, Inc., Syracuse, New York. Its Individual Artist Commission was made possible with funds from the Decentralization Program, a regrant program of the New York State Council on the Arts with the support of Governor Andrew Cuomo and the New York State Legislature. My Commission was administered by CNY Arts, Inc. and due to their generous support, I have turned over the ownership of this book to the Oswego County Pioneer Search and Rescue Team. All profits from the book's sales will go toward the financial support of the team.

RESOURCES

The Adirondacks, PBS Home Video, 2008.

Banks, Clarisse. "A Lesson Remembered." *New York Teacher*. March 24, 1999.

Barrett, Charlotte K. *A Visitor's Guide to Camp Santanoni, Adirondack Great Camp and National Historic Landmark*. Albany, New York: Adirondack Architectural Heritage, 2013.

Bennett, Howard. "Search and Rescuer Team Training Pays Off, Saving a Hunter's Life." *Oswego County Weeklies*, December 5, 1995.

Delaney, Barbara and Dunn, Russell. *Adirondack Trails with Tales*. Delmar, New York: Black Dome Press Corp., 2009.

Denver, John. "The Eagle and the Hawk." John Denver and Michael Taylor. Warner/Chappell Music, Inc. 1971. CD

Engel, Robert; Kirschenbaum, Howard; Malo, Paul. *Santanoni: From Japanese Temple to Life at an Adirondack Great Camp*. Keeseville, New York: Adirondack Architectural Heritage Book, 2000.

Federman, Adam. "Lost." *Adirondack Life,* October 2010.

Jackson, Melanie K. "Boy Fell through Ice Before Rescue." *Post-Standard* , January 21, 1996.

Larkin, Ralph. "Oswego Volunteers Create Search and Rescue Team." *Environmental Quality News*. The New York State Department of Environmental Conservation, June-July, 1973.

Lehman, Don. "Forty Years Later, Case of Missing Boy Remains an Adirondacks Mystery." *Poststar.com*, July 15, 2011.

Oswego Public Library archives.

PuLSAR, newsletter of The Oswego County Pioneer Search and Rescue Team. Various issues.

Rein, Richard. "Inspired By a Dog That Came Back, Lisa Teifer Searches for Three Men Lost in the Wilds. *People,* March 12, 1979.

Smith, Amanda M. "The Beauty and Danger of the Adirondacks." *All Points North* website, Winter 2012 issue.

"Starving Dog Encourages Plane Crash Searchers." *The Auburn Citizen,* January 12, 1979.

Stites, Karen A. "Little Boy Lost: The Mystery of Douglas Legg." *The Sun Community News & Printing,* September 14, 2016.

VanLaer, Scott. "Crashed in the Wilderness." *New York State Conservationist,* December 2013.

Warren, John. "A Short History of Adirondack Airplane Crashes." *Adirondack Almanack,* November 18, 2009.

Web:
adirondack.net/hiking/safety
dec.ny.gov
murderpedia.org/male.L/l/lent-lewis
nysforestrangers.com
oswegocounty.com/sheriff/allen
oswegocountytoday.com/its-wooly-worm-racing-at-its-hottest
syracuse.com
ussartf.org/dogs_search_rescue
websoilsurvey.nrcs.usda.gov
wikipedia.org

ABOUT THE AUTHOR

Jim Farfaglia lives in and writes about the history and culture of Upstate New York. In 2011, after a fulfilling career directing a children's camp and advocating for youth, Farfaglia transitioned to focusing on his lifelong interest in writing. Splitting his time between poetry and what he calls "story-driven nonfiction," Jim also enjoys helping others fulfill their dream of writing a book. Visit his website at www.jimfarfaglia.com.

Back Cover Photo:

Picture taken at the Fulton Public Library on June 17, 2016 by library staff person Janelle Wallace.
Seated, l to r: Howard Bennett, Burnetta Bennett, Nancy Crombach, Huey Parrow.
Standing, l to r: Jim Farfaglia, Jeannie Parrow, Barbara Bartholomew, Roger Fox, Dale Currier, Steve Ives, Jim Crombach.

Interior Book Photographs:

Images used in this book are courtesy of The Oswego County Pioneer Search and Rescue Team with the following exceptions:

pages 10, 21 and 26: Gary Carter
pages 42 and 45: Barbara Bartholomew
page 52: Charles Blount family
page 54: Earl Lockwood
page 63: Brenda LaMay
pages 71, 77, 106 and 144: Burnetta and Howard Bennett
page 140: Bonnie Sommers
page 146: Thom and Patty Benedetto
page 154: Jim Farfaglia
page 196: New York State United Teachers